Early Families of
Berks, Bucks

and

Montgomery Counties
Pennsylvania

Keith A. Dull

HERITAGE BOOKS
2007

HERITAGE BOOKS

AN IMPRINT OF HERITAGE BOOKS, INC.

Books, CDs, and more—Worldwide

For our listing of thousands of titles see our website
at
www.HeritageBooks.com

Published 2007 by
HERITAGE BOOKS, INC.
Publishing Division
65 East Main Street
Westminster, Maryland 21157-5026

Other books by the author:

Early Families of Berks, Bucks and Montgomery Counties, Pennsylvania

Early Families of Lancaster, Lebanon and Dauphin Counties, Pennsylvania

Early Families of Somerset and Fayette Counties, Pennsylvania

Early Families of York County, Pennsylvania, Volume 1

Early Families of York County, Pennsylvania, Volume 2

Early German Settlers of York County, Pennsylvania, Revised Edition

International Standard Book Number: 978-1-58549-419-4

Contents

Sources

These genealogies were compiled from research conducted at the Allen County Public Library, Fort Wayne, Indiana; the Huntington County Public Library, Huntington, Indiana; the Indiana State Library, Indianapolis, Indiana; and the York County, Historical Society, York, Pennsylvania.

The following court records were consulted:

Bucks County, Pennsylvania, wills, tax lists, and deeds.
Berks County, Pennsylvania, wills, tax lists, and deeds.
Fayette County, Pennsylvania, wills, tax lists, and deeds.
Lehigh County, Pennsylvania, wills, tax lists, and deeds.
Montgomery County, Pennsylvania, wills, tax lists, and deeds.
Northampton County, Pennsylvania, wills, tax lists, and deeds.
Philadelphia County, Pennsylvania, wills, tax lists, and deeds.
Somerset County, Pennsylvania, wills, tax lists, and deeds.
York County, Pennsylvania, wills, tax lists, and deeds.
Allen County, Ohio, wills.
Fairfield County, Ohio, wills, and tax lists.
Mercer County, Ohio, wills, and tax lists.
Brooke County, Virginia, wills.
Miami County, Ohio, wills and tax lists.
Shelby County, Ohio, wills and tax lists.
Muskingum County, Ohio, wills.
Williams County, Ohio, wills.
Defiance County, Ohio, wills.
Hunterdon County, New Jersey, wills, and tax lists.
Middlesex County, New Jersey, tax lists.
Franklin County, Missouri, tax lists.
Fort Bend County, Texas, wills.

The following church records were consulted:

Records of the Reformed Congregation in Lower Saucon Township, Northampton County.
Dryland Church (Northampton County).
First Reformed Church of Easton, Pennsylvania.
St. Peter's (Northampton County).
German Evangelical Lutheran of Easton (Northampton

County).
Stone Church (Northampton County).
Mt. Bethel Church (Northampton County).
Records of Reverend Daniel Schumacher.
Augustus Trappe Church (Montgomery County)
New Goshenhoppen Congregation (Montgomery County)
St. Paul's (Montgomery County, Upper Hanover Township).
New Hanover Church (Montgomery County).
Falkner Swamp Church (Montgomery County).
Old Goshemhoppen Church (Montgomery County).
Indian Creek Church (Montgomery County).
Indianfield Church (Montgomery County).
Great Swamp Congregation (Lehigh County).
St. Paul's (Blue) Church (Lehigh County).
Evangelical Lutheran Congregation in Upper Milford Township
(Lehigh County).
Zion's Church (Lehigh County).
Zion's Church (Zionsville, Lehigh County).
Reformed Congregation in Lower Milford Township (Lehigh
County).
Oley Hill Church (Berks County).
Longswamp (Berks County).
Moslem Church (Berks County).
DeLong's Church (Berks County).
Records of Johan Caspar Stoever.
Atolheo Church (Berks County).
Mertz Church (Berks County).
Allemangel Church (Berks County).
Rosenthal Church (Berks County).
St. Michael's and Zion in Philadelphia.

The following census records were consulted:

Berks County, Pennsylvania.
Bucks County, Pennsylvania.
Fayette County, Pennsylvania.
Montgomery County, Pennsylvania.
Northampton County, Pennsylvania.
Philadelphia County, Pennsylvania.
Somerset County, Pennsylvania.
Westmoreland County, Pennsylvania.

Allen County, Ohio.
Defiance County, Ohio.
Fairfield County, Ohio.
Licking County, Ohio
Mercer County, Ohio.
Miami County, Ohio.
Montgomery County, Ohio.
Muskingum County, Ohio.
Shelby County, Ohio.
Williams County, Ohio.
Allen County, Indiana.
Marshall County, Indiana.
Fort Bend County, Texas.

The following books were consulted:

18th Century Emigrants from German Speaking Lands to North America, Vol. I & II by Annette K. Burgert.
18th Century Emigrants From Northern Alsace to America by Annette K. Burgert.
Palatine Families of New York.
Swingle, Swengel and Swingley by Jane Cassedy.

Information from the following researchers contributed to portions of this book:

Roger Sims
Craig Bailey
Coleen Eagen

Abbreviations

b. = born
d. = died
m. = married

Johannes Abraham Baehli

Johannes Abraham[1a] m. Anna Maria. He was probably the Johannes Bolle that immigrated to America on the ship *Mortonhouse* on Aug. 24, 1728. He was residing in Berks County, Albany Township, Pennsylvania, in 1754. It is uncertain what religion he belonged to before he immigrated to America, because most of his children underwent adult Lutheran baptisms in Berks County. He was probably of Swiss descent, because that name is prevalent there. Johannes and Anna Maria disappear from the records of Berks County after the baptism of their son Abraham in 1763. Johannnes and Anna Maria were the parents of the following children:

Annastass[1.1a], b. about 1728, and baptized by Reverend Daniel Schumacher on Jan. 28, 1755.

Frantz[1.2a], b. in 1730.

Daniel[1.3a], b. about 1732.

Jacob[1.4a], b. on Sep. 1, 1734.

Peter[1.5a], b. about 1738.

Johan Nickel[1.6a], b. about 1740.

Johann Abraham[1.7a], b. in 1742.

Carl Ludwig[1.8a], b. about 1744.

Frantz Baehli

Frantz[1.2a] was baptized by Reverend Daniel Schumacher on May 25, 1755, and m. Christina about 1752. Frantz d. in Albany Township in Mar. 1805. Frantz and Christina had the following children in Albany Township:

Johan Andreas[1.2.1a], b. in 1753, and baptized by Reverend Daniel Schumacher on May 25, 1755. He was sponsored by Andreas and Maria Margaretha Hagenbuch.

Johan Martin[1.2.2a], b. in 1754, and baptized by Reverend Daniel Schumacher on May 25, 1755. He was sponsored by Andreas and Maria Margaretha Hagenbuch.

Maria Magdalena[1.2.3a], b. on May 12, 1756, and baptized by Reverend Daniel Schumacher on June 24, 1756. She was sponsored by Reverend Daniel Schumacher and Magdalena Stebelton.

Johan Daniel[1.2.4a], b. on Apr. 17, 1758, baptized at Allemangel Lutheran Church on Apr. 17, 1760, and sponsored by his uncle and aunt, Daniel and Rosina Baehli.

Johannes[1.2.5a], b. on Mar. 12, 1764, baptized at Ziegel's Lutheran Church on Apr. 8, 1764, and sponsored by Frid and Agnes Hard.

Christina Barbara$^{1.2.6a}$, b. on May 23, 1766, baptized at
Allemangel Lutheran Church on Sep. 21, 1766, and sponsored by
Tobias and Barbara Stebelton.

Johan Martin Baehli
Johan Martin$^{1.2.2a}$ m. Magdalene, and had the following son in
Berks County:

Michael$^{1.2.2.1a}$, b. on Mar. 6, 1795, baptized at Rosenthal
Lutheran on May 24, 1795, and sponsored by Michael and Eva
Hagenbuch.

Johan Daniel Baehli
Johan Daniel$^{1.2.4a}$ m. Elisabeth (b. in 1763), and had the
following daughter in Berks County:

Mary Magdalene$^{1.2.4.1a}$, b. on Dec. 18, 1783, baptized at
Rosenthal Lutheran Church, and sponsored by Jacob Gerhart and wife.

Daniel Baehli
Daniel$^{1.3a}$ m. Anna Rosina (Hoell). He resided in Berks
County, Windsor Township, Pennsylvania, in 1754, 1757, 1759, and
1761. About 1765, Daniel and his brother, Jacob moved to York
County, Shrewsbury Township, Pennsylvania. In 1779 and 1780, Daniel
had 100 acres, two horses and two cattle; in 1781, 100 acres, two
horses and four cattle; in 1782, 100 acres, two horses, and five cattle;
and in 1783, he had 100 acres and two inhabitants. Anna Rosina's
maiden name is presumed to be Hoell because Daniel and Rosina
appeared on as sponsors on numerous baptisms of the Hoell family at
Zion's Moselem Church in Richmond Township. Daniel d. in
Shrewsbury Township in Jan. 1811, and Anna Rosina in May 1815.
Daniel's will was written on June 5, 1798, and probated by Rosina
Baehli and Henry Ruhl on Jan. 21, 1811. Rosina's will was written on
Mar. 28, 1815, and probated on May 2, 1815 by Henry Ruhl and
George Frederick. The beneficiaries of Rosina's estate were Jacob
Baehli, Henry Baker, Lydia Baker, Rosina Baker, and Henry Ruhl.
Daniel and Rosina may have had the following children in Berks
County, Windsor Township, Pennsylvania:

Eva$^{1.3.1a}$, It has not been proven, but it is possible that Daniel
had a daughter named Eva, because a Rosina, Lydia and Henry Baker
were the beneficiaries of Anna Rosina Baehli's will.

Eva Baehli

Eva[1.3.1a] may be the Eva that m. Jacob Becker/Baker. His will was written on Jan. 6, 1808, probated in Shrewsbury Township on Feb. 6, 1808, and executed by Georg Gantz and Henry Ruhl. Jacob and Eva had the following children:

Anna Maria[1.3.1.1a], b. on Feb. 19, 1798, baptized at Ziegler's on Mar. 13, 1798, and sponsored by Philip and Anna Maria Stambach. An Rosina[1.3.1.2a], b. on Oct. 4, 1799, baptized at Fissel's, and sponsored by Daniel and Rosina Baehli. Lydia[1.3.1.3a]; Jacob[1.3.1.4a]; Henry[1.3.1.5a].

Jacob Baehli

Jacob[1.4a] was baptized by Reverend Daniel Schumacher on Oct. 29, 1755, sponsored by Anthony and Elisabeth Pettersheimer. He was on the tax lists of Albany Township in 1754, 1758, and 1759. In 1758, he is listed as poor. He m. Anna Maria, had one daughter, and then m. Eva Elisabetha, daughter of Hans Peter and Eva Elisabetha (Kunckel) Kleinfelter, in Berks County, Pennsylvania, about 1759/60. Eva was b. in Florsbach, Hessen, Germany, in 1732.[1]

Jacob Baehli moved to York County, Shrewsbury Township, Pennsylvania, with his brother Daniel in 1765. Jacob was a weaver and yeoman. In 1779, he had 70 acres, two horses, and one head of cattle; in 1780 and 1781, 100 acres, two horses, and three cattle; in 1782, he had 50 acres, two horses, and three cattle; and in 1783, 100 acres and four inhabitants. During the Revolutionary War, Jacob served as a Private in the York County, Militia, Captain John Ehrman's Company in 1776 and 1778. Eva Elisabetha d. in Shrewsbury Township on June

---

[1] She previously m. Johan Gottleib Volck about 1754. Gottleib d. in Berks County, Ruscombe Manner Township, in 1759. Gottleib and Eva Elisabetha had the following daughter in Ruscome Manner Township: Elisabetha, b. on July 22, 1755, baptized at Mertz Church in Rockland Township on Aug. 31, 1755, and sponsored by Michael and Elizabeth Homan. She was mentioned in the 1812 will of her stepfather, Jacob Baehli, as Elizabeth Folk. I believe she may be Elisabetha Volck (Folk), wife of Wentel Heiss/Heuss, because they appear on numerous baptisms of the Baehli family. Wentel d. in Shrewsbury Township. His will was written on Mar. 11, 1815, probated on July 13, 1816, and executed by Daniel Heiss and Peter Kleinfelter. Wentel and Elisabetha had the following children: Henry; Jacob (m. Elisabetha, and had a daughter Eva, b. June 14, 1796, baptized at Fissel's, and sponsored by Eva Heiss, single); Eve; Daniel; George; Margaret; John.

24, 1809, and Jacob on Aug. 1, 1812. They are buried in Fissel's cemetery. Jacob was the father of the following children:

Anna Catharina[1.4.1a], b. on Feb. 12, 1758.

Jacob[1.4.2a], b. about 1760.

George[1.4.3a], b. on Dec. 13, 1762.

Margaretha Barbara[1.4.4a], b. on July 23, 1764.

Anna Barbara[1.4.5a], b. on Apr. 17, 1766.

Anna Rosina[1.4.6a], b. on Mar. 27, 1769.

Susanna[1.4.7a], b. about 1771.

Johannes[1.4.8a], b. about 1773.

Anna Catharina Baehli

Anna Catharina[1.4.1a] was baptized by Reverend Daniel Schumacher on Apr. 2, 1758, and sponsored by Conrad Bielmann and Catherina Grimmen. It has not been confirmed, but she probably m. Michael, son of Adam and Catharina Roser. Michael was a Private in the Sixth Company, Seventh Battalion in 1778-80, and the Eighth Company, Fifth Battalion as a Corporal 1782-83 during the Revolutionary War. He had a Land Draft called *Roseborough*, consisting of 27 3/4 acres in Shrewsbury Township, on the Maryland line on Oct. 29, 1786. In 1783, he resided in Codorus Township. He was later considered a yeoman of Baltimore County, Maryland. Michael and Catharina had the following children:

Catharina[1.4.1.1a], b. on Apr. 4, 1782, baptized at Fissel's on May 18, 1782, and sponsored by her grandparents, Adam and Anna Catherina Roser.

Elisabetha[1.4.1.2a], b. on Mar. 8, 1785, baptized at Fissel's on May 1, 1785, and sponsored by Jacob and Susanna Baehli.

Eva[1.4.1.3a], b. on Dec. 10, 1791, baptized at Fissel's, and sponsored by Georg Baehli and wife.

Anna Rosina[1.4.1.4a], b. on Jan. 20, 1793, baptized at Fissel's, and sponsored by Daniel and Rosina Baehli.

Jacob Baehli

Jacob[1.4.2a] m. Susanna about 1784. Jacob resided in Codorus Township with 10 acres, and one horse in 1779; 10 acres, and one head of cattle in 1780; 10 acres, one horse, and two cattle in 1781 and 1782; and 10 acres and five inhabitants in 1783. Jacob moved to Lycoming County, Elmsport, Pennsylvania, between 1812 and 1817, where Susanna d. before 1817, and Jacob d. in 1829. After Susanna's death, Jacob m. Elizabeth Conrad, widow of Michael Fisher. Michael d. in

1799. Elizabeth was b. in 1760. Jacob and Susanna were the parents of the following children, b. in Codorus Township:

Anna Eva[1.4.2.1a], b. on Sep. 7, 1784, baptized at Fissel's on Sep. 14, 1784, and sponsored by her uncle and aunt, Henry and Margaretha Ruhl. She m. George Markel at Christ's Lutheran Church of York on Feb. 22, 1803 (this may have been her cousin, Eva).

Jacob[1.4.2.2a], b. in Apr. 1787.

Elisabeta[1.4.2.3a], b. on May 7, 1788, baptized at Fissel's on May 23, 1788, and sponsored by Wentel and Elisabetha Heuss.

Anna Barbara[1.4.2.4a], b. on Jan. 3, 1790, baptized at Fissel's in 1790, sponsored by her uncle and aunt, Bernhard Hamsher and wife.

Catherina[1.4.2.5a], b. about 1792, and m. Johannes (b. 25 Aug. 1792), son of Michael and Elizabeth (Conrad) Fisher. He d. in Lycoming County before 1845, and her will was probated in Lycoming County, Washington Township, on July 29, 1845.

Johannes[1.4.2.6a], b. on Aug. 7, 1794, baptized at Fissel's, and sponsored by his great uncle and aunt, Daniel and Rosina Baehli.

Susanna[1.4.2.7a], b. on May 22, 1796, baptized at Fissel's, sponsored by Jacob and Susanna Kerchner.

Lulisabini[1.4.2.8a], b. on Aug. 31, 1798, baptized at Fissel's, and sponsored by Hannes and Lulisabini Groh.

Jacob Baehli

Jacob[1.4.2.2a] m. Christina, daughter of Michael and Elizabeth (Conrad) Fisher, of Carroll County, Bachman's Valley, Maryland, and d. on Sep. 28, 1846. She was b. in Baltimore County, Maryland, on Mar. 30, 1794, and d. on June 30, 1876. They had the following children:

David[1.4.2.2.1a] resided in Marion County, Indiana, in 1853.

Sarah[1.4.2.2.2a], b. in 1815, and d. in York County on Mar. 26, 1887.

Jacob[1.4.2.2.3a], b. on Nov. 25, 1822, m. Sevilla Hess, and d. on Oct. 10, 1878.

Christina[1.4.2.2.4a], b. on Dec. 11, 1831, m. William Trump in 1853, and d. on Apr. 4, 1909.

John[1.4.2.2.5a], m. Elizabeth.

Susanna[1.4.2.2.6a], m. Charles Myhart.

Eleanora[1.4.2.2.7a], m. Benjamin Smith.

Elizabeth[1.4.2.2.8a], m. Moses Allen.

Henry[1.4.2.2.9a] resided in Wellsville, Ohio, in 1852.

George[1.4.2.2.10a], m. Ellen Trump.

Leah[1.4.2.2.11a].
Rebecca[1.4.2.2.12a], m. Adam Benner.

George Baehli

George[1.4.3a] m. Margaretha daughter of Peter and Anna Margaretha (Rudolph) Gerberich, about 1781, and Catharine Eberhart in York County on June 9, 1800. Margaretha d. about 1799/1800. In 1779, George had 100 acres, two horses, and one head of cattle in Shrewsbury Township; in 1780 and 1781, 100 acres, two horses, and three cattle; in 1782, 100 acres, two horses, and five cattle; and in 1790, one male over 16, three males under 16, and five females. George was a Private in the Revolutionary War. He was drafted into the York County, Militia in July 1776, and served in Captain Long's Company and Col. Swope's Battalion for three months. He marched from York to Lancaster, and then to Philadelphia, Trenton, and Brunswick. He then marched to Amboy and Newark, and then was discharged in Oct. 1776. He was drafted again in the fall of 1782. He served in Captain Furry's Company under Major Austin. He was assigned to guard (at Camp Security, York) British prisoners taken with Cornwallis for three months. He applied for pension in Jan. 1834. George d. in Codorus Township on Nov. 24 (23), 1843, and his estate was administered in Jan. 1845. George resided with Henry Baehli in later years. George and Margaretha had the following children, in Shrewsbury Township:

Peter[1.4.3.1a], b. about 1782.
Elisabeth[1.4.3.2a], b. about 1783, and m. Jacob Kerchner.
John[1.4.3.3a], b. about 1785.
Jacob[1.4.3.4a], b. about 1787.
Eve[1.4.3.5a], b. about 1789.
Margaret[1.4.3.6a], b. about 1790.
George[1.4.3.7a], b. in 1802.
Henry[1.4.3.8a], b. in 1808.

Peter Baehli

Peter[1.4.3.1a] m. Christina, daughter of Frederick Froesher, and d. in 1854. She was b. in 1781, and d. in 1853. They had the following children:

Catharina[1.4.3.1.1a], baptized at St. Jacob's Lutheran Church in York County on Apr. 30, 1803.
John[1.4.3.1.2a], b. in 1814, m. Mary Ann (1834-1910), and d. in 1881.

Petrus$^{1.4.3.1.3a}$, baptized at St. Jacob's on Aug. 8, 1819, m. Sarah Ann (1825-1888), and d. in 1898.

George Baehli

George$^{1.4.3.7a}$ m. Juliana (1804-1894), and d. in 1876. They had the following children:

Susan Ann$^{1.4.3.7.1a}$, b. in 1830.

Rebecca$^{1.4.3.7.2a}$, b. in 1839.

John$^{1.4.3.7.3a}$, b. in 1839.

George$^{1.4.3.7.4a}$, b. in 1843.

Jacob S.$^{1.4.3.7.5a}$, b. in 1844, and m. Elizabeth Kline.

Henry Baehli

Henry$^{1.4.3.8a}$ m. Mary, daughter of Christian and Susanna (Lau) Rohrbaugh, and d. in Shrewsbury Township on Jan. 20, 1892. She was b. on Dec. 1, 1816, and d. in Shrewsbury Township on Apr. 26, 1857. They had the following children:

Jesse R.$^{1.4.3.8.1a}$, b. on Jan. 5, 1836, and m. Sarah Brenneman.

Jacob R.$^{1.4.3.8.2a}$, b. on May 15, 1839, m. Sarah Markel, and d. in Codorus Township on Oct. 10, 1911.

Samuel R.$^{1.4.3.8.3a}$, b. on Mar. 23, 1841. He m. Christina, daughter of George B., and Nancy (Brenneman) Merckel, on Aug. 4, 1864, and d. in York County on Aug. 13, 1910. He is buried in Zion Church cemetery. She was b. on Dec. 28, 1848, and d. on Apr. 10, 1913.

Mary Ann R.$^{1.4.3.8.4a}$, b. in 1843, and d. on Nov. 7, 1920. She is buried in Fissel's cemetery.

John R.$^{1.4.3.8.5a}$, b. on July 4, 1847, and d. on Mar. 3, 1878. He is buried in Fissel's cemetery.

Sarah$^{1.4.3.8.6a}$, b. in 1849.

Henry R.$^{1.4.3.8.7a}$, b. on march 12, 1853, and d. on Nov. 13, 1926. He is buried in Fissel's cemetery.

Levi R.$^{1.4.3.8.8a}$, b. on Mar. 12, 1856, m. Ellen C., and d. on July 12, 1918. He is buried at St. Jacob's.

Margaretha Barbara Baehli

Margaretha Barbara$^{1.4.4a}$ m. Heinrich, son of Frederick and Maria Elisabetha (Bahn) Ruhl. He was baptized at Christ's Lutheran Church of York on Feb. 13, 1763, and sponsored by his grandparents, Henry and Eva Bahn. Heinrich m. Margaretha Barbara, daughter of

Jacob and Eva Elisabetha (Kleinfelter) Baehli, at he First Reformed Lutheran Church of York on Sep. 24, 1782. Margaretha was b. on July 23, 1764, baptized in Albany Township, Berks County, Pennsylvania, at the Allemangel Lutheran Church on Sep. 2, 1764, and sponsored by Andreas Kunckell and Margaretha Barbara Probst. Henry was a yeoman with 100 acres in Shrewsbury Township in 1783. He received Pleasant Ridge from his father in 1802, which he in turn deeded to his son, Johannes[1.4.4.2a], on Jan. 26, 1811, along with the tract of 2Q,299 supra, which was patented to Henry on June 25, 1810. In 1828, he and his sister-in-law, Rosina (Baehli) Ruhl's, family moved to Ohio. Henry settled in Sandusky Township, Richland County, where he d. between Jan. 5, and Mar. 9, 1830. Margaret d. sometime after Jan. 1830. They were the parents of the following children, who were b. in Shrewsbury Township:

Johan Jacob[1.4.4.1a], b. on Aug. 21, 1783, baptized at Fissel's on Sep. 14, 1783, and sponsored by his grandparents Jacob and Elisabeth Baehli. Johan Jacob d. sometime before 1797.

Johannes[1.4.4.2a], b. on Nov. 18, 1785. He was baptized at Fissel's on Dec. 18, 1785, and sponsored by his father's uncle and aunt, Johannes and Helena Ruhl. Johannes m. Catherina on Dec. 23, 1809. She was b. on Dec. 3, 1791, and d. in Shrewsbury Township on June 18, 1882. Johannes was a blacksmith, and received Pleasant Ridge, and tract of 2Q,299 supra from his father in 1811. Johannes sold part of the land of 2V,420 supra to John Grove on July 26, 1817, and Johannes bought the tract of 3C,266 supra from John and Elizabeth Grove on Apr. 1, 1825. John bought 8 acres and 51 perches in Shrewsbury Township from Daniel and Isabella Kauffelt on June 7, 1834. Johannes d. in Shrewsbury Township on Feb. 19, 1858, and is buried beside his wife in the Lutheran cemetery.

Elisabetha[1.4.4.3a], b. on Jan. 9, 1788, and m. Johannes Gerberich.

Henrich[1.4.4.4a], b. on Aug. 10, 1792, baptized at Fissel's about 1792, and sponsored by his uncle and aunt, Johannes Baehli and wife. He d. in Shrewsbury Township on Dec. 28, 1815, and was buried in Lischy's Reformed Church cemetery.

Michael[1.4.4.5a], b. in 1795. He m. Rebecca Richey in Shrewsbury Township, York County, Pennsylvania, on Apr. 18, 1822. He received "one-third of middle one-third half section" of his father's land from his father's will. Rebecca d. sometime before 1850, and Michael resided in Crawford County, Jackson Township, Ohio, in 1850.

Jacob[1.4.4.6a], b. on Jan. 7, 1797. He received the "privilege of
living on, clearing, and improving" his father's land after his mother's
death. Jacob d. in Crawford County, Galion, Ohio, on Aug. 8, 1842. He
m. Catherine Fate.

Eva[1.4.4.7a], b. on July 17, 1800. She was baptized at Fissel's
about 1800, and sponsored by her uncle and aunt, Johann and
Margareta Baehli. She m. Jacob Nunemaker about 1822. He was b. in
York County, Codorus Township, Pennsylvania, in 1800 to Jacob and
Anna Maria Nunemaker. He was baptized at Steltz Union (Bethlehem)
Church in Jan. 1800, and sponsored by Solomon Nunemaker and wife.
Eva d. sometime before Jan. 5, 1830 in York County, Shrewsbury
Township. In her father's will, each of her sons was given fifty dollars
upon attaining their twenty-first birthday. Jacob was residing in
Shrewsbury Township in 1850 with his second wife.

Susanna[1.4.4.8a], b. about 1802. She m. Johan Adam, son of
Adam and Maria Barbara Hoffman. He was b. in Codorus Township on
Apr. 11, 1781. They resided in Codorus Township until 1838, when
they moved to Richland County (now Morrow), Perry Township, Ohio.
Adam d. on May 22, 1848, and is buried in North Woodbury Lutheran
cemetery.

Mary[1.4.4.9a], b. on May 4, 1804, and m. Georg Ruhl[1.4.6.8a].

Lydia[1.4.4.10], b. about 1806. She was unmarried in 1830, and
received "one-third of land on middle one-third half section cut off
North end by an east-west line, two cows, bureau, bed, two iron pots"
from her father's will. She may have been the Lydia Ruhl, b. in 1810,
residing in Shrewsbury Township, York County, Pennsylvania, with
Ese Geisey and Jacob and Christian Smith in 1850.

Anna Barbara Baehli

Anna Barbara[1.4.5a] was baptized at St. Jacob's on May 10,
1766, and sponsored by Ludwig Hahnawaldt and Anna Barbara
Gerberich. She m. Barnet Hamschear in Trinity Reformed Church of
York, Pennsylvania, on Dec. 24, 1780. Barnet d. in Shrewsbury
Township in 1792. Barnet and Barbara had the following children in
Shrewsbury Township:

Barnet[1.4.5.1a], b. in 1783.

Margaretha[1.4.5.2a], b. in 1786.

Eva[1.4.5.3a], b. in 1787.

Heinrich[1.4.5.4a], b. in 1790.

Johannes[1.4.5.5a], b. on May 15, 1791, baptized at Fissel's on
June 5, 1791, and sponsored by his uncle, Hannes Baehli (single).

Anna Rosina Baehli

Anna Rosina[1.4.6h] m. Johan Georg, son of Johannes and
Helena (Schenck) Ruhl. He was baptized at St. Jacob's on July 30,
1765, and sponsored by his uncle and aunt, Georg Ruhl and Rosina
Schenck. He was confirmed on May 3, 1784, and m. Anna Rosina,
daughter of Jacob and Eva Elisabetha (Kleinfelter) Baehli, in York
County, Pennsylvania, in 1786. Anna Rosina was b. in Shrewsbury
Township on Mar. 27, 1769, baptized at St. Jacob's on May 28, 1769,
and sponsored by her uncle and aunt, Daniel and Anna Rosina Baehli.
Georg was a yeoman in Codorus Township, and he purchased 140
acres, 27 perches there on Mar. 12, 1787 from Jacob and Maria
Catherina Noll. On Mar. 24, 1795, Georg and Rosina deeded to Philip
Ruhl, three tracts in Codorus Township: (a) 60 acres 127 perches
surveyed to Martin Anthony in 1767, called *Hard Scoffle*; (b) 79 acres
60 perches surveyed to Martin Anthony in 1768, called *Hog's Manor*;
(c) 50 acres warranted to Georg Ruhl on Apr. 5, 1788. In Feb. 1794,
Georg signed an agreement for the founding of a union congregation at
New Freedom in Codorus Township, called Steltz Union (Bethlehem)
Church (the actual church building was erected about 1801). During
the War of 1812, Georg served as a Private in the York County Militia.
Georg and Rosina lived in the borderland region between Codorus
Township, and Baltimore County, Mine Run Hundred, Maryland, and
appeared on census and tax record records of both areas, but their
sons indicate that they were b. in Baltimore County, Maryland. Georg
and Rosina moved to Mine Run Hundred in Maryland in 1795, and
Georg d. there on Mar. 15, 1815. His will was probated in Baltimore
County, Maryland, and he is buried in Steltz cemetery in York County,
Pennsylvania, beside his parents. In his will, he mentions his land in
Ohio, where Rosina, and her sons, Johannes[1.4.6.4a] and Georg[1.4.6.8a],
moved to in 1828. The journey was made by team with the family of
Rosina's brother-in-law, Henry Ruhl. During the trip they cut a portion
of the road to Mansfield, Ohio, and after their arrival lived in a covered
wagon until they cleared a site to build a cabin. Rosina d. on Dec. 8,
1855, and is buried in North Woodbury Lutheran Church cemetery.
Georg and Rosina were the parents of the following children:

Elisabetha[1.4.6.1a], b. on Feb. 2, 1787, baptized at Fissel's on
Feb. 26, 1787, and sponsored by her parents.

Eve[1.4.6.2a], b. about 1790, and m. Jacob, son of Jacob and
Anna Maria (Heibele) Dick, before 1815. Jacob was b. in Shrewsbury
Township on Oct. 10, 1784, baptized at Fissel's on Nov. 14, 1784, and
sponsored by his parents.

Caterina[1.4.6.3a], b. about 1793.

Johannes[1.4.6.4a], b. on Dec. 14, 1796. He was baptized at
Steltz Union in Dec. 1796, and sponsored by his uncle and aunt,
Johannes and Margaretha Gerberich. He m. Susannah Blossner in
York County, about 1820. She was b. in York County on Jan.
30, 1802, and d. in Morrow County, Perry Township, Ohio, on Apr. 7, 1895.
Johannes was a farmer in Perry Township, where he d. on Mar. 12,
1874. They are buried in Shauck cemetery.

Maria[1.4.6.5a], b. in 1799, baptized at Steltz Union on Dec. 27,
1799, and sponsored by Johannes Huber.

Johan Jacob[1.4.6.6a], b. in 1802. He was baptized at Steltz
Union on Oct. 22, 1802, and sponsored by his grandfather, Jacob
Baehli. Initially, he remained in Baltimore County, Maryland, after his
mother and brothers headed west. Jacob resided in Mine Run
Hundred, District 6 in 1850, and moved to Morrow County, Perry
Township, Ohio, in the 1860s. His son, Adam[1.4.6.6.1a], moved to Perry
Township in the 1850s. Jacob was a farmer and a wagonmaker. He m.
Elizabeth sometime prior to 1831. She was b. in Pennsylvania in 1805,
and d. in Richland County, Troy Township, Ohio, in 1882. In 1880,
Elizabeth was residing in Troy Township with Ellen Ruhl, a 32 year old
tailoress, who was b. in Maryland and her parents b. in Pennsylvania.
Ellen's relationship to this family has not been established. Jacob d. in
Morrow County, Perry Township, in 1875, and is buried beside his wife
in Shauck cemetery.

Susanna[1.4.6.7a], b. about 1804.

Georg[1.4.6.8a], b. on July 6, 1806. He was baptized at Steltz
Union on Aug. 8, 1806, and sponsored by Jacob Nunnemacher and
wife. He m. his first cousin, Mary[1.4.4.9a], daughter of Henry and
Margaret (Baehli) Ruhl, in York County, Pennsylvania, on Nov. 16,
1826. Mary received one hundred dollars from her father's will. Georg
and Mary moved with their families to North Woodbury, Ohio, in 1828,
and erected a cabin with a puncheon floor. Their farm consisted of 160
acres on NE 1/2 of Section 19 Range 19 W Township 19 N. They lived
in the cabin for some time before finally clearing the land, and building
the home, which he later sold to his brother's son-in-law, Norman
Merwine, when he left Ohio. Georg sold eight lots from his farm for
the village of Woodbury, and donated one to the United Brethren
Church. He farmed in Perry Township until 1863, when he engaged in
trade at different places, first at West Point, Ohio, then at Galion,
Ohio. About 1865/66, he moved his family to Marshall County, Indiana,
and settled first at Bourbon and then on a small farm in Green

Township, just southwest of Argos, Indiana. In Indiana, he worked as a farmer, and carpenter. He was Justice of the Peace for many years as well as the Assessor and Trustee of Green Township. He was a member, and elder of the Evangelical Lutheran Church. Mary d. in Green Township on May 9, 1870, and Georg m. Mary Ann Newhouse in Marshall County, on Dec. 11, 1872. Mary Ann d. on Dec. 22, 1921. In 1867, George converted from the Lutheran faith to the Methodist Episcopal Church. Georg d. on June 2 (3), 1890, and is buried beside his first wife, in Gilead cemetery.

Susanna Baehli

Susanna$^{1.4.7a}$ probably m. Jacob Kerchner about 1787, but it has not been confirmed. After Susanna's death, Jacob m. Elisabetha$^{1.4.3.2h}$, daughter of Georg and Margaretha (Gerberich) Baehli, at Christ's Lutheran Church of York on June 14, 1803. Jacob d. in York County, Pennsylvania, prior to May 13, 1828, when the probate was begun on his estate. Jacob had the following children in Shrewsbury Township:

Johannes$^{1.4.7.1a}$, b. in Oct. 1791, baptized at Fissel's in Nov. 1791, sponsored by Jacob and Elisabeth Stehli.

Eva$^{1.4.7.2a}$, b. on July 9, 1794, baptized at Fissel's on July 30, 1794, sponsored by Wentel and Elisabeth Heuss. She m. Ludwig Krebs.

Jacob$^{1.4.7.3a}$, b. in 1797. He m. Anna Mary, daughter of Peter Lau, and Catharine Rohrbach, before 1850. Anna Mary was b. in 1794, and d. before 1835. Jacob d. in 1872.

Rosina$^{1.4.7.4a}$, b. in 1800, and m. James Thompson.

Elizabeth$^{1.4.7.5a}$, b. about 1802, and m. Henry Hetrick.

George$^{1.4.3.2.1a}$, b. about 1804.

Margaret$^{1.4.3.2.2a}$, b. about 1806, and m. George Trouett.

Catharine$^{1.4.3.2.3a}$, b. about 1807.

Susanna$^{1.4.3.2.4a}$, b. about 1809.

John B.$^{1.4.3.2.5a}$, b. on Apr. 21, 1812. He m. Elizabeth (Sep. 20, 1819-Mar. 6, 1894), daughter of Adam and Anna Behler, and d. on May 8, 1880.

Henry$^{1.4.3.2.6a}$, b. about 1814. He is probably the Henry Kerchner that m. Christina Lenden in York County, Hanover, St. Matthew's Lutheran Church on Jan. 7, 1847.

Lydia$^{1.4.3.2.7a}$, b. about 1816.

Charles$^{1.4.3.2.8a}$, b. about 1818. He m. Mary Ann.

Johannes Baehli

Johannes[1.4.8a] d. in Codorus Township in Aug. 1841. His will was written on Feb. 4, 1841, and probated on Aug. 21, 1841 by John Ruhl and Jacob Kerschner. Johannes m. Margaretta and had the following daughter:

Mary[1.4.8.1a], m. ____ Moyer.

Peter Baehli

Peter[1.5a] m. Margaretha and had the following children in Berks County, Albany Township:

Anna Rosina[1.5.1a], baptized on Aug. 1, 1762, by Reverend Daniel Schumacher.

Johan Abraham[1.5.2a], baptized on Dec. 30, 1764, by Reverend Daniel Schumacher.

Johan Nickel Baehli

Johan Nickel[1.6a] m. Catharina, and had the following daughter in Berks County, Greenwich Township, Pennsylvania:

Catharina[1.6.1a], b. on Mar. 15, 1763.

Johann Abraham Baehli

Johann Abraham[1.7a] was baptized on Apr. 28, 1763 at Rosenthal Lutheran Church, and sponsored by his brother, Jacob Baehli. Abraham m. Catharina, who d. about 1770, and then m. Margaretha in 1770. Abraham moved to Frederick County, Middletown, Maryland, with his brother, Carl Ludwig, about 1770. Abraham had the following children (the first three, b. in Albany Township):

Johan Peter[1.7.1a], baptized at Allemangel Lutheran Church on June 3, 1764, and sponsored by Peter and Anna Elisabeth Scheibeli.

Johan Abraham[1.7.2a], b. on Sep. 21, 1766, baptized at Allemangel Lutheran Church on Oct. 12, 1766, and sponsored by Peter and Anna Elisabeth Scheibeli.

Maria Margaretha[1.7.3a], b. on Mar. 26, 1769, and baptized at Allemangel Lutheran Church on Apr. 9, 1769.

Wilhelm[1.7.4a], b. on June 1, 1771, and baptized at Middletown on Sep. 25, 1771.

Carl Ludwig Baehli

Carl Ludwig[1.8a] m. Anna Elisabeth. They moved to Frederick County, Middletown, Maryland, with Carl's brother, Abraham, in 1770. Carl Ludwig and Anna Elisabeth had the following children:

Jacob[1.8.1a], baptized on Jan. 30, 1766 at Berks County, Reading, Pennsylvania.

Daniel[1.8.2a], b. on Apr. 18, 1773, baptized at the Evangelical Reformed Church of Frederick, Maryland, on May 30, 1773, and sponsored by Daniel and Catherine Hauwet.

Susanna[1.8.3a], b. on Feb. 25, 1779.

****

Johann Tiehl Bohn

Johann Tiehl[1b] m. Anna Marien Sponheimer, and had the following son:

Peter Tilmann[1.1b], b. in Boos on Jan. 1, 1677.

Peter Tilmann Bohn

Peter Tilmann[1.1b] m. Anna Christina, daughter of Johann Herman Ebert on May 16, 1702, and Maria Elisabetha (Ebert) Muller. Peter and his son, Henrich immigrated to America on the ship *Loyal Judith* on Nov. 25, 1740. Peter had the following children:

Johan Philipp[1.1.1b], b. about 1703.

Johan Frederich[1.1.2b], b. about 1705.

Anna Elisabetha[1.1.3b], b. about 1707.

Maria Katharina[1.1.4b], b. about 1709.

Sara Konradina[1.1.5b], b. about 1711.

Anna Maria Jakobina (by second wife)[1.1.6b], b. about 1720.

Johanna Margaretha[1.1.7b], b. about 1722.

Johan Henrich[1.1.8b], b. in 1724, and m. Eve.

Johan Peter[1.1.9b], b. about 1726, and m. Catharina Kamp.

Johan Konrad[1.1.10b], b. about 1728.

Johan Henrich Dielboen/Thielbon

Henry[1.1.8b] was b. in Unkenbach, Pfalz, Germany, in 1724, and immigrated to America on the ship *Loyal Judith* on Nov. 25, 1740. He m. Eve, and d. in Berks County, Rockland Township, Pennsylvania, in June 1785. They had the following son in Rockland Township (and may have had a son, Johann, who resided in Frederick County, Maryland):

Henry[1.1.8.1b], baptized in DeLong's Reformed Church on June 30, 1765, and sponsored by Henry Sowah and wife.

Henry Dilbone

Henry[1.1.8.1b] m. Barbara, daughter of John and Margaret (Terfen-Rench) Millhouse, in Lancaster County, Pennsylvania, in 1801. She was b. in Maryland in 1770. They moved to Miami County, Piqua, Ohio, where they were massacred by Indians on Aug. 19, 1813. They had the following children in Miami County, Spring Creek Township, Ohio:

John[1.1.8.1.1b], b. in 1806.
Margaret[1.1.8.1.2b], b. in 1808.
Priscilla[1.1.8.1.3b], b. in 1810.
William[1.1.8.1.4b], b. on Jan. 28, 1813.

William Dilbone

William[1.1.8.1.4b] m. Lydia, daughter of Henry and Mary (Benham) Baltzell, in Miami County, Troy, Ohio, on Feb. 25, 1831. She was b. in Hamilton County, Ohio, on Mar. 26, 1813, and d. in Mercer County, Dublin Township, Ohio, on Mar. 12, 1897. Henry, son of Peter and Saville Baltzell, was b. in Washington County, Pennsylvania, on July 12, 1791, and d. in Mercer County, Ohio, in 1867. Henry m. Mary Benham in Hamilton County, Ohio, on Nov. 9, 1811. She was b. in Hamilton County, Ohio, on Feb. 9, 1796, and d. in Van Wert County, Ohio, in 1860. Henry served in Captain Luther Leonard's Company in the War of 1812. Peter, son of Henry and Maria Margaretha Baltzell, was b. in Frederick County, Maryland, on Jan. 9, 1764, m. Saville Crepps (Mar. 9, 1766-Sep. 25, 1854) in 1785, and d. in Hamilton County, Springfield Township, Ohio, on Apr. 3, 1834. Henry, son of Hans Peter and Anna Barbara Baltzell, was b. in Klingen, Germany, in 1735, m. Mary Margaretha (1741-1821), daughter of Henry and Margaret Alexander in Frederick County, Maryland, on Nov. 2, 1760, and d. in Hamilton County, Sycamore Township, Ohio, in 1821. Hans Peter, son of Benedict and Anna Barbara Batzell, was b. in Klingen, Bavaria, about 1704, m. Anna Barbara (1705-Jan. 27, 1744, Thaleischweiler), arrived at Philadelphia on the ship *St. Andrew* on Aug. 18, 1750, and resided in Frederick County, Maryland, in 1778. Benedict Baltzell d. in Klingen in 1714, and his wife, Anna Barbara, d. there in 1737. William Dilbone served as Justice of the Peace for Dublin Township from 1858 to 1863. William d. in Dublin Township on Jan. 14, 1878. They are buried in Mount Olive cemetery. They moved to Mercer County, Ohio, between 1837 and 1842. They had the following children:

Priscilla[1.1.8.1.4.1b], b. in 1832, and m. Lucins Daring in Mercer County on Feb. 14, 1853, and Bird Methune.

John[1.1.8.1.4.2b], b. on Jan. 17, 1834. He m. Almira, daughter of Garrison and Sarah Caroline (Everett) Roebuck, in Mercer County on Oct. 10, 1858. She was b. in Dublin Township on Jan. 5, 1840, and d. there in 1903. John d. in Dublin Township on June 10, 1912.

Henry[1.1.8.1.4.3b], b. in 1835.

Mary Jane[1.1.8.1.4.4b], b. in Aug. 1837, and m. Jefferson Everett, and Josiah, son of Peter Dull, sometime after 1889. She resided in Dublin Township in 1900.

Margaret[1.1.8.1.4.5b], b. in Aug. 1837.

Louisa[1.1.8.1.4.6b], b. in Jan. 1842, and m. John, son of Peter and Catharina (Schlater) Dull.

Isaac Newton[1.1.8.1.4.7b], b. on Dec. 10, 1843. He m. Eliza J. about 1864 and Nancy Ann Estill about 1885. Eliza was b. on Oct. 1, 1836. Nancy was b. in Van Wert, Ohio, on Jan. 5, 1861, and d. there on Jan. 10, 1929. They are buried in Mount Olive cemetery. Isaac worked at the sawmill, and d. in Van Wert County, Ohio, on July 14, 1922.

David[1.1.8.1.4.8b], b. in 1845. He m. Sally, and resided in Mason County, Illinois.

Charles Wesley[1.1.8.1.4.9b], b. on Aug. 14 (24), 1849. He m. Matilda Ann, daughter of Josiah Dull, in Mercer County on Aug. 14, 1872, and d. in Mercer County, Rockford, Ohio, on Sep. 19, 1920. Matilda d. on June 28, 1911. They are buried in Riverside cemetery.

William[1.1.8.1.4.10b], b. about 1851, m. Rebecca Rhodes, and resided in Wells County, Indiana.

****

Hans Peter Doll

Hans Peter[1c] had the following son at Erzweiler, Ulmet Parish, Palatinate, Germany:

Johannes Peter[1.1c], b. in 1642.

Johannes Peter Doll

Johannes Peter[1.1c] m. Gertraut, daughter of Hans Peter and Margaretha Riek, at Ulmet on May 2, 1666. She was b. at Ulmet on Feb. 13, 1641/42, and d. there in Dec. 1723. Johannes Peter d. at Ulmet on Oct. 14, 1717. They had the following children at Ulmet:

Christoffel[1.1.1c], b. on July 6, 1671.
Anna Elisabetha[1.1.2c], b. on June 8, 1674.
Casper[1.1.3c], b. in 1676.
Anna Margaretha[1.1.4c], b. about 1678.
Philip[1.1.5c], b. in 1680.
Johannes Christian[1.1.6c], b. in 1682.

Christoffel Doll

Christoffel[1.1.1c] m. Sara Catharina, daughter of Johann Peter and Anna Maria (Kappel) Schuch, at Erzweiler on Mar. 2, 1703/04. She was b. at Rathsweiler, Palatinate, baptized at Baumholder, Rheinland, on Jan. 19, 1690, and d. in Bucks County, Tohickon Township, Pennsylvania, on Apr. 3, 1760. She was buried at Tohickon Union Church Apr. 4. Johann Peter and Anna Maria Schuch, had a son, Johann Christian, who was b. on May 4, 1690, and later immigrated to America. Christoffel and his family set out for America on the ship *Samuel.* Christoffel d. en route, and the rest of the family arrived at Philadelphia in 1739 (except for two sons who immigrated to America in 1737). Christoffel and Sara had the following children at Ulmet:
Anna Maria Margaretha[1.1.1.1c], b. in Nov. 1705.
Anna Catharina[1.1.1.2c], b. on Mar. 14, 1707/08.
Johann Peter[1.1.1.3c], b. on Sep. 22, 1709, and d. in 1714.
Johann Christian[1.1.1.4c], b. in 1712.
Johann Peter[1.1.1.5c], b. on Jan. 20, 1714/15.
Maria Engel[1.1.1.6c], b. on Sep. 15, 1717.
Johann Abraham[1.1.1.7c], b. on Apr. 14, 1720.
Johann Caspar[1.1.1.8c], b. on Feb. 1, 1721/22.
Johann Nickel[1.1.1.9c], b. on May 8, 1725.
Infant[1.1.1.10c], b. on July 3, 1729.

Anna Maria Margaretha Doll

Anna Maria Margaretha[1.1.1.1c] m. Johan Peter, son of Jacob and Anna Catharina Mumbauer, in Erzweiler on June 12, 1727. He was baptized in Erzweiler/Irtzweiler on Mar. 3, 1697. Peter and Margaretha immigrated to America on the ship *Samuel* in 1739. They had the following children:
Johan Christian[1.1.1.1c], d. in 1729, aged 3/4 years.
Johan Christian[1.1.1.2c], baptized on June 27, 1732.
Johan Peter[1.1.1.3c], baptized on Apr. 24, 1735.
Johan Georg Christian[1.1.1.4c], baptized on June 10, 1736.

Johann Christian Doll

Johann Christian[1.1.1.4c] m. Maria Catharina, daughter of
Simon and Anna Elisabetha (Mumbauer) Drumm, at Erzweiler on Oct.
21, 1734. She was b. in Irtzweiler on June 30, 1716. Her grandparents
were Johan Christian and Catharina (Diel) Drumm, and Jacob and
Anna Catharina Mumbauer. Her great grandparents were Adam
Drumm and Nickel Diel. Christian Doll immigrated to America with his
brother, Johann Peter, in 1737. In 1739, he purchased 150 acres
adjoining John Rhinberry in Northampton County on the Hockendaqua
Creek from Ludwig Erb. In 1746, he signed to create the Township of
Allen (now Millcreek) in Northampton County. On July 20, 1749, he
was warranted 25 acres on the Hockendaqua adjoining his other land.
In July 1752, he received a warrant for 25 acres on the Forks of the
Delaware adjoining Frederick Altamouse and Nicholas Dull. On Jan. 12,
1753, he was warranted land adjoining Rowland Smith on Hockendaqua
Creek. On June 18, 1754, he (?Christian Doll, Jr.) was warranted 20
acres adjoining Peter Doll in the Blue Mountains. Johann Christian was
naturalized in 1755, and resided in Philadelphia (now Montgomery)
County, Gwynedd Township, Pennsylvania. He purchased 50 acres in
Philadelphia County on Feb. 22, 1737, 200 acres on Mar. 14, 1743, and
50 acres on Apr. 25, 1750. In 1763, Christian's land is mentioned in
Moore Township. Christian d. between 1763 and 1771, and before
1771, his widow m. Ludwig Erb. On Oct. 31, 1775 (patent date (Nov. 7,
1775), Ludwig and Catharina Erb, as assignees of Christian Doll's
heirs, sold Christian's Northampton County land to Abraham Storver
for 700 £ (he later sold it to Casper Erb). Johann Christian and Maria
Catharina had the following children:

Christian[1.1.1.4.1c], b. on Aug. 12, 1742.

Johannes[1.1.1.4.2c], b. about 1750, was a single freeman in
Moore Township in 1768, and was presented by his stepfather, Ludwig
Erb, in Northampton County, Allen Township, Kreidersville Stone
Church in 1771. He served in Captain Peter Rundio's Flying Camp
Company in 1776, was taken prisoner at the Capture of Fort
Washington, and d. in a New York Church that the British were using
as a prison on Jan. 4, 1777. This John m. Catharine, and had an
administration bond granted in Northampton County on May 13, 1777.
The bondsman was Nicholas and Samuel Kern of Moyamensing in
Montgomery County. It mentioned 50 acres of land.

Elizabeth[1.1.1.4.3c], b. about 1752, and presented by his
stepfather, Ludwig Erb, in Northampton County, Allen Township,
Kreidersville Stone Church in 1771.

Christian Doll

Christian[1.1.1.4.1.1c] m. Elizabeth Dotterer in Montgomery County in 1769. He was taxed in Bucks County, Springfield Township, in 1778. He was a Captain during the Revolutionary War, and d. on Sep. 27, 1820. They had the following children:

Christian[1.1.1.4.1.1c], b. on Dec. 18, 1770.
Sybila[1.1.1.4.1.2c], b. on July 27, 1772.
Mary[1.1.1.4.1.3c], b. on Feb. 15, 1776.
Elizabeth[1.1.1.4.1.4c], b. on Dec. 20, 1777.
John[1.1.1.4.1.5c], b. on Sep. 23, 1779.
Hannah[1.1.1.4.1.6c], b. on Sep. 12, 1781.
Catherine[1.1.1.4.1.7c], b. on July 16, 1787.

Johann Peter Doll

Johann Peter[1.1.1.5c] m. Margaretha. He arrived at Philadelphia with his brother, Johann Christian, in the ship *Samuel* on Aug. 30, 1737. He settled in Bucks (Northampton in 1752) County, Pennsylvania, and in Oct. 1746, obtained a warrant for 50 acres adjoining William Torbert from Jacob Deemer and Christian Young. In Nov. 1746, he received an application for 50 acres adjoining William Teetor on a branch of the Lehigh. In 1746, he was a signer of a petition to form the Township of Allen (now Millcreek). In 1752, his land is mentioned as being in the Lee Swamp above the Forks of the Delaware, and is 1754, it is mentioned as bordering the Blue Mountains. In 1754, Peter was a Schoolmaster it Northampton (now Lehigh) County, Macungie, and in 1755, he was a Captain in the French and Indian War. Sometime during the winter of 1755/56, Peter and Margaretha moved to Northampton County, Moore Township.

On Dec. 14, 1755, Captain Solomon Jennings and Captain (Peter) Doll, with their commands passed through Nazareth on route to the Hoeth farm with orders to search for and bury the dead, after the Indians had massacred the family of Frederick Hoeth, at the Hoeth farm about 12 miles east from Gnadenhutten on Pocho Pocho Creek. Doll and Jennings returned five days later to the Rose Inn just east of Nazareth. On Jan. 15, 1756, Peter's house and barn were reported burnt by the Indians. The family may have sought refuge at Macungie, which would explain the baptism of a son there in Oct. 1756. Peter's name appears on Powell relief lists from Indian attacks during this period (1755/56), while his brother, Nicholas (of Saccon and Shippach Townships), was listed as contributing relief to the victims of these raids. In the summer of 1757, a peace treaty was made with the

Indians at Easton, but the Indians continued to make depredations in the area. By Sep. 1757, Peter had erected a blockhouse in Moore Township, and was quartering soldiers evacuated from Fort Norris on Sep. 27. On Oct. 5, 1757, Peter's name appears on a petition to the government for men and ammunition to defend themselves, and there property. The blockhouse was situated about a mile and a half north-northwest of Klecknersville, Pennsylvania, on the banks of the Hockendauqua Creek. It was 20 miles away from both, Dupui's house on the Delaware River, and Teed's Blockhouse near Wind Gap, and was situated 8 miles from Lehigh Gap. It was located on the road running along the base of the road running along the base of the Blue Mountains, three eights of a mile west of Scholl's Mill. The blockhouse was garrisoned in Jan. 1758, served at an outpost of Fort Lehigh, had two barracks added to serve the garrison, and no stockade. On Feb. 5, 1758, Lt. Snyder of Captain Davis' Company was on duty at the blockhouse with twenty-five men, sixteen province arms, nine private arms, forty lbs. of powder, fifty lbs. of lead, four months provisions, ten cartridges, and Jacob Levan was serving as the commissary for the station. The blockhouse was mentioned in Mar. of 1758, when Major James Burd made his tour of inspection. On Wednesday, Mar. 1, 1758, Burd reported that he found Lt. Snyder and 23 undisciplined men, 15 lbs of powder, 30 lbs lead, no blankets, and 8 province arms bad. Lt. Humphries relieved Lt. Snyder that morning, and Snyder went to his post over Susquehanna. Burd was informed that the magistrate had ordered the farmers should not assist the troops unless the officers immediately pay, and the soldiers should not take regimentals, as it only puts money in their officers pockets. Burd also found a sergeant confined on account of mutiny, ordered a regimental court martial, and marched to the Nazareth Stockade at 10 a.m.

Peter Doll was appointed guardian of Johannes, son of Johan Nickel and Maria Margaretha Heil in Moore Township in Sep. 1762. In 1761, he paid 1 shilling tax in Northampton County, Lehigh Township, and in 1762, sold his land on the branch of the Hockendauqa Creek to Jacob Rees/Ries. Peter was taxed in Lehigh Township in 1763 and 1764. He moved to Montgomery County, Providence Township, Pennsylvania, where he was taxed from 1769 to 1779. A son, John was taxed in Providence Township in 1769, but was gone by 1774. Peter and Margaretha had the following children:

Leonard[1.1.1.5.1c], b. about 1738, and m. Margaretha, daughter of Georg and Elisabeth Stoltz of Northampton County, Plainfield, in Bucks County, Tohickon Township, Pennsylvania, on Oct. 15, 1760. He was a Second Lieutenant in Lewis's Pennsylvania Battalion of the Flying Camp in July-Dec. 1776. He was taxed in Northampton County, Lehigh Township, in 1761, and in Plainfield Township from 1762-1764. He was taxed in Montgomery County, Providence Township, in 1774 and 1779.

Catharina$^{1.1.1.5.2c}$, b. about 1740. She has not been proven as a daughter of Peter.

Eva$^{1.1.1.5.3c}$, b. about 1742. She has not been proven as a daughter of Peter.

Casper$^{1.1.1.5.4c}$, b. on June 11, 1748 (near Skippack in Montgomery County (this is where he was living at the time of his marriage, and the Revolution, and may not necessarily be his birth place (if it is, he may be a son of Christian). He was taxed in Montgomery County, Providence Township, Pennsylvania, from 1774 to 1780.

John$^{1.1.1.5.5c}$, b. on May 20, 1753.

Anna Maria$^{1.1.1.5.6c}$, b. at Macungie in Aug. 1754, baptized at Zion's Lutheran Church on Aug. 25, 1754, and sponsored by Jacob and Anna Maria Wetzel (her mother is Magdalena on the baptism).

Johann Christophel$^{1.1.1.5.7c}$, baptized at Zion's Lutheran Church on Oct. 30, 1756, and sponsored by Peter Federolff, Jr., and Maria Margaretha, daughter of _____.

Johan Jurg$^{1.1.1.5.8c}$, b. in Moore Township about 1758.

Elisabeth$^{1.1.1.5.9c}$, b. in Moore Township on Apr. 15, 1760.

Catharina Dull

Catharina$^{1.1.1.5.2c}$ m. Frederick Hesser in Bucks County, Tohickon Township, Pennsylvania, on Oct. 12, 1760. Frederick was b. in 1736, and d. about 1790. He served as a Private in the Revolutionary War. They had the following children:

Johannes$^{1.1.1.5.2.1c}$, b. on Aug. 10, 1761, baptized at Augustus Trappe Lutheran Church in Montgomery County, Pennsylvania, on Sep. 6, 1761, and sponsored by his parents.

Eve Dull

Eva$^{1.1.1.5.3c}$ m. Henry Hauser in Bucks County, Tohickon Township, Pennsylvania, on Nov. 3, 1761, and had the following daughter:

Elizabeth$^{1.1.1.5.3.1c}$, b. about 1771, and baptized in Northampton County, Lower Nazareth Township, Dryland Church in 1771.

Casper Doll

Casper[1.1.1.5.4c] m. Hannah Catherine Mathieu in Montgomery County, New Hanover, Pennsylvania, on Sep. 20, 1774. She was b. at New Hanover on Feb. 21, 1758, and d. in Mifflin County, McVeytown, Pennsylvania, on Feb. 21, 1826. Casper was taxed in Montgomery County, Providence Township, Pennsylvania, from 1774 to 1780. He was a Captain during the Revolutionary War, and d. at McVeytown on July 23, 1829. Casper and Hannah had the following children:

Catherine[1.1.1.5.4.1c], b. on Aug. 8, 1775, and d. in June 1838. She m. Benjamin Walters.

Daniel[1.1.1.5.4.2c], b. on May 17, 1777, baptized by Reverend Henry Melchior Muhlenberg, and d. before 1830. He m. Elizabeth Stanley.

Elisabeth[1.1.1.5.4.3c], b. on Mar. 9 (7), 1779, baptized by Henry Melchior Muhlenberg, and d. in 1844. She m. Casper Cosmer.

John[1.1.1.5.4.4c], b. on July 8, 1781.

Libby[1.1.1.5.45c], b. about 1783, and d. in 1833.

Hannah Catherine[1.1.1.5.4.6c], b. on Feb. 26, 1786, and d. on Feb. 25, 1837. She m. Mehlor Ruth.

Sybel[1.1.1.5.4.7c], b. on Aug. 22, 1788, and d. before 1830. She m. Abraham Copeland.

Casper[1.1.1.5.4.8c], b. on Dec. 25, 1791.

Mary[1.1.1.5.4.9c], b. on Jan. 1, 1796, and d. before 1830. She m. Isaiah Van Zandt.

George[1.1.1.5.4.10c], b. on July 17, 1797.

Benjamin Mathieu[1.1.1.5.4.11c], b. on May 11, 1799, and d. before 1830. He m. Nancy Younkin.

Joseph[1.1.1.5.4.12c], b. on Jan. 7, 1804, and d. in 1847. He m. Jane Barkley, Jane Laird, and Martha Price.

John Dull

John[1.1.1.5.4.4c] m. Margaret Betty. She was b. in Pennsylvania in 1786. They were residing in Carroll County, Pittsburg, Indiana, in Oct. 1855. They had the following children:

James C.[1.1.1.5.4.4.1c], b. in 1810.

Casper[1.1.1.5.4.4.2c], b. in 1815.

Benjamin[1.1.1.5.4.4.3c], b. in Ohio in 1820, and m. Martha. She was b. in Ohio in 1820. They were residing in Carroll County, Indiana, in 1850.

Margaret[1.1.1.5.4.4.4c], b. in Ohio in 1826.

Mary$^{1.1.1.5.4.4.5c}$, b. in Ohio in 1828.
Daniel$^{1.1.1.5.4.4.6c}$, b. in Ohio in 1830.

James C. Dull

James C.$^{1.1.1.5.4.4.1c}$ m. Margaret. She was b. in Ohio in 1815. They resided in Carroll County, Indiana, in 1850. They had the following children:

Sarah$^{1.1.1.5.4.4.1.1c}$, b. in Ohio in 1836.
Hannah$^{1.1.1.5.4.4.1.2c}$, b. in Ohio in 1838.
Nancy Jane$^{1.1.1.5.4.4.1.3c}$, b. in Ohio in Mar. 1840. She m. Bowen Wesley Speece in Carroll County, Indiana, on Oct. 27, 1859. Bowen was b. in Montgomery County, Dayton, Ohio, in Mar. 1830, and d. in Jasper County, Carthage, Missouri, on Jan. 18, 1915. Nancy d. in Carthage, Missouri, sometime after 1910.
Rebecca$^{1.1.1.5.4.4.1.4c}$, b. in Ohio in 1844.
Lydia$^{1.1.1.5.4.4.1.5c}$, b. in Ohio in 1848.

Casper Dull

Casper$^{1.1.1.5.4.4.2c}$ m. Mary A. She was b. in Ohio in 1818. They resided in Carroll County, Indiana, in 1850. They had the following children:

Ruthie$^{1.1.1.5.4.4.2.1c}$, b. in Carroll County, Indiana, in 1849.

Casper Dull

Casper$^{1.1.1.5.4.8c}$ m. Jane Junkin. He was a keelboatman on the Juniata River, and d. in McVeytown, Pennsylvania, in Aug. 1874. They had the following children:

James T.$^{1.1.1.5.4.8.1c}$, b. about 1812.
Hannah C.$^{1.1.1.5.4.8.2c}$, b. about 1814, and m. Vance Criswell.
Daniel M.$^{1.1.1.5.4.8.3c}$, b. about 1816, and resided at Lewistown, Pennsylvania.
Nancy T.$^{1.1.1.5.4.8.4c}$, b. about 1818, and m. George Macklin.
Margaret E.$^{1.1.1.5.4.8.5c}$, b. about 1820, and m. Samuel Horning.
Andrew I.$^{1.1.1.5.4.8.6c}$, b. about 1822.
C. Penrose$^{1.1.1.5.4.8.7c}$, b. about 1824, and was the proprietor of the Sand Mines.
Joseph F.$^{1.1.1.5.4.8.8c}$, b. about 1826.

George Dull

George[1.1.1.5.4.10c] m. Lydia Postlewait. He resided in Tippecanoe County, Lafayette, Indiana, in Oct. 1855. They had the following daughter:

Hannah[1.1.1.4.3.10.1c].

John Dull

John[1.1.1.5.5c] m. Elisabeth, daughter of Andreas and Catharina Barbara (Bourgey) Boudemont, in Washington County, Maryland, about 1777. John served as a Corporal in the Washington County, Maryland, Militia under Captain Henry Boteler during the Revolution. John and Elisabeth resided at Washington County, Root's Hill, near Eakles Mills, Maryland, until late 1782. In 1783, John was taxed in Somerset County, Milford Township, Pennsylvania. In 1785, he had 150 acres. He purchased land on Scrub Glade in 1787. He was Supervisor of the Roads and Highways for Milford Township in 1800. He served in the Milford Militia on Feb. 5, 1789. He resided near New Centerville, and was a trapper, trader, hunter, and farmer on Coxes Creek Glades. John d. in Milford Township on Nov. 20, 1835, and Elisabeth on Oct. 22, 1843. They are buried in New Centerville cemetery. They had the following children:

Johannes[1.1.1.5.5.1c], b. in Oct. 1778.

Catherine[1.1.1.5.5.2c], b. in 1780.

Peter[1.1.1.5.5.3c], b. on June 15, 1782.

Elisabeth[1.1.1.5.5.4c], b. on Sep. 17 (8), 1784.

Margaretha[1.1.1.5.5.5c], baptized at Samuel's Lutheran Church on Apr. 26, 1785.

Andreas[1.1.1.5.5.6c], b. on Feb. 28, 1786, and baptized at Samuel's Church on July 31, 1787.

Frederick[1.1.1.5.5.7c], b. on Sep. 28, 1787.

Magdalena[1.1.1.5.5.8c], b. in 1790.

Simon[1.1.1.5.5.9c], b. about 1792.

George[1.1.1.5.5.10c], b. on Mar. 15, 1794.

Susan[1.1.1.5.5.11c], b. in 1795, and m. John Whipkey.

Johannes Dull

Johannes[1.1.1.5.5.1c] m. Hannah, daughter of Johan Georg and Anna Catharina Lenhart, in Somerset County, Pennsylvania, about 1799. She was b. in York County, Newbury Township, Pennsylvania, in 1780. He was b. in Washington County, Root's Hill, near Eakles Mills, Maryland, in Oct. 1778. About 1814, John and Hannah moved to

Fayette County, Salt Lick Township, Pennsylvania, near Champion, and in 1832, moved to Stark County, Sugar Creek Township, Ohio, near Wilmont. In Stark County, John entered 320 acres of land. John d. from Asiatic Cholera on Sep. 20, 1834, and Hannah d. from the same disease on Sep. 27, 1834. They are buried in Weimer Church cemetery. A stone was erected several years after their death by their son, Elias, but the bronze plaque which held the inscription was melted down for the war effort. Johannes and Hannah had the following children:

Peter$^{1.1.1.5.5.1.1c}$, b. on June 4, 1800.

Anna Maria$^{1.1.1.5.5.1.2c}$, b. on Mar. 1, 1802.

Joseph$^{1.1.1.5.5.1.3c}$, b. on Feb. 9, 1804.

Philipena "Phebe"$^{1.1.1.5.5.1.4c}$, b. on Mar. 7, 1806.

John$^{1.1.1.5.5.1.5c}$, b. on Jan. 15, 1808.

Infant$^{1.1.1.5.5.1.6c}$, b. about 1810.

Infant$^{1.1.1.5.5.1.7c}$, b. about 1812.

Elizabeth$^{1.1.1.5.5.1.8c}$, b. on June 4, 1813.

Lenhart$^{1.1.1.5.5.1.9c}$, b. on Aug. 11, 1815.

Jacob$^{1.1.1.5.5.1.10c}$, b. on May 1, 1817.

Johannah$^{1.1.1.5.5.1.11c}$, b. on May 11, 1819.

Elias$^{1.1.1.5.5.1.12c}$, b. on Feb. 3, 1822, and baptized at Good Hope Lutheran Church on June 26, 1822.

Catherine$^{1.1.1.5.5.1.13c}$, b. on Dec. 27, 1824, and baptized at Good Hope Lutheran Church.

Peter Dull

Peter$^{1.1.1.5.5.1.1c}$ m. Catharina, daughter of Samuel and Elisabetha Barbara (Robinson) Schlater, in Fayette County, Pennsylvania, in 1824. She was b. in Fayette County, Salt Lick Township, Pennsylvania, on Sep. 30, 1804, baptized at Good Hope Lutheran Church on Oct. 21, 1804, and sponsored by Abraham and Catharina Dumbauld. Peter moved to Stark County, Ohio, with his father in 1832, and, in 1840, moved to Mercer County, Dublin Township, Ohio, settling just northeast of Shane's Crossing. He purchased 161 acres in section six in 1840, and sold it to his brothers-in-law, W. R. and P. Schlater, in 1841 to purchase 183 acres in section ten. In 1842, 1853, and 1855, he purchased land in section three. From 1867 to 1882, Peter deeded all of his land in section three to Josiah, Thomas, William Dull, and Nancy Jane Hooks. In 1882, Peter sold the home farm (consisting of 100 acres) in section ten to Nancy Jane Hooks, and the remaining 83 acres to William Dull. From 1882 till his death, Peter resided with his daughter, Nancy Jane Hooks. Peter farmed northeast of Shane's Crossing until his death on Apr. 7, 1888. Catherine was b. in Fayette County, Salt Lick Township, Pennsylvania, on Sep. 30, 1804, d. on Oct. 8, 1882, and is buried beside Peter in Ridge cemetery in Van Wert County, Ohio. They had the following children:

Jerimyah[1.1.1.5.5.1.1.1c], b. on Mar. 1, 1826, and baptized at Good Hope Lutheran Church on July 8, 1827. He m. Cynthia Ann, daughter of William and Catharine (Harp) Frysinger, in Van Wert County, Ohio, on Dec. 8, 1853, and Sarah Ann (Shaffer) Putman in Mercer County on Apr. 10, 1862. Cynthia was b. in 1831, d. in Dublin Township in 1859, and is buried in the Old Frysinger cemetery. Jeremiah enlisted on Sep. 7, 1864, and was killed in the Civil War in Chatham County, Savannah, Georgia, on Jan. 30, 1865. He is buried in Laurel Grove cemetery in Georgia.

Mary[1.1.1.5.5.1.1.2c], b. on May 14, 1827, baptized at Good Hope Lutheran Church, and m. Hugh Dobson in Mercer County on Sep. 7, 1848. She d. in Dublin Township on Jan. 4, 1850, and is buried in Ridge cemetery.

Josias[1.1.1.5.5.1.1.3c], b. on Mar. 5, 1830, baptized at Good Hope on July 31, 1830, and sponsored by his mother. He m. Mary Ann, daughter of Abraham and Martha Miller, in Mercer County on Nov. 10, 1854, and Mary Jane, daughter of William and Lydia (Baltzell) Dilbone, about 1889/90. Mary Ann was b. in Ohio in 1836, and d. of Typhoid in Dublin Township on Oct. 31, 1889. Mary Jane was the widow of Jefferson Everett. She was b. Miami County, Ohio, in Aug. 1837, and was alive in 1900. Josiah d. in Dublin Township on Aug. 13, 1909. They are buried in Mount Olive cemetery.

Hanna[1.1.1.5.5.1.1.4c], b. on July 10, 1831, baptized at Good Hope on Aug. 27, 1831, and sponsored by her parents. She d. before 1836.

Lucinda[1.1.1.5.5.1.1.5c], b. on Feb. 8, 1833, and m. Seth Temple in Van Wert County, Ohio, on Dec. 2, 1852. He was b. in 1824, and d. in Van Wert County, Liberty Township, Ohio, on Aug. 15, 1863. Lucinda d. in Liberty Township on Sep. 20, 1861, and is buried beside her husband in Ridge cemetery.

Samuel[1.1.1.5.5.1.1.6c], b. on Mar. 17, 1834, and brought a load of horses for his father, by way of rail to Viroqua, Wisconsin, in 1851. He sold all but two teams, which he traded for land in Vernon County, Bad Ax, Wisconsin. He m. Mary O'Leary in Vernon County, Bad Ax, Wisconsin, in Sep. 1856. Samuel sold the land in Bad Ax, and purchased land on North Clayton, where he raised his family. Later he turned the farm over to his son, John, and moved to Readstown, Wisconsin. After a short stay, they returned to North Clayton. He d. in Vernon County, North Clayton, Wisconsin, on Apr. 21, 1918.

Hannah$^{1.1.1.5.5.1.1.7c}$, b. on Mar. 10, 1836, and d. in Mercer/Van Wert County, Ohio, on Sep. 21, 1899. She m. Lafayette Frazier in Mercer County on Apr. 5, 1849. He was b. in 1818, and d. in 1899.

Catherine$^{1.1.1.5.5.1.1.8c}$, b. on Mar. 10, 1836, and m. Alfred Frysinger in Mercer County on Sep. 5, 1857. He was b. in Ohio in 1834. Catherine d. in Mercer County, Dublin Township, in 1907.

John$^{1.1.1.5.5.1.1.9c}$, b. on Feb. 8, 1837, and m. Susan, daughter of George and Katherine A. (Stophlet) Roebuck, in Mercer County on Jan. 1, 1860, and Louisa, daughter of William and Lydia (Baltzell) Dilbone, in Mercer County on Dec. 23, 1866. Susan d. in Dublin Township on Aug. 9, 1863, and is buried in Roebuck cemetery. Louisa d. in Dublin Township in 1913. John d. in Dublin Township on Nov. 27, 1897. John and Louisa are buried in Mt. Olive cemetery. John had a 40 acre farm on the Louis Godfrey Reserve in Dublin Township.

William S.$^{1.1.1.5.5.1.1.10c}$, b. on Mar. 15, 1840, and m. Martha Shindeldecker in Mercer County on Aug. 18, 1861. She was b. on Oct. 22, 1838, and d. in Mercer County, Dublin Township, Ohio, on Mar. 24, 1925. He d. in Van Wert County, Ohio City, Ohio, on Feb. 22, 1913. He is buried in Woodlawn cemetery.

Franklin$^{1.1.1.5.5.1.1.11c}$, b. in 1843, and m. Jane Miller in Mercer County on Mar. 12, 1863. In the 1880s, they resided in Hamilton County, Cincinnati, Ohio, and Clermont County, Goshen, Ohio.

Nancy Jane$^{1.1.1.5.5.1.1.12c}$, b. on May 12, 1848, and m. Abraham Hooks in Mercer County on Feb. 29, 1872. He was b. in Dublin Township on Dec. 28, 1851, and d. in Allen County, Lima, Ohio, on Feb. 8, 1913. She d. in Lima on Jan. 8, 1901.

Phoebe$^{1.1.1.5.5.1.1.13c}$, b. on Mar. 15, 1849, and d. on Jan. 27, 1853. She is buried in Ridge cemetery.

Anna Maria Dull

Anna Maria$^{1.1.1.5.5.1.2c}$ m. Heinrich, son of Samuel and Elisabeth Barbara (Robinson) Schlater in Fayette County, Pennsylvania, in 1821. Henry was b. in Fayette County, Salt Lick Township, Pennsylvania, on Mar. 14, 1803, baptized at Good Hope Lutheran Church on May 15, 1803, and sponsored by his parents. He d. in Tuscarwas County, Wayne Township, Ohio, in 1847. Anna Maria

d. in Davies County, Indiana, in 1882. In 1850, Anna Maria resided in Tuscarwas County, Ohio. They had the following children:

Samuel[1.1.1.5.5.1.2.1c], b. on Jan. 3, 1825, and baptized at Good Hope Lutheran Church.

Catharina[1.1.1.5.5.1.2.2c], b. on Dec. 9, 1826, baptized at Good Hope on July 8, 1827, and m. Crawford Arford in Tuscarwas County, Ohio, on Mar. 3, 1850.

Hanna[1.1.1.5.5.1.2.3c], b. on Nov. 21, 1828, baptized at Good Hope on July 5, 1829, and sponsored by Johannes and Hanna Dull.

Phebe Ann[1.1.1.5.5.1.2.4c], b. in 1835, and m. James M. Smith in Mercer County, Ohio, on Aug. 16, 1855.

Joseph Dull

Joseph[1.1.1.5.5.1.3c] m. Elizabeth Isabell, daughter of Frederick and Christina (Wolfe) Dumbauld, in Fayette County, Pennsylvania, on Mar. 29, 1827. She was b. in Fayette County, Pennsylvania, on Oct. 30, 1807, and d. in Licking County, Ohio, on Mar. 21, 1881. Joseph d. in Licking County, Liberty Township, Ohio, on Oct. 17, 1891. They had the following children:

Phebe[1.1.1.5.5.1.3.1c], b. in Fayette County, Salt Lick Township, Pennsylvania, on Jan. 7, 1829, and m. Elisha T. P. Brooks.

Christina[1.1.1.5.5.1.3.2c], b. in Fayette County, Salt Lick Township, Pennsylvania, on June 3, 1831, baptized at Good Hope Lutheran Church on Aug. 27, 1831, and sponsored by Frederich and Susanna Dumbauld. She m. Joseph Perkins Brooks. He was b. in Licking County, Ohio, on May 29, 1831, and resided in Erie County, Sandusky, Ohio, in 1917.

Johannah[1.1.1.5.5.1.3.3c], b. in Stark County, Sugar Creek Township, Ohio, on Aug. 1, 1833, and m. Jackson Stephens in Licking County, Ohio, on July 17, 1853. Joannah d. on Mar. 22, 1898.

Uriah[1.1.1.5.5.1.3.4c], b. in Stark County, Sugar Creek Township, Ohio, on Nov. 15, 1835, and m. Oelands/Lindy Ramsey. Uriah d. on Aug. 31, 1909.

Nancy[1.1.1.5.5.1.3.5c], b. in Ohio on June 17, 1838, and m. Jared Anderson.

John[1.1.1.5.5.1.3.6c], b. in Ohio on Mar. 23, 1841, and m. Mary Tippett.

Elias[1.1.1.5.5.1.3.7c], b. in Ohio on Oct. 10, 1843, and m. Caroline Wright. She was b. in 1851.

Charlotte[1.1.1.5.5.1.1.3.8c], b. in Ohio on June 15, 1848, and m. Allen Stanbach/Stanbaugh on June 23, 1875. She d. in Stark County, Sugar Creek Township, Ohio.

Lucenia Jane[1.1.1.5.5.1.1.3.9c], b. in Ohio on June 15, 1848, and d. in Ohio on Aug. 18, 1856.

Phillipena Dull

Phillipena "Phebe"[1.1.1.5.5.1.4c] m. Johannes, son of Samuel and Elisabeth Barbara (Robinson) Schlater, in Fayette County, Pennsylvania, about 1824. He was b. in Fayette County, Salt Lick Township, Pennsylvania, on Feb. 13, 1800, baptized at Good Hope Lutheran Church on Mar. 30, 1800, and sponsored by John Robinson and wife. They moved to Stark County, Ohio, before 1831, and Van Wert County, Ohio, about 1836. John d. in Van Wert County, Liberty Township, Ohio, on Sep. 22, 1845, and Phebe d. there on Aug. 11, 1887. They had the following children:

Joseph[1.1.1.5.5.1.4.1c], b. in 1825, and m. Maria. They resided in Van Wert County, Liberty Township, Ohio, in 1850. He was Mayor of Van Wert from 1862 to 1866, and managed the America House Tavern.

Mary A.[1.1.1.5.5.1.4.2c], b. in 1826.

Nancy[1.1.1.5.5.1.4.3c], b. about 1828, and m. O. W. Rose in Van Wert County, Ohio, on Jan. 8, 1849.

Sarah[1.1.1.5.5.1.4.4c], b. on Nov. 26, 1829, and m. Abraham Balyeat in Van Wert County, Ohio, on May 13, 1852. He was b. in 1823, and d. in 1881. Sarah d. in Van Wert County, Pleasant Township, Ohio, on Jan. 19, 1894.

Polly[1.1.1.5.5.1.4.5c], b. on Dec. 16, 18(30), and d. in Stark County, Sugar Creek Township, Ohio, on Mar. 17, 18(33). She is buried in Weimer cemetery.

Catherine[1.1.1.5.5.1.4.6c], b. in 1830, and m. R. Conn.

Hannah[1.1.1.5.5.1.4.7c], b. in 1833, and m. Z. A. Smith. They resided in Kansas.

Judith[1.1.1.5.5.1.4.8c], b. in 1835, and m. Robert Bruce Encill. They resided in Kosciusko County, Warsaw, Indiana.

Benjamin F.[1.1.1.5.5.1.4.9c], b. on July 5, 1837, and m. Delilah Fortney in Van Wert County, Ohio, on Apr. 21, 1861. She was b. in 1843, and d. in 1883.

Elizabeth[1.1.1.5.5.1.4.10c], b. on Feb. 7, 1840, and m. George F. Edson in Van Wert County, Ohio, on Mar. 29, 1857.

Jane$^{1.1.1.5.5.1.4.11c}$, b. in 1841, and m. William Henry McGough.

Samuel$^{1.1.1.5.5.1.4.12c}$, b. in 1844.

John$^{1.1.1.5.5.1.4.13c}$, b. in 1846.

John Dull

John$^{1.1.1.5.5.1.1.5c}$ m. Mary Jane Harbaugh in 1829 (?). She was b. in Pennsylvania on Feb. 17, 1813, and d. in Van Wert County, Wilshire Township, Ohio, on Nov. 20, 1882. John d. in Wilshire Township on Aug. 28, 1849. They had the following children:

Elisabeth Anna$^{1.1.1.5.5.1.1.5.1c}$, b. on Oct. 27, 1827, baptized at Good Hope Lutheran Church on June 6, 1828, and sponsored by her parents.

Lydia$^{1.1.1.5.5.1.1.5.2c}$, b. in Fayette County, Salt Lick Township, Pennsylvania, in 1830, and d. in 1915. She m. Samuel Krick.

Franklin Benjamin$^{1.1.1.5.5.1.1.5.3c}$, b. in Stark County, Sugar Creek Township, Ohio, in 1832, and m. Rebecca Jane Walters in Van Wert County on Dec. 21, 1854. She was b. on Jan. 31, 1837, and d. in Wilshire Township on Sep. 30, 1894. Franklin d. in Wilshire Township in 1910.

Sarah$^{1.1.1.5.5.1.1.5.4c}$, b. in Stark County, Sugar Creek Township, Ohio, in 1834, and m. John Smith.

Joseph$^{1.1.1.5.5.1.1.5.5c}$, b. in Stark County, Sugar Creek Township, Ohio, in 1836.

George A.$^{1.1.1.5.5.1.1.5.6c}$, b. in Van Wert County, Wilshire Township, Ohio, on Sep. 27, 1841, and d. on Sep. 3, 1849.

John$^{1.1.1.5.5.1.1.5.7c}$, b. in Wilshire Township about 1843.

Louisa Jane$^{1.1.1.5.5.1.1.5.8c}$, b. in Wilshire Township in 1845, and d. in 1923. She m. Conrad Ault.

Mary J.$^{1.1.1.5.5.1.1.5.9c}$, b. in Wilshire Township on Aug. 23, 1849, and d. on Mar. 23, 1851.

Lenhart Dull

Lenhart$^{1.1.1.5.5.1.1.9c}$ m. Susannah Ream in Van Wert County, on Feb. 17, 1842. She was b. on May 10, 1824, and d. in Tuscarwas County, New Philadelphia, Ohio, on Nov. 10, 1924. After Lenhart's death, Susannah m. his brother, Elias (between 1900 and 1906). Lenhart d. in Van Wert County, Wilshire Township, Ohio, on May 8, 1892. They had the following children in Wilshire Township:

Celesta$^{1.1.1.5.5.1.1.9.1c}$, b. on Dec. 2, 1844, and m. Edward W. Robinson. Celesta d. in 1937.

James Monroe$^{1.1.1.5.5.1.1.9.2c}$, b. on Jan. 23, 1846, and m. Martha Ann Lintermoot in Van Wert County on May 17, 1868. She was b. in 1851, and d. in 1916. Monroe d. in Van Wert County on June 6, 1916.

Thomas Jefferson$^{1.1.1.5.5.1.1.9.3c}$, b. Apr. 7, 1848, and m. Mary Ursula Exline. She was b. in 1848, and d. in 1918.

George Washington$^{1.1.1.5.5.1.1.9.4c}$, b. on June 2, 1850, and d. in 1892. He m. Evaline Pickering in Mercer County on Mar. 7, 1875.

Franklin Pierce$^{1.1.1.5.5.1.1.9.5c}$, b. on Jan. 31, 1855, and m. Hattie E. Martin in Van Wert County on Jan. 6, 1881. She was b. in 1862.

James Buchanan$^{1.1.1.5.5.1.1.9.6c}$, b. on July 11, 1857, and m. Serena Lintermoot. She was b. in Ohio in Nov. 1863. James d. in Mercer County, Black Creek Township, Ohio, in 1945.

Lafayette Jackson$^{1.1.1.5.5.1.1.9.7c}$, b. on Apr. 15, 1861, and d. in 1945. He m. Cora McKillip in Mercer County on Aug. 8, 1883, and Thursa Randels.

Joseph Elmore$^{1.1.1.5.5.1.1.9.8c}$, b. on Aug. 8, 1863, and m. Augusta Krumboltz and Frances Krumboltz.

Isabella$^{1.1.1.5.5.1.1.9.9c}$, b. on Aug. 20, 1865, and m. Victor Miller.

Arabella$^{1.1.1.5.5.1.1.9.10c}$, b. on Sep. 5, 1866, and m. Frank Cushwa/Cushman.

Mary C.$^{1.1.1.5.5.1.1.9.11c}$, b. on Mar. 5, 1871, and m. Frank Estell.

Jacob Dull

Jacob$^{1.1.1.5.5.1.1.10c}$ m. Harriet Ream in Van Wert County on Nov. 18, 1846. She was b. in Ohio on July 1, 1828, and d. in Van Wert County, Wilshire Township, Ohio, on Apr. 12, 1914. Jacob d. in Wilshire Township on Aug. 15, 1904. They had the following children in Wilshire Township:

Sylvester$^{1.1.1.5.5.1.1.10.1c}$, bon in June 1846, and m. Rebecca Exline.

Amos$^{1.1.1.5.5.1.1.10.2c}$, b. in Mar. 1851, and m. Emily E. Stewart in Van Wert County on Mar. 8, 1873. She was b. in 1845.

Mariah Isabell$^{1.1.1.5.5.1.1.10.3c}$, b. in 1855.

Samuel$^{1.1.1.5.5.1.1.10.4c}$, b. in Jan. 1858, and m. Martha J.. She was b. in 1856.

Franklin Monroe$^{1.1.1.5.5.1.1.10.5c}$, b. on Apr. 3, 1860, and d. on Dec. 15, 1860.

Margaret S.$^{1.1.1.5.5.1.1.10.6c}$, b. in 1861.
Uriah$^{1.1.1.5.5.1.1.10.7c}$, b. in 1875.
Jacob A.$^{1.1.1.5.5.1.1.10.8c}$, b. in 1878.

Johannah Dull

Johannah$^{1.1.1.5.5.1.1.11c}$ m. William Agler in Van Wert
County on Mar. 21, 1847. He was b. in Stark County, Sugar Creek
Township, Ohio, in 1824, and d. in Van Wert County in 1904. Johannah
d. in Van Wert County in 1894. They had the following children in Van
Wert County:

Mahala$^{1.1.1.5.5.1.1.11.1c}$, b. in 1848, and d. 1851.

Emily Clara$^{1.1.1.5.5.1.1.11.2c}$, b. on Jan. 6, 1850, and m. John
William Lewellen in Van Wert County on Jan. 2, 1870. He was b. in
1844, and d. in 1929. Emily d. in Montgomery County, Lewiston,
Michigan, on Jan. 5, 1933.

Valentine$^{1.1.1.5.5.1.1.11.3c}$, b. in 1852, and m. Mary Elizabeth
Knight. She was b. in 1857, and d. in 1898. Valentine d. 1898.

Joseph R.$^{1.1.1.5.5.1.1.11.4c}$, b. in 1854.

Naomi$^{1.1.1.5.5.1.1.11.5c}$, b. in 1856, and m. Jacob Kraugh. He
was b. in 1857, and d. in 1929. She d. in 1930.

Celestia$^{1.1.1.5.5.1.1.11.6c}$, b. in 1859, and d. in 1876.

William$^{1.1.1.5.5.1.1.11.7c}$, b. in Jan. 1862.

Willis McKey$^{1.1.1.5.5.1.1.11.8}$, b. in Jan. 1862, and m. Mary
Sabina, daughter of Joshua and Elmira (Medaugh) Wagers, on July 4,
1888. She was b. in 1864, and d. in 1954. He d. in 1953.

Elias Dull

Elias$^{1.1.1.5.5.1.1.12c}$ m. Jane Walters in Van Wert County on
Sep. 3, 1850 and Susannah Ream, widow of his brother, Lenhart,
between 1900 and 1907. Jane was b. on Aug. 31, 1823, and d. in
Wilshire Township on Apr. 25, 1900. Elias d. there on Sep. 3, 1907.
They had the following children in Wilshire Township:

Harriet Ellen$^{1.1.1.5.5.1.1.12.1c}$, b. on July 1, 1853, and m.
John Lorenzo Hileman in Van Wert County on May 5, 1870. He was b.
in 1848, and d. in 1918.

Hannah Lucretia$^{1.1.1.5.5.1.1.12.2c}$, b. on Sep. 4, 1854, and m.
William Sylvania, son of Ephraim and Jane (Schlater) Medaugh, in Van
Wert County, Ohio, on Aug. 7, 1873. She d. in Paulding County,
Paulding, Ohio, on Sep. 11, 1882. William d. in Wilshire Township on
June 6, 1882.

John Wesley[1.1.1.5.5.1.1.12.3c], b. on Mar. 6, 1855, and m.
Mary Armand Bay in Van Wert County on Dec. 2, 1875. She was b. in
1855. He d. in Wilshire Township in 1929.
William Walters[1.1.1.5.5.1.1.12.4c], b. on Mar. 4, 1857, and m.
Mary E. Shaffer. He d. in Wilshire Township on Nov. 19, 1909.
Rebecca Jane[1.1.1.5.5.1.1.12.5c], b. on Feb. 4, 1860, and m.
Charley Blish in Van Wert County in 1882.
Mary Rosetta[1.1.1.5.5.1.1.12.6c], b. on Nov. 11, 1865, and m.
Wirt A. Belden. Mary d. in Wilshire Township on July 9, 1890.

Catherine Dull

Catherine[1.1.1.5.5.1.1.13c] m. Peter Brubaker in Van Wert
County on Nov. 26, 1844. He was b. in Franklin County, Pennsylvania,
on May 19, 1814, and d. in Van Wert County, Liberty Township, Ohio,
on July 12, 1898. Catherine d. there on July 28, 1909. They had the
following children in Liberty Township:
George E.[1.1.1.5.5.1.1.13.1c], b. in 1846.
Elizabeth[1.1.1.5.5.1.1.13.2c], b. in 1847.
Naaman[1.1.1.5.5.1.1.13.3c], b. on Dec. 12, 1849, and m. Ellen
Lintermoot. She was b. in 1856.
Elmira[1.1.1.5.5.1.1.13.4c], b. on Nov. 18, 1851, and d. on Sep. 2,
1853.
Eleanor[1.1.1.5.5.1.1.13.5c], b. in 1854.
Willis[1.1.1.5.5.1.1.13.6c], b. in 1857.
Annete[1.1.1.5.5.1.1.13.7c], b. in 1859, and m. ____ Smith.
Mary D.[1.1.1.5.5.1.1.13.8c], b. in July 1861, and m. Solomon,
son of Isaac and Sophia (Mihm) Putman, in Van Wert County, Ohio, in
1880.
Hannah D.[1.1.1.5.5.1.1.13.9c], b. in 1864.
William[1.1.1.5.5.1.1.13.10c], b. in 1866.

Catherine Dull

Catherine[1.1.1.5.5.2c] m. John H. Pile. He was b. in
Washington County, Hagerstown, Maryland, on Aug. 17, 1775, and d.
in Somerset County, Milford Township, Pennsylvania, in 1845.
Catherine d. in Milford Township on Oct. 23, 1860. They had the
following children in Milford Township:
George[1.1.1.5.5.2.1c], b. on Feb. 10, 1797.
John[1.1.1.5.5.2.2c], b. about 1799, and m. Salome/Margaret
Knable.

Joseph$^{1.1.1.5.5.2.3c}$, b. on Apr. 4, 1804, and d. in Milford Township on Feb. 24, 1877. He m. Mary Barkman. She was b. in 1804, and d. in 1870.

Jonathan$^{1.1.1.5.5.2.4c}$, b. on Aug. 2, 1805, and d. in Somerset County, Sculton, Pennsylvania, on Sep. 7, 1889. He m. Catherine. She was b. in 1820, and d. in 1896.

Henry$^{1.1.1.5.5.2.5c}$, b. about 1807.

Jacob$^{1.1.1.5.5.2.6c}$, b. about 1809.

Samuel$^{1.1.1.5.5.2.7c}$, b. on Sep. 23, 1811.

Peter$^{1.1.1.5.5.2.8c}$, b. about 1812, and d. sometime before 1845.

David$^{1.1.1.5.5.2.9c}$, b. about 1815, and d. sometime before 1845.

Elias$^{1.1.1.5.5.2.10c}$, b. on June 29, 1816, and m. Mary. She was b. in 1816, and they resided in Somerset County, Jefferson Township, Pennsylvania.

Elizabeth$^{1.1.1.5.5.2.11c}$, b. on Jan. 25, 1818.

Daniel Barnetta$^{1.1.1.5.5.2.12c}$, b. on Jan. 11, 1819, and d. in Milford Township on Apr. 18, 1879. He m. Sarah Bearl. She was b. in 1818, and d. in 1888.

Absalom$^{1.1.1.5.5.2.13c}$, b. on Feb. 6, 1822, and m. Delilah. She was b. in 1833.

George Pile

George$^{1.1.1.5.5.2.1c}$ m. Salome, daughter of Andreas and Anna Elisabetha (Lenhart) Putman. She d. in Milford Township on Oct. 1, 1891, and George d. there on Mar. 15, 1894. They had the following children in Milford Township:

Rosanna$^{1.1.1.5.5.2.1.1c}$, b. in 1821, and d. in 1916. She m. William Moore and John L. Gardner. William was b. in 1811, and d. in 1852. John was b. in 1830.

Andrew$^{1.1.1.5.5.2.1.2c}$, b. about 1823.

Josiah$^{1.1.1.5.5.2.1.3c}$, b. in 1825, and d. in 1868. He m. Margaret Kooser. She was b. in 1828, and d. in 1911.

Mary$^{1.1.1.5.5.2.1.4c}$, b. about 1827, and m. Franklin King.

Jeremiah$^{1.1.1.5.5.2.1.5c}$, b. in 1829, and d. in 1926. He m. Susan Stough and Ida Lowry. Susan was b. in 1836, and d. in 1882.

Solomon$^{1.1.1.5.5.2.1.6c}$, b. in 1831, and d. in 1917. He m. Sarah King. She was b. in 1837, and d. in 1908.

Samuel Pile

Samuel[1.1.1.5.5.2.7c] m. Elizabeth Cable, daughter of Peter and Sarah (Cable) Dumbauld. She d. in Licking County, Bennington Township, Ohio, on Sep. 7, 1885, and Samuel d. there on May 25, 1882. They had the following children in Fayette County, Salt Lick Township, Pennsylvania:

Sarah E.[1.1.1.5.5.2.7.1c], b. on Oct. 28, 1833, baptized at Good Hope Lutheran Church on June 11, 1837, and sponsored by Petrus Dumbauld. She m. Henry S. Beider on Aug. 8, 1855. He was b. in Fayette County, Pennsylvania, on July 11, 1832, and d. in Licking County, Jonestown, Ohio, in 1915. Sarah d. there in 1902.

Ananias[1.1.1.5.5.2.7.2c], b. and d. in 1834.

Clarissa Clara[1.1.1.5.5.2.7.3c], b. on Jan. 11, 1836, and m. Henry Jackson Crotinger. He was b. in Licking County, Burlington Township, Ohio, in 1835, and d. there in 1857. Clarissa d. at Jonestown, Ohio, on June 26, 1911.

Catherine Ann[1.1.1.5.5.2.7.4c], b. on July 25, 1838, and m. William Henry Barrick. He was b. in Licking County, Burlington Township, Ohio, and d. in Bennington Township on Jan. 30, 1920. Catherine d. in Bennington Township on Apr. 13, 1874.

Austin[1.1.1.5.5.2.7.5c], b. on Aug. 24, 1840, and d. in Licking County, Bennington Township, Ohio, on Nov. 11, 1906. He m. Kate Hurd in 1876. She was b. in June 1855, and d. in Bennington Township in 1923.

Amanda[1.1.1.5.5.2.7.6c], b. on June 30, 1842, and m. Joseph Runnels in Licking County, Ohio, in 1864. He was b. in Ohio on Dec. 11, 1837, and d. in Licking County, Liberty Township, Ohio, on Dec. 5, 1917. Amanda d. in Liberty Township on Mar. 10, 1904.

Peter Dull

Peter[1.1.1.5.5.3c] m. Eva K. Knable in Somerset County, Pennsylvania, in 1804. She was b. on Mar. 31, 1790, and d. in Somerset County, Milford Township, Pennsylvania, on Sep. 19, 1861. Peter d. in Milford Township on Dec. 15, 1854. They had the following children in Milford Township:

John[1.1.1.5.5.3.1c], b. on Oct. 17, 1805.

George[1.1.1.5.5.3.2c], b. on Jan. 30, 1808.

Elizabeth[1.1.1.5.5.3.3c], b. on May 26, 1810.

Jacob[1.1.1.5.5.3.4c], b. on Dec. 3, 1812, and m. Catherine McCormick. She was b. in 1822.

Mary[1.1.1.5.5.3.5c], b. about 1814, and m. ____ Brant.

Peter[1.1.1.5.5.3.6c], b. on Sep. 23, 1816.

Anthony[1.1.1.5.5.3.7c], b. on Nov. 26, 1818, and d. in 1895. He m. Polly. She was b. in 1811, and d. in 1881.

Daniel[1.1.1.5.5.3.8c], b. on Apr. 19, 1822, and d. on Oct. 21, 1870. He m. Margaret King. She was b. in 1827, and d. in 1870.

Sarah Salome[1.1.1.5.5.3.9c], b. on Mar. 28, 1825, and d. on Sep. 18, 1883. She m. George Brant. He was b. in 1825, and d. in 1913.

Christina[1.1.1.5.5.3.10c], b. on Nov. 20, 1827, and m. Daniel Ressler and Jacob Brooks.

Catherine[1.1.1.5.5.3.11c], b. in Mar. 1828.

Samuel H.[1.1.1.5.5.3.12c], b. on Nov. 13, 1831, and d. on July 28, 1878. He m. Cassandra Walter in Somerset County on Dec. 9, 1852. She was b. in 1830, and d. in 1878.

John Dull

John[1.1.1.5.5.3.1c] m. Mary K. Hartzell in Somerset County on May 18, 1826. She was b. in 1806, and d. in 1841. They had the following children:

George Alexander[1.1.1.5.5.3.1.1c], b. in 1827.

Hiram[1.1.1.5.5.3.1.2c], b. in 1828.

Elizabeth Catherine[1.1.1.5.5.3.1.3c], b. in 1830.

Simon Peter[1.1.1.5.5.3.1.4c], b. in 1832.

Mary[1.1.1.5.5.3.1.5c], b. in 1833, and d. in 1920. She m. Singleton Kimmel. He was b. in 1827, and d. in 1906.

George Dull

George[1.1.1.5.5.3.2c] m. Catherine Walter. She was b. in 1805, and d. in 1865. George d. in 1880. They had the following children:

Daniel W.[1.1.1.5.5.3.2.1c], b. in 1829, and m. Rebecca, daughter of George and Eva (Putman) Barron. She was b. in 1827, and d. 1893. Daniel d. in 1891.

Uriah[1.1.1.5.5.3.2.2c], b. in 1831, and m. Margaret Kooser.

Julia[1.1.1.5.5.3.2.3c], b. in 1833, and d. in 1894. She m. David L. Colbern. He was b. in 1827, and d. in 1868.

Jacob[1.1.1.5.5.3.2.4c], b. in 1835, and d. in 1902.

Harriet[1.1.1.5.5.3.2.5c], b. in 1837.

Romanus[1.1.1.5.5.3.2.6c], b. in 1839, and d. in 1865.

William[1.1.1.5.5.3.2.7c], b. in 1841, and m. Louise Sipe.

Rebecca[1.1.1.5.5.3.2.8c], b. in 1843, and m. Solomon Davis.

John[1.1.1.5.5.3.2.9c], b. in 1846, and d. in 1917. He m. Jane Bailey.

Mary$^{1.1.1.5.5.3.2.10c}$, b. in 1848, and d. in 1891. She m. Hiram
C. Sipe.
Lucinda$^{1.1.1.5.5.3.2.11c}$, b. in 1850, and m. Alexander Brooks.

Elizabeth Dull

Elizabeth$^{1.1.1.5.5.3.3c}$ m. Jonathan, son of Daniel Sechler, and
d. on May 14, 1883. He was b. in Milford Township in 1800, and d.
there in 1869 (70). They had the following children:

Harriet$^{1.1.1.5.5.3.3.1c}$, m. John Mason.

Daniel$^{1.1.1.5.5.3.3.2c}$.

Juliana$^{1.1.1.5.5.3.3.3c}$, m. Joseph Siebert.

Barbara$^{1.1.1.5.5.3.3.4c}$, b. on June 20, 1837, m. George F., son
of Samuel K. and Mary (Flich) Kimmel, on Apr. 12, 1861. He was b. in
Somerset County, Milford Township, on Dec. 30, 1837.

George$^{1.1.1.5.5.3.3.5c}$, m. Minerva Boucher and Catherine
(Knogey) Reese. George served in the Civil War. Minerva d. on May
23, 1891.

Elizabeth$^{1.1.1.5.5.3.3.6c}$ m. Samuel Kuhlman and Herman
Kreager.

Joseph$^{1.1.1.5.5.3.3.7c}$.

Peter Dull

Peter$^{1.1.1.5.5.3.6c}$ m. Catherine Weller. She was b. in 1823,
and d. in 1907. Peter d. on Mar. 31, 1885. They had the following
children:

Martha$^{1.1.1.5.5.3.6.1c}$, m. ____ Critchfield;
Samantha$^{1.1.1.5.5.3.6.2c}$, m. ____ Fritz; Susan$^{1.1.1.5.5.3.6.3c}$, d. in
1884; Minerva$^{1.1.1.5.5.3.6.4c}$, m. ____ Reid; Albertha$^{1.1.1.5.5.3.6.5c}$;
Elmira$^{1.1.1.5.5.3.6.6c}$; R. H.$^{1.1.1.5.5.3.6.7c}$; I. P.$^{1.1.1.5.5.3.6.8c}$; John
W.$^{1.1.1.5.5.3.6.9c}$, d. in 1884; William L.$^{1.1.1.5.5.3.6.10c}$.

Elisabeth Dull

Elisabeth$^{1.1.1.5.5.4c}$ m. Jacob Sipe. Elisabeth d. in Somerset
County, Pennsylvania, in 1824. They had the following children in
Somerset County:

Christina$^{1.1.1.5.5.4.1c}$, b. in Aug. 1815.

Joseph$^{1.1.1.5.5.4.2c}$, b. on Mar. 9, 1816.

Michael$^{1.1.1.5.5.4.3c}$, b. on May 11, 1818.

Jacob$^{1.1.1.5.5.4.4c}$, b. on Aug. 21, 1820, and d. at New
Centerville, Pennsylvania, in 1887. He m. Sarah Chorpenning.

Sarah$^{1.1.1.5.5.4.5c}$, b. about 1822.

Christina Sipe

Christina[1.1.1.5.5.4.1c] m. Jonas Shultz. He was b. in 1815, and d. in 1883. Christina d. in Somerset County on Aug. 16, 1905. They had the following children:

Sarah[1.1.1.5.5.4.1.1c], b. in 1837, and m. Daniel Barklay. He was b. in 1837, and d. in 1907. Sarah d. in 1927.

Mary Anne[1.1.1.5.5.4.1.2c], b. in 1838, and d. in 1851.

Joseph Sipe

Joseph[1.1.1.5.5.4.2c] m. Mary Friedline in Somerset County on Sep. 9, 1836. She was b. in 1818. They had the following daughters:

Joanna[1.1.1.5.5.4.2.1c], b. in 1844.

Elizabeth[1.1.1.5.5.4.2.2c].

Frederick Dull

Frederick[1.1.1.5.5.7c] resided in Somerset County, Upper Turkeyfoot Township, Pennsylvania. He had the following sons:

Jacob[1.1.1.5.5.7.1c], b. in Somerset County, Pennsylvania, in 1804, and d. in Preston County, West Virginia, in 1881.

Abraham[1.1.1.5.5.7.2c], b. in Somerset County, Pennsylvania, and d. in Preston County, West Virginia.

Magdalena Dull

Magdalena[1.1.1.5.5.8c] m. Christian Speicher, and had the following children in Somerset County, Pennsylvania:

Sarah[1.1.1.5.5.8.1c], b. on Oct. 24, 1814, and d. on Feb. 28, 1831.

John[1.1.1.5.5.8.2c], b. on Dec. 6, 1816.

Joseph[1.1.1.5.5.8.3c], b. on May 18, 1817.

Samuel[1.1.1.5.5.8.4c], b. on Feb. 11, 1823.

Francis[1.1.1.5.5.8.5c], b. on Sep. 12, 1825.

Aaron[1.1.1.5.5.8.6c], b. on May 7, 1827.

Peter[1.1.1.5.5.8.7c], b. on Apr. 5, 1829.

Mary Ann[1.1.1.5.5.8.8c], b. on Mar. 5, 1831, and d. on June 28, 1836.

Christian[1.1.1.5.5.8.9c], b. on Mar. 25, 1833, and d. on Apr. 13, 1834.

George Dull

George[1.1.1.5.5.10c] m. Christina, daughter of Frederick G. and Catherine (Patton) Younkin. She was b. in Milford Township on Aug.

15, 1795, baptized at Sanner Lutheran Church on Feb. 23, 1797, and d. in Milford Township on July 9, 1881. George d. in Milford Township on Mar. 27, 1852. They are buried in New Centerville cemetery. They had the following children in Milford Township:

Sabina[1.1.1.5.5.10.1c], b. about 1814, and d. in 1896.

Elizabeth[1.1.1.5.5.10.2c], b. on Apr. 9, 1815, and m. Jonathan Cable Dumbauld.

Catherine[1.1.1.5.5.10.3c], b. on Oct. 6, 1817, and d. in Milford Township on Oct. 5, 1843.

Frederick[1.1.1.5.5.10.4c], b. on Jan. 29, 1819.

Mary Ann[1.1.1.5.5.10.5c], b. about 1820.

Lucinda[1.1.1.5.5.10.6c], b. about 1820, and m. Jacob Howenstein.

John Rhees[1.1.1.5.5.10.7c], b. on Feb. 1, 1821, and d. in Black Hawk County, Waterloo, Iowa. He m. Caroline Howenstein on Sep. 16, 1841.

Gertrude Junta[1.1.1.5.5.10.8c], b. on Mar. 11, 1823.

William[1.1.1.5.5.10.9c], b. on May 20, 1825, and d. in Milford Township on Jan. 8, 1908. He m. Margaret Flick. She was b. in 1830.

Sarah Ann[1.1.1.5.5.10.10c], b. on Oct. 11, 1827, and m. Samuel Saylor.

Marion[1.1.1.5.5.10.11c], b. on June 3, 1830.

Juliana Christine[1.1.1.5.5.10.12c], b. on Sep. 8, 1833, and d. on Sep. 5, 1889. She m. Jesse Sweitzer.

Josiah[1.1.1.5.5.10.13c], b. on Dec. 22, 1835.

Harriet[1.1.1.5.5.10.14c], b. on Aug. 18, 1837.

Frederick Dull

Frederick[1.1.1.5.5.10.4c] d. in Somerset County, Ursina, Pennsylvania, on May 10, 1896. He m. Margaret Fadley in Somerset County on Sep. 6, 1840. She was b. on Oct. 13, 1822, and d. in Lower Turkeyfoot Township on Feb. 27, 1899. They had the following children in Lower Turkeyfoot Township, Ursina:

Sarah[1.1.1.5.5.10.4.1c], b. in 1841, and m. Jacob J. Rush on June 12, 1859.

Freeman[1.1.1.5.5.10.4.2c], b. about 1843.

Christina[1.1.1.5.5.10.4.3c], b. on Apr. 28, 1845, and m. Samuel Baley.

Barbary[1.1.1.5.5.10.4.4c], b. on Apr. 28, 1845, and d. before 1852.

John[1.1.1.5.5.10.4.5c], b. in 1847.

Barbara Ellen[1.1.1.5.5.10.4.6c], b. on July 15, 1852, and m. Albert Ream about 1870, Samuel Brougher in Somerset County on Feb. 2, 1879, and ____ Crosson about 1887. Barbara d. in Somerset County, Upper Turkeyfoot Township, on May 3, 1938. Samuel was b. in Upper Turkeyfoot Township on Sep. 2, 1937, and d. there on Jan. 29, 1886.

Ann[1.1.1.5.5.10.4.7c], b. about 1854, and m. Bruce Harnett.

George[1.1.1.5.5.10.4.8c], b. about 1856.

Frederick Wilson[1.1.1.5.5.10.4.9c], b. about 1858, and m. Candace Conn.

Mary M.[1.1.1.5.4.10.4.10c], b. about 1860, and m. James Sanbour.

Harris H.[1.1.1.5.4.10.4.11c], b. about 1862.

Mary Ann Dull

Mary Ann[1.1.1.5.5.10.5c] m. Jacob Critchfield, and d. in Somerset County, Rockwood, Pennsylvania. He was b. in Milford Township on Mar. 10, 1830. They had the following children:

Oliver[1.1.1.5.5.10.5.1c], m. Rohama Knepper.

John M.[1.1.1.5.5.10.5.2c], b. in Milford Township on July 29, 1851, and m. Anna, daughter of John and Martha (Lobe) Hay, in Somerset County on Feb. 2, 1875. She was b. in Milford Township on Mar. 1, 1856.

Louisa[1.1.1.5.5.10.5.3c], m. Jacob Critchfield.

Emma[1.1.1.5.5.10.5.4c], m. Watson Schrock.

Minerva[1.1.1.5.5.10.5.5c], m. Edward Hoover.

Anna M.[1.1.1.5.5.10.5.6c], m. Edward Spangler.

Eleanora[1.1.1.5.5.10.5.7c], b. on Mar. 22, 1871, and m. Charles, son of Lewis J. and Elizabeth (Walker) Knepper in Somerset County, Pennsylvania, on Apr. 15, 1897. He was b. in Brother's Valley Township on Aug. 9, 1870, and d. in Somerset County on June 1, 1894. Eleanora d. in Somerset County on Aug. 1, 1889.

Edward S.[1.1.1.5.5.10.5.8c], m. Kate Ferman.

William W.[1.1.1.5.5.10.5.9c], m. Sadie Braham.

Josiah Dull

Josiah[1.1.1.5.5.10.13c] m. Elizabeth Gilbert/Ross in 1857. Josiah d. in Cerro Gordo County, Rockwell, Iowa, in 1909. They had the following children:

Emma[1.1.1.5.5.10.13.1c], b. in Black Hawk County, Waterloo, Iowa, in 1859.

Flora$^{1.1.1.5.5.10.13.2c}$, b. in Waterloo, Iowa, in 1861.
Frederick$^{1.1.1.5.5.10.13.3c}$, b. in Waterloo, Iowa, in 1863, and
d. in South Dakota in May 1929.
Louis Augusta$^{1.1.1.5.5.10.13.4c}$, b. in Waterloo, Iowa, in 1866.
Charles Albert$^{1.1.1.5.5.10.13.5c}$, b. in Waterloo, Iowa, in 1872.
Martha Mae$^{1.1.1.5.5.10.13.6c}$, b. in Rockwell, Iowa, on May 22,
1880.
Guy Hornea$^{1.1.1.5.5.10.13.7c}$, b. in Rockwell, Iowa, in 1884.

Johan Caspar Doll

Johann Caspar$^{1.1.1.8c}$ m. Margaret (daughter of Adam Dietz?),
and d. in Northampton County, Plainfield, Pennsylvania, on Feb. 11,
1793. She was b. in 1724, and d. in Northampton County, Plainfield,
Pennsylvania, on Apr. 26 (22), 1790. They were buried in Plainfield
Reformed Church cemetery. In 1747, Casper purchased 151.5 acres in
the Blue Mountains of Northampton County. In 1755, they were
sponsors to a baptism in Petersville Church Emmanuel in Moore
Township. Caspar was appointed guardian of Maria Margaretha,
Susannah and Maria Elisabetha, daughters of Johan Nickel and Maria
Margaretha Heil in Moore Township in Sep. 1762. In 1763, he was an
elder in the Plainfield Reformed Church, and was taxed in Plainfield
from 1761, till his death. In 1774, he was the Commissioner of Safety.
In 1785, he purchased 80 acres in Plainfield Township, and in 1791, he
purchased 60 acres from Christian Bender. Casper and Margaret had
the following children:
Georg$^{1.1.1.8.1c}$, b. on Feb. 11, 1744.
Maria$^{1.1.1.8.2c}$, b. about 1746, and m. ___ Young.
Sara Margaretha$^{1.1.1.8.3c}$, b. on July 22, 1748, sponsored by
Nicholas Doll at her baptism, m. ___ Schneider, and had Jacob,
Johannes, and Susanna.
Anna$^{1.1.1.8.4c}$, b. on May 16, 1751, m. Peter Kuchlein, and
had a son, Jacob. Peter was b. in Germany on Nov. 8, 1722, and d. in
Pennsylvania on Nov. 27, 1789.
Elizabeth$^{1.1.1.8.5c}$, b. on Feb. 22, 1754, m. ___ Engel, and
had Henrich, Johannes, and Susannah.
Anna Catharina$^{1.1.1.8.1.6c}$, b. in Bucks County, Tohickon
Township, Pennsylvania, on Jan. 1, 1757, baptized at Tohickon Union
Church on Feb. 22, 1757, and sponsored by Jost and Christina
Edelman. She m. ___ Stechel.

Georg Doll

Georg$^{1.1.1.8.1c}$ m. Hannah (?daughter of Peter Metz?), and d. in Northampton County in 1783. In 1786, Hannah is taxed in Northampton County, Hamilton Township. They baptized the following children in Northampton County, Pennsylvania:

Elizabeth$^{1.1.1.8.1.1c}$, baptized on Aug. 7, 1775.
John$^{1.1.1.8.1.2c}$, baptized on Dec. 24, 1775.

Maria Doll

Maria$^{1.1.1.8.2c}$ is probably the Anna Maria that m. Johan Henrich Jung/Young, and had the following children baptized at St. Peter's Lutheran Church in Plainfield, Northampton County (unless otherwise noted):

Maria Engel$^{1.1.1.8.2.1c}$, b. on Feb. 24, 1766.
Catharina$^{1.1.1.8.2.2c}$, b. on Aug. 14, 1768.
Susanna$^{1.1.1.8.2.3c}$, b. on Sep. 14, 1775.
Magdalena$^{1.1.1.8.2.4c}$, b. on June 22, 1778.
Veronica$^{1.1.1.8.2.5c}$, b. on Mar. 12, 1780.
Johan Henrich$^{1.1.1.8.2.6c}$, b. on July 18, 1781.
Georg Henrich$^{1.1.1.8.2.7c}$, b. on May 14, 1783, and baptized at Dryland Church in Nazareth Township.
Veronica$^{1.1.1.8.2.8c}$, b. on Feb. 8, 1785.
John Daniel$^{1.1.1.8.2.9c}$, b. on Apr. 1, 1785, and baptized at Dryland Church in Nazareth Township.
Johann Mattheus$^{1.1.1.8.2.10c}$, b. on Feb. 24, 1787, and baptized at the Stone Church, Northampton County, Allen Township, Kreidersville.

Elizabeth Doll

Elizabeth$^{1.1.1.8.5c}$ is probably the Elizabeth that m. Christopher Engel, and had the following children baptized at St. Peter's in Plainfield (unless otherwise noted):

Henry$^{1.1.1.8.5.1c}$, b. on Feb. 3, 1780.
Susanna$^{1.1.1.8.5.2c}$, b. on June 29, 1782, and baptized at the First Reformed Church of Easton.
John$^{1.1.1.8.5.3c}$, b. on Nov. 18, 1784.
Georg$^{1.1.1.8.5.4c}$, b. on Dec. 8, 1787.

Johan Nickel Doll

Johan Nickel$^{1.1.1.9c}$ m. Margaretha. In 1739, he purchased 100 acres adjacent John Shook and Joseph Martz in the area of Bucks

County that became Northampton County, Pennsylvania. In 1746, he purchased 100 acres on the Forks of the Delaware adjacent to his other land. In 1752, he was a sponsor with Casper's wife in Upper Saucon Township. He was taxed in Northampton County, Plainfield Township, from 1761 to 1766. They had the following children:

Susanna Margaret[1.1.1.9.1c], b. on Sep. 24, 1759, and baptized in Bucks County, Tohickon Township, Tohickon Union Church Oct. 26, 1759. She was sponsored by Peter Doll and wife.

Martin[1.1.1.9.2c], b. about 1762. He has not been confirmed as a son.

Elizabeth[1.1.1.9.3c], baptized at Northampton County, Plainfield, Pennsylvania, on Apr. 1, 1764.

Johan Frederick[1.1.1.9.4c], baptized at Plainfield on Aug. 31, 1766.

Martin Doll

Martin[1.1.1.9.2c] m. Elisabeth. He resided in Northampton County, Moore Township, Pennsylvania, in Aug. 1793, and York County, Chanceford Township, Pennsylvania, in 1798. They had the following children:

John[1.1.1.9.2.1c], b. in Moore Township on Feb. 12, 1788, baptized at Kreidersville (Stone) Church on Mar. 23, 1788, and sponsored by Gertrude Flick.

Susanna[1.1.1.9.2.2c], b. on Feb. 24, 1791, baptized at Kreidersville on Apr. 3, 1791, and sponsored by Christian Esch and Barbara Bartholemi.

Elisabeth[1.1.1.9.2.3c], b. in York County, Chanceford Township, on Aug. 5, 1800, baptized at Stehli's Union Church on Aug. 24, 1800, and sponsored by Jacob Arner.

Anna Elisabetha Doll

Anna Elisabetha[1.1.2c] m. Johan Christian, son of Adam Drumm, at Ulmet, Germany, on Feb. 26, 1696/97. Johan Christian was b. at Ulmet on Oct. 14, 1665, and d. there on Mar. 8, 1730/31. They had the following children at Ulmet:

Maria Margaretha[1.1.2.1c], baptized on Apr. 7, 1700, and m. Johan Daniel Staudt.

Christina Barbara[1.1.2.2c], baptized on Sep. 8, 1703, and m. Johan Peter Klein.

Johannes Adam[1.1.2.3c], baptized on Dec. 9, 1705.

Maria Elisabetha[1.1.2.4c], baptized on May 17, 1708, and d. in 1714.

Johan Peter[1.1.2.5c], baptized on Mar. 18, 1711, and d. in 1714.

Anna Maria[1.1.2.6c], baptized on June 13, 1713, and m. Johan Adam Albert on Apr. 24, 1731.

Johann Georg[1.1.2.7c], baptized on Jan. 16, 1716.

Johann Abraham[1.1.2.8c], baptized on Sep. 1, 1718.

Johannes Adam Drum

Johannes Adam[1.1.2.3c] arrived at Philadelphia on the ship *Samuel* in 1737 with his cousins, Peter and Christian Doll. Adam m. Maria Gertraud, daughter of Peter Bier, at Ulmet, Germany, on Jan. 22, 1732/33. She was b. at Ulmet on Apr. 2, 1704, and d. sometime after 1757. Adam was killed by Indians in Berks County, Albany Township, Allemangel, Pennsylvania, on June 22, 1757. The Indians also took his wife, and their 19 year old son prisoner. When his wife escaped, one of the Indians threw a tomahawk, and cut her badly in the neck. They had the following children:

Johan Christian[1.1.2.3.1c], baptized on Apr. 17, 1735.

George A.[1.1.2.3.2c], b. in Albany Township in 1738, and m. Maria Catherine Strasser in Berks County, Pennsylvania, in 1759. George d. in Fairfield County, Ohio, on Oct. 19, 1808. Maria Catherine d. in Fairfield County, about 1817.

Anna Margaretha Doll

Anna Margaretha[1.1.4c] m. Johan Jacob, son of Peter Mack of Oberalben, at Irtzweiler/Ulmet on Apr. 5, 1701, and immigrated to America on the ship *Glasgow* in 1738. Jacob was b. Sep. 4, 1675, and d. in Ulmet on Nov. 4, 1723. She settled in Montgomery County, New Goshenhoppen, Pennsylvania. They had the following children baptized at Ulmet:

Anna Catharina[1.1.4.1c], baptized on May 12, 1702.

Johan Nickel[1.1.4.2c], baptized on July 18, 1704.

Sara Elisabetha[1.1.4.3c], baptized on Jan. 3, 1707, and m. Jacob, son of Simon Mann, in Oberalben on Jan. 10, 1732.

Johan Peter[1.1.4.4c], baptized on May 11, 1710, and was buried at New Goshenhoppen on Nov. 24, 1767.

Anna Juliana[1.1.4.5c], baptized on Mar. 20, 1713, and m. Johan Peter May in Montgomery County, Pennsylvania, at Red Hill Lutheran Church on Mar. 30, 1741.

Johan Jacob[1.1.4.6c], baptized on Nov. 24, 1715, and d. on May 23, 1717.

Anna Maria[1.1.4.7c], baptized on July 23, 1719.

Anna Catharina[1.1.4.8c], baptized on Mar. 1, 1722.

****

Valentine Doll

Valentine[1c(b)] d. in Northampton County, Salisbury Township, in 1758, and his will was probated on Oct. 24, 1758. He had the following children:

Nicholas[1.1c(b)], b. about 1749, and was a single man in Northampton Town in 1776. Valentine Dull's will mentions eldest son, Nicholas. Nicholas was taxed in Salisbury Township in 1776.

Auqualla[1.2c(b)], b. about 1751, and was a laborer in Salisbury Township in 1772 (he has not been proven as a son).

****

Johannes Doll

Johannes[1c(c)] resided in Lichtenberg, and later Ulmet Parish. He had the following children:

Christophorus[1.1c(c)], b. in 1699, and confirmed at Ulmet in 1715. He immigrated to America on the ship *Samuel* in 1739. He received a warrant for 200 acres on a tract on the Little Lehigh Creek in Philadelphia (now Berks) County, Longswamp Township, on Dec. 17, 1739. This land was surveyed on Apr. 11, 1740. Christophorus's will was written on June 24, 1751, and probated on July 25, 1751. He left everything to his siblings.

Johann Philips[1.2c(c)], b. in 1712, and confirmed at Ulmet in 1728.

Margaretha Catharina[1.3c(c)], confirmed at Pfeffelbach-Thallichtenberg in 1730, and was alive in Mar. 1763.

Maria Elisabetha[1.4c(c)], m. Joseph Biere of Horbach in Lichtenberg on Jan. 23, 1731, and immigrated to America on the ship *Samuel* in 1739.

Barbara[1.5c(c)], was alive in Mar. 1763.

Johann Philips Doll

Johann Philips[1.2c(c)] immigrated to America on the ship *Samuel* in 1739, and m. Margaretha. They had the following children in Berks County, Longswamp Township, Pennsylvania:

Johann Henrich[1.2.1c(c)], baptized at Longswamp on June 11, 1764, and sponsored by Heinrich Bieri.

Maria Magdalena[1.2.2c(c)], baptized at Longswamp on Apr. 21, 1776, and sponsored by Henrich Bieri.

****

Jacob Engel

Jacob[1d] m. Maria Barbara. He resided in Montgomery County, Douglas Township, Pennsylvania, in 1769, with 117 acres, 4 horses, and 3 cattle. They had the following children:

Elisabeth[1.1d], b. about 1730, and m. Johan Michael Stophlet.

Gertraudt[1.2d], b. about 1732, and m. Johan Philip Lauterbach at Falkner Swamp on Oct. 31, 1751.

Agnes[1.3d], b. about 1734, and m. Jacob Bleiler at Falkner Swamp on Feb. 25, 1755.

Johan Heinrich[1.4d], b. about 1742.

Catharina Christina[1.5d], b. on Feb. 2, 1748, and baptized at New Hanover Lutheran Church, in Montgomery County, New Hanover Township, Pennsylvania.

Johan Heinrich Engel

Johan Heinrich[1.4d] m. Catharina. He resided in Montgomery County, Douglas Township, Pennsylvania, in 1769, with 150 acres, 2 horses, and 2 cattle. He d. in Berks County, Colebrookdale, Pennsylvania. His will was written on Mar. 24, 1808, and probated on Jan. 6, 1809. They had the following children:

Georg[1.4.1d], b. about 1761.

Anna Margareth[1.4.2d], b. on Oct. 25, 1763, and baptized at New Hanover Lutheran Church in Montgomery County.

Catharina[1.4.3d], baptized at Falkner Swamp Lutheran Church in Montgomery County, New Hanover Township, on Mar. 31, 1766.

Jacob[1.4.4d], b. about 1768.

Henrich[1.4.5d], b. about 1770.

Anna Maria[1.4.6d], b. about 1771.

Elizabeth[1.4.7d], b. on Aug. 16, 1772, and baptized at Falkner Swamp.

Susanna$^{1.4.8d}$, b. about 1774.

Johannes$^{1.4.9d}$, b. on Sep. 29, 1776, and baptized at Falkner Swamp.

Magdalena$^{1.4.10d}$, b. on Jan. 23, 1776, and baptized at Falkner Swamp.

Margaretha$^{1.4.11d}$, b. on Nov. 16, 1778, and baptized at Falkner Swamp.

Peter$^{1.4.12d}$, b. about 1781.

Catharina Elisabeth$^{1.4.13d}$, b. on Oct. 8, 1784, and baptized at Falkner Swamp. She m. Leonard Hartranft.

Georg Engel

Georg$^{1.4.1d}$ m. Elisabetha, and had the following children:

Johanes$^{1.4.1.1d}$, b. on Mar. 28, 1782, and baptized at St. Paul's Lutheran Church in Upper Hanover Township.

Georg$^{1.4.1.2d}$, b. on Jan. 13, 1784, and baptized at St. Paul's Lutheran Church in Upper Hanover Township.

Michael$^{1.4.1.3d}$, b. on Apr. 7, 1787, and baptized at St. Paul's.

Johann Friedrich$^{1.4.1.4d}$, b. on Oct. 10, 1789, and baptized at St. Paul's.

Peter$^{1.4.1.5d}$, b. on Jan. 10, 1792, and baptized at St. Paul's.

Johann Adam$^{1.4.1.6d}$, b. on May 26, 1794, and baptized at St. Paul's.

Samuel$^{1.4.1.7d}$, b. on Aug. 13, 1796, and baptized at St. Paul's.

Catharina Engel

Catharina$^{1.4.3d}$ m. Conrad Schuman, and had the following children:

Anna Maria$^{1.4.3.1d}$, b. on Dec. 18, 1784, and baptized at Falkner Swamp Lutheran Church in New Hanover Township.

Elizabeth$^{1.4.3.2d}$, b. on Apr. 3, 1789, and baptized at Falkner Swamp.

Jacob Engel

Jacob$^{1.4.4d}$ m. Elizabeth Bucher at Falkner Swamp on Aug. 19, 1783, and had the following children:

Jacob$^{1.4.4.1d}$, b. on Apr. 6, 1787, and baptized at Falkner Swamp.

Maria Catharine$^{1.4.4.2d}$, b. on Dec. 5, 1788, and baptized at Falkner Swamp.

John Gabriel[1.4.4.3d], b. on Jan. 30, 1791, and baptized at Falkner Swamp.

Anna Maria[1.4.4.4d], b. on Dec. 1, 1794, and baptized at Falkner Swamp in New Hanover Township.

Henry[1.4.4.5d], b. on Dec. 28, 1796, and baptized at Falkner Swamp.

Elizabeth[1.4.4.6d], b. on Apr. 11, 1799, and baptized at Falkner Swamp.

Henrich Engel

Henrich[1.4.5d] m. Elisabeth, and had the following children:

Joseph[1.4.5.1d], b. on Jan. 2, 1790, and baptized at Emanuel Lutheran Church, Montgomery County, Pottsgrove Township, Pottstown, Pennsylvania.

Catherine[1.4.5.2d], b. on May 5, 1799, and baptized at Emanuel Lutheran Church, Montgomery County, Pottsgrove Township, Pottstown, Pennsylvania.

Anna Maria Engel

Anna Maria[1.4.6d] m. Conrad Bucher at Falkner Swamp on Apr. 2, 1791, and had the following children:

Henry[1.4.6.1d], b. on Jan. 3, 1792, and baptized at Falkner Swamp in New Hanover Township.

George[1.4.6.2d], b. on Jan. 1, 1794, and baptized at Falkner Swamp in New Hanover Township.

Sebastian[1.4.6.3d] b. on Feb. 27, 1796, and baptized at Falkner Swamp in New Hanover Township.

Daniel[1.4.6.4d], b. on Sep. 20, 1798, and baptized at Falkner Swamp in New Hanover Township.

Susanna Engel

Susanna[1.4.8d] m. Berhardt Gilbert, and had the following children:

Henry[1.4.8.1d], b. on Sep. 24, 1791, and baptized at New Hanover Lutheran Church in New Hanover Township.

Magdalena[1.4.8.2d], b. on Feb. 2, 1797, and baptized at New Hanover.

Johannes Engel

Johannes[1.4.9d] m. Susanna, and had the following child:

John$^{1.4.8.1d}$, b. on Mar. 21, 1798, and baptized at Falkner Swamp in New Hanover Township.

****

Johann Rudolph Geri

Johann Rudolph^{1e} was b. in Switzerland, m. Elisabetha, and had the following children in Hirschland/Drulingen, Alsace, France:

Johann Adam$^{1.1e}$, b. on Nov. 6, 1718.

Anna Magdalena$^{1.2e}$, b. on Feb. 22, 1719/20.

Jacob$^{1.3e}$, b. on May 9, 1721.

Johann Adam Geri

Johann Adam$^{1.1e}$ m. Anna Barbara before 1748, and Magdalena Heinli in Lehigh County, Pennsylvania, on May 8, 1758, and d. in Berks County, Longswamp, Pennsylvania, in Nov. 1786. He was a shoemaker. He immigrated to America on the ship *Robert and Alice* on Sep. 3, 1739. He is presumed to have had the following daughter:

Elisabeth$^{1.1.1e}$, who was a sponsor at the baptism of Elisabeth Carl at Longswamp in 1752.

Jacob Geri

Jacob$^{1.3e}$ m. Anna Margaretha Gertrude, daughter of Johan Valentine and Anna Maria (Zugk) Griesemer. She was b. in Hessen, Starkenberg, Lampertheim, Germany, on May 15, 1728, and d. in Montgomery County, Upper Hanover Township, Pennsylvania, on Feb. 8, 1802. Jacob immigrated to America on the ship *Robert and Alice* on Sep. 3, 1739, was a "Redemptioner," and paid for his passage to the new world by working for Valentine Griesemer. He was a tile maker, and operated "Geri's Ziegel Huette." He owned 600 acres of land located partially in Montgomery County, Upper Hanover Township, and partially in Berks County, Hereford Township. Jacob d. in Upper Hanover Township on Feb. 25, 1808. They had the following children in Upper Hanover Township (baptized at the New Goshenhoppen Reformed Congregation):

Anna Maria$^{1.3.1e}$, baptized on Oct. 26, 1746, and m. August Johannes Hillegas in Montgomery County on Mar. 3, 1767.

Catharina$^{1.3.2e}$, baptized on Mar. 25, 1749, and m. Michael Hillegas and John Wagner.

Johan Adam$^{1.3.3e}$, b. in 1752.

Jacob$^{1.3.4e}$, b. on Feb. 11, 1754.

Elisabetha[1.3.5e], b. about 1756.
Johannes[1.3.6e], baptized on June 3, 1759.
Rebecca[1.3.7e], b. about 1761.
Johan Georg[1.3.8e], b. on Jan. 9, 1763, baptized at St. Paul's Lutheran Church, and d. before Oct. 24, 1797.
Johan Petrus[1.3.9e], b. on Jan. 25, 1769.
Johan Michaelus[1.3.10e], b. on July 13, 1771, and m. Maria Nuss at Oley Hill Church in Berks County on Aug. 2, 1796.

Johan Adam Geri

Johan Adam[1.3.3e] m. Barbara Weiller in Montgomery County on June 11, 1776, and d. before Oct. 24, 1797. They had the following children:

Barbara[1.3.3.1e], b. about 1778, and baptized at Great Swamp Reformed Lutheran Church in Lehigh County.
A. Margreth[1.3.3.2e], b. on Oct. 23, 1782, and baptized at Great Swamp Reformed Lutheran Church in Lehigh County.
Johan Georg[1.3.3.3e], b. on Feb. 11, 1787, and at the New Goshenhoppen Reformed Congregation.
Valentine[1.3.3.4e], b. on Apr. 29, 1789, baptized at DeLong's Reformed Church on June 1, 1789, and sponsored by Peter Gehry and Maria Elisabetha Bernhard.
Catharina[1.3.3.5e], b. on Mar. 5, 1791, baptized at Longswamp Reformed Church in Berks County, and sponsored by Jacob and Catharina Lang.

Jacob Geri

Jacob[1.3.4e] m. Elisabetha Lauer at Falkner Swamp in Montgomery County on May 15, 1781, and Margareth about 1796, and d. in Upper Hanover Township on Sep. 28, 1828. He had the following children baptized at the New Goshenhoppen Reformed Congregation (except the last):

Jacob[1.3.4.1e], b. on May 31, 1782.
Peter[1.3.4.2e], b. on Nov. 23, 1783.
Sarah[1.3.4.3e], b. on Apr. 15, 1785, and baptized at Zion's Reformed Church in Lehigh County.
Catharina[1.3.4.4e], b. on Jan. 15, 1787.
Johannes[1.3.4.5e], b. on June 30, 1787.
Anna[1.3.4.6e], b. on July 31, 1792.
John[1.3.4.7e], b. on Sep. 9, 1792.

Daniel[1.3.4.8e], b. on Aug. 4, 1796, baptized at Oley Hill Church in Berks County on Aug. 28, 1796, and sponsored by Balthasar and Barbara Bohm.

Johannes Geri

Johannes[1.3.6e] m. Susanna Wigner in Montgomery County, Pennsylvania, on May 11, 1784, and had the following children (baptized at New Goshenhoppen Reformed Congregation):

Samuel[1.3.6.1e], baptized at Longswamp Reformed Church in Berks County on Mar. 25, 1785, and sponsored by Jacob and Gertrude Geri. He m. Susanna Schlicher, and d. on Sep. 4, 1848. She was b. on Oct. 15, 1789, and d. on May 29, 1861.

Catherine[1.3.6.2e], b. on Jan. 15, 1787, baptized on Feb. 15, 1787, m. George Carl, and d. on Nov. 25, 1875. He was b. on Sep. 28, 1789, and d. on Dec. 10, 1874.

Anna Maria[1.3.6.3e], b. on Oct. 16, 1790, m. John Schlicher, and d. on Dec. 9, 1857. He was b. on Mar. 14, 1780, and d. on July 31, 1846.

John W.[1.3.6.4e], b. on Oct. 19, 1792, m. Catherine Glausen, and d. on Sep. 5, 1878. She was b. on Jan. 1, 1799, and d. on Feb. 7, 1884.

George[1.3.6.5e], b. on Apr. 6, 1794, m. Sarah Carl on Nov. 15, 1838, and d. on Feb. 14, 1857. She was b. on Feb. 20, 1819, and d. on Mar. 21, 1844.

Susanna[1.3.6.6e], b. on Jan. 24, 1795, m. Henry Graber, and d. on July 26, 1850. He was b. on Sep. 24, 1789, and d. on Mar. 30, 1859.

Anna[1.3.6.7e], b. on Jan. 31, 1797, m. John Heilig, and d. in Allentown, Pennsylvania, on Apr. 22, 1857. He was b. on Apr. 19, 1795, and d. on Apr. 22, 1869.

Charles[1.3.6.8e], b. on Jan. 31, 1797, and d. in 1867.

Rebecca[1.3.6.9e], b. about 1800, and m. John Sassaman.

Sarah[1.3.6.10e], b. about 1802, and m. Sebastian Glaes.

Polly[1.3.6.11e], b. about 1804, m. _____ Willouer, and resided in Montgomery County, Pennsylvania.

Lydia[1.3.6.12e], b. on Jan. 6, 1806, m. Amos Antrim on Dec. 25, 1825, and d. on Sep. 19, 1879. He was b. on Aug. 26, 1804, and d. on Apr. 13, 1877.

****

Johan Valentine Griesemer

Johan Valentine[1f] m. Anna Maria Margaretha Kern in
Lampertheim on July 12, 1712, Anna Maria Zugk in Hessen
Starkenburg, Lampertheim, Germany, on May 25, 1723, and Barbara
before 1773. Johan Valentine was b. in Alsace, France, on Jan. 4,
1687/88, and d. in Berks County, Hereford Township, Pennsylvania, on
June 3, 1773. He arrived at Philadelphia on the ship *Thistle* on Aug.
29, 1730. Barbara d. in Hereford Township about Oct. 1776. Johan
Valentine had the following children:

Casper[1.1f], b. Feb. 24, 1715.

Johan[1.2f], b. in 1717.

Johan Jacob[1.3f], b. in Lampertheim on Feb. 27, 1724/25.

Anna Margaretha Gertrude[1.4f], b. in Lampertheim on May 15,
1728, and m. Jacob Geri.

Johan Leonhard[1.5f], baptized at New Goshenhoppen in
Montgomery County, Upper Hanover Township, Pennsylvania, on June
11, 1732.

Maria Elisabetha[1.6f], b. in Upper Hanover Township on Jan.
19, 1733/34, baptized on Mar. 25, 1734, and sponsored by Maria
Elisabetha Steinmanerin.

Maria Catherina[1.7f], b. in Upper Hanover Township on June 6,
1736.

Maria Barbara[1.8f], b. about 1737, and m. Johan Peter Cabel in
Montgomery County on Mar. 22, 1757.

Jacob Wilhelm[1.9f], b. about 1739, and m. Anna Catharina,
daughter of Johannes and Magdalena Hahlman, in Montgomery County
on Jan. 18, 1759. She d. in Upper Hanover Township in Feb. 1800.

Casper Griesemer

Casper[1.1f] immigrated to Pennsylvania in 1730, and d. in
Berks County, (buried in Swartzwald), Pennsylvania, on Mar. 1, 1794.
He m. Elisabetha, and baptized the following child at the New
Goshenhoppen Reformed Congregation:

Son[1.1.1f], baptized on Apr. 7, 1746.

Johan Griesemer

Johan[1.2f] m. Anna Maria Bruner, and d. in Lehigh County,
Lower Milford Township, Pennsylvania, Oct. 10, 1789. They had the
following son:

Felix[1.2.1f], b. about 1749, and baptized at Great Swamp
Reformed Church in Lehigh County.

Johannes$^{1.2.2f}$, b. about 1750.
Abraham$^{1.2.3f}$, b. about 1760.

Johannes Griesemer

Johannes$^{1.2.2f}$ m. Catharina, daughter of Hans Adam and
Maria Margaretha (Hahlman) Hillegas, in Montgomery County on May
5, 1772, and had the following children:
      Solomon$^{1.2.2.1f}$, b. on Dec. 7, 1772, and baptized at Zion
Reformed Lutheran Church in Lehigh County, Allentown,
Pennsylvania.
      Johan Friedrich$^{1.2.2.2f}$, b. on Mar. 5, 1773, and baptized at
the New Goshenhoppen Reformed Congregation in Montgomery
County.
      Anna Maria$^{1.2.2.3f}$, b. on Oct. 4, 1774, and baptized at Zion
Reformed Church in Lehigh County.
      Johannes$^{1.2.2.4f}$, b. on July 14, 1776, and baptized at
Chestnut Reformed Congregation, Lehigh County, Lower Milford
Township, Pennsylvania.
      Eva Catharina$^{1.2.2.5f}$, b. on Aug. 14, 1778, and baptized at
Chestnut Reformed Congregation in Lehigh County.
      Peter$^{1.2.2.6f}$, b. on Oct. 16, 1781, and baptized at Great
Swamp Reformed Lutheran Church in Lehigh County.
      Elisabeth$^{1.2.2.7f}$, b. on Dec. 7, 1783, and baptized at the New
Goshenhoppen Reformed Congregation.
      Adam$^{1.2.2.8f}$, b. on Jan. 31, 1786, and baptized at St. Paul's
Lutheran Church in Montgomery County.

Abraham Griesemer

Abraham$^{1.2.3f}$ m. Catharina, and baptized the following
children at Zion Reformed Church, Lehigh County, Allentown,
Pennsylvania:
      Elizabeth$^{1.2.3.1f}$, b. on Oct. 19, 1783.
      Hannah$^{1.2.3.2f}$, b. on Apr. 11, 1786.
      Solomon$^{1.2.3.3f}$, b. on Apr. 6, 1788.
      Catharina$^{1.2.3.4f}$, b. on June 17, 1792.
      Lydia$^{1.2.3.5f}$, b. on Dec. 28, 1794.
      Maria Magdalena$^{1.2.3.6f}$, b. on June 16, 1797.
      Salome$^{1.2.3.7f}$, b. on Oct. 19, 1799.

Johan Leonhard Griesemer

Johan Leonhard[1.5f] m. Elizabeth Lefebre, and d. in Upper
Hanover Township on Jan. 5, 1821. They baptized the following
children at the New Goshenhoppen Reformed Congregation:
Johannes[1.5.1f], b. on Feb. 27, 1762.
Johannes Georg[1.5.2f], b. in 1767.
Margaretha[1.5.3f], b. on Jan. 17, 1770.
Susanna[1.5.4f], b. on Jan. 14, 1773.
Jacobus[1.5.5f], b. on Nov. 28, 1774.
Abraham[1.5.6f], b. on Apr. 16, 1777. He may be the Abraham
that was b. on Mar. 11, 1776, and d. in Berks County, Pennsylvania, on
Mar. 12, 1798.

Johannes Griesemer

Johannes[1.5.1f] m. Anna Barbara, and had the following
children:
Heinrich[1.5.1.1f], b. on Mar. 20, 1784, and baptized at St.
Paul's Lutheran Church.
Johan Jacobus[1.5.1.2f], b. on July 18, 1787, and baptized at the
New Goshenhoppen Reformed Congregation.
Jonathan[1.5.1.3f], b. on Nov. 13, 1792, and baptized at the New
Goshenhoppen Reformed Congregation.

Maria Catharina Griesemer

Maria Catherina[1.7f] m. Johannes Cunius (Cimius), and d. in
Berks County, Pennsylvania, on Sep. 5, 1816. They baptized the
following children at the New Goshenhoppen Reformed Congregation:
Wilhelm[1.7.1f], b. on Jan. 24, 1755.
Johannes[1.7.2f], b. on Dec. 15, 1756.
Johan Nicolaus[1.7.3f], baptized on Apr. 15, 1759.
Anna Maria[1.7.4f], b. on Mar. 14, 1759.
Anna Margaretha[1.7.5f], b. on July 20, 1761, and baptized on
Aug. 9, 1761.
Catharina[1.7.6f], b. on Sep. 27, 1763.
Johannes[1.7.7f], b. on Oct. 7, 1765.
Johan Phillip[1.7.8f], b. on Dec. 6, 1770.
Elisabetha[1.7.9f], b. on Nov. 6, 1772.

****

Peter Heilmann

Peter[1g] m. Maria, and had the following children baptized at Oberoewisheim, Karlsruhe, Baden, Germany:

Maria[1.1g], b. on June 9, 1644, and baptized on June 16, 1644.

Anna Barbara[1.2g], b. on Feb. 5, 1655.

Eva Barbara[1.3g], b. on Mar. 20, 1657.

Hans Martin[1.4g], b. on June 5, 1659.

Hans Martin Heilmann

Hans Martin[1.4g] m. Anna Barbara, daughter of Marquard and Otilia (Raub) Boeb, in Oberoewisheim, Karlsruhe, Baden, on Nov. 14, 1682, and had the following children baptized there:

Anna Barbara[1.4.1g], b. on Feb. 11, 1684.

Eva Otilia[1.4.2g], b. on Feb. 21, 1687.

Johannes (Hans Martin)[1.4.3g], b. on Mar. 3, 1688, and baptized on June 22, 1688.

Johannes Hahlman/Heilmann

Johannes[1.4.3g] m. Anna Maria Catharina Burkhard in Nordheim, Neckarkreis, Wuertemburg, on Apr. 30, 1709, Anna Magdalena Weyberger in Nordheim on July 1, 1727, and possibly Elisabetha before 1745. He immigrated to America on the ship *Loyal Judith* on Sep. 25, 1732. He d. in Montgomery County, Salford Township, Pennsylvania, on Oct. 11, 1748. His will was written on Sep. 6, 1748. He was said to be from Beyond Schuylkill in 1747. They had the following children (in Nordheim before 1733 (?in Skippack Township/baptized at Augustus Evangelical Lutheran Church, Trappe in Upper Providence Township)):

Hans Martin[1.4.3.1g], baptized on May 16, 1709, and immigrated to America with his father in 1732.

Maria Margaretha[1.4.3.2g], baptized on May 10, 1713, and m. Hans Adam Hillegas.

Hans Michael[1.4.3.3g], baptized on Mar. 19, 1715, and d. in 1715.

Hans Michael[1.4.3.4g], b. on Feb. 27, 1716, baptized on June 4, 1716, and was the executor of his father's will.

Jerg Adam[1.4.3.5g], baptized on Feb. 2, 1720, m. Elisabetha. He was named in his father's will.

Johannes[1.4.3.6g], baptized on Apr. 27, 1728, and d. in 1728.

Johannes[1.4.3.7g], b. in 1729, baptized on Aug. 25, 1729, and confirmed on May 7, 1747, age 18. He was named in his father's will.

He m. Maria Barbara, daughter of Johan Martin Plieninger of
Nordheim, in Philadelphia County, Pennsylvania, on May 15, 1753.
    Johan Conrad[1.4.3.8g], baptized on Apr. 3, 1731.
    Johannes Baltesar[1.4.3.9g], b. on Mar. 21, 1735/36, baptized at
Augustus Trappe Lutheran Church on Apr. 11, 1736, and sponsored by
Johan Georg Riser and Maria Sybilla Weinbergerin. He was confirmed
on Apr. 14, 1754, age 18. He was sponsored by his step-brother
Michael. Baltesar's mother was Magdalena.
    Magdalena[1.4.3.10g], b. in 1738, and confirmed on Apr. 14,
1754, age 16. She was sponsored by her brother Michael.
    Anna Catharina[1.4.3.11g], b. about 1740, m. Jacob Wilhelm
Griesemer in Montgomery County on Jan. 18, 1759, and d. in Upper
Hanover Township in Feb. 1800. In her will, she names the children of
her sister, Mary Margaret, wife of Adam Hillegas, deceased.
    Johann Peter[1.4.3.12g], b. in Apr. 1744, and baptized at
Augustus Trappe Lutheran in May 1744.
    Johann Stephanus[1.4.3.13g], b. on Apr. 15, 1746, and baptized
at Augustus Trappe Lutheran on May 12, 1746. His mother was
Elisabetha.

Hans Michael Hahlman

    Hans Michael[1.4.3.4g] m. Anna Maria, and baptized the
following children at Augustus Evangelical Lutheran:
    Elissabetda[1.4.3.4.1g], b. on Dec. 3, 1742, baptized at Augustus
Trappe Lutheran on Apr. 21, 1743, and sponsored by Johan Wendel
and Anna Katarina Ernst.
    Maria Margaretha[1.4.3.4.2g], b. on Aug. 9, 1746, baptized on
Sep. 2, 1746, and sponsored by Melchior Heiter.
    Margaretha[1.4.3.4.3g], b. on Oct. 11, 1747, baptized on Dec. 1,
1747, and sponsored by Johan Wendel and Margaretha Ernst.
    Catharina[1.4.3.4.4g], b. on Dec. 24, 1749, baptized on Mar. 1,
1750, and sponsored by her parents.
    Friedrich[1.4.3.4.5g], b. on Nov. 6, 1756, baptized on Jan. 1,
1757, and sponsored by his parents.

Jerg Adam Hahlman

    Jerg Adam[1.4.3.5g] m. Elisabeth Dufrene in Montgomery
County in Feb. 1744/45, and baptized the following children at
Augustus Evangelical Lutheran:
    Johannes[1.4.3.5.1g], b. on July 2, 1745, baptized at Augustus
Trappe Lutheran on Aug. 15, 1745, and sponsored by Wendel Ernst.

Michael$^{1.4.3.5.2g}$, b. on June 18, 1748, baptized on Oct. 1, 1748, and sponsored by Michael Heilman and wife.

Catharina$^{1.4.3.5.3g}$, b. on Sep. 25, 1750, baptized on Feb. 1, 1751, and sponsored by her parents.

****

Marquard Boeb/Bob

Marquard^{1h} m. Otilia Raub, and had the following children baptized at Oberoewisheim, Karlsruhe, Baden, Germany:

Hans Martin$^{1.1h}$, baptized on Oct. 27, 1653.

Maria Barbara$^{1.2h}$, baptized on Oct. 29, 1656.

Anna Barbara$^{1.3h}$, baptized on Mar. 31, 1661, and m. Hans Martin Heilmann.

****

Johannes Herb

Johannes^{1i} m. Judita, and d. in Berks County, District Township, Pennsylvania, before 1759. Johannes had a land warrant in Philadelphia for 150 acres in Sep. 1734. They had the following children:

Catherina$^{1.1i}$, b. about 1723, and m. Michael Jacks in Berks County, Goshenhoppen Catholic Church on Dec. 26, 1745.

Abraham$^{1.2i}$, b. about 1725.

Jacob$^{1.3i}$, b. about 1727.

Susanna$^{1.4i}$, b. about 1728, and m. Johan Conrad Lorsbach at Falkner Swamp on Nov. 17, 1748.

Johanna Elisabetha$^{1.5i}$, b. in Nov. 1732.

Johannes$^{1.6i}$, b. about 1735.

Abraham Herb

Abraham$^{1.2i}$ m. Gartroudt about 1749, and d. in Berks County, Hereford Township, Pennsylvania, in Sep. 1779. He had a land warrant in Philadelphia for 150 acres on Sep. 12, 1734. Gartroudt d. after 1779. They had the following children in Hereford Township:

Abraham$^{1.2.1i}$, b. in 1748, and baptized at New Hanover Lutheran Church in Montgomery County on Oct. 28, 1759.

Elizabeth$^{1.2.2i}$, b. about 1751.

Mary Angela$^{1.2.3i}$, b. about 1753, and m. Francis Hartman in Berks County, Bally on Dec. 28, 1775.

Gertraudt[1.2.4i], b. in 1755.
Sabina[1.2.5i], b. about 1757.
Susanna[1.2.6i], b. about 1759.

Abraham Harp

Abraham[1.2.1i] m. Susanna Fucks in Berks County,
Pennsylvania, about 1768, Sibilla Wachst at Falkner Swamp in
Montgomery County on Apr. 24, 1780, and Anna Fucks about 1782. He
was a cordwainer. Abraham had the following children in Berks County
(baptized at Oley Hill):

Susanna[1.2.1.1i], b. on July 20, 1769, baptized on Oct. 8, 1769,
and sponsored by Willhelm and Maria Elizabeth Reichart.

Anna Margaretha[1.2.1.2i], b. on Jan. 1, 1783, baptized on Mar.
9, 1783, and sponsored by Heinrich and Margaretha Frey.

Catharine[1.2.1.3i], b. on Dec. 12, 1784, baptized on Feb. 13,
1785, and sponsored by Andreas and Catharine Nestor. She may be the
Catherine that m. John Frohnhauser at New Hanover Lutheran on
Feb. 3, 1807.

Susanna[1.2.1.4i], b. on Nov. 22, 1786, baptized on Apr. 1, 1787,
and sponsored by Christian Geres and Susanna Herb.

Anna Maria[1.2.1.5i], b. on Apr. 2, 1797, baptized on July 30,
1797, and sponsored by Johannes and Elizabeth Wachter.

Gertraudt Herb

Gertraudt[1.2.4i] m. Phillip Weller (1754-Feb. 15, 1828), and d.
in 1855. Phillip was a Private in the Revolutionary War. They had the
following children (baptized at Oley Hill):

Catharine[1.2.4.1i], b. on Jan. 2, 1783, baptized on Mar. 9, 1783,
and sponsored by George and Catharine Mayer.

Maria[1.2.4.2i], b. on Dec. 8, 1784, baptized on Mar. 25, 1785,
and sponsored by Fredrich Reitenauer and Susanna Herb.

Peter[1.2.4.3i], b. on Dec. 16, 1788, baptized on Mar. 29, 1789,
and sponsored by Peter and Elizabeth Weller.

George[1.2.4.4i], b. on Jan. 2, 1791, baptized on Apr. 10, 1791,
and sponsored by Abraham and Anna Herb.

Jacob Herb

Jacob[1.31i] m. Maria Catherina. She was b. in 1730, and d. after
1806. Jacob was a cordwainer, and had 118 acres in District Township.
Jacob d. in Berks County, District Township, Pennsylvania, on Oct. 11,

1806. They had the following children in District Township (baptized at Oley Hill unless otherwise noted):

Johan Jacob[1.3.1i], b. on Feb. 22, 1754, baptized on Mar. 24, 1754, and sponsored by Jacob and Maria Elizabetha Hauck. (A Jacob and Elisabetha Herb had Jorg Jacob on Apr. 13, 1754, and baptized at New Hanover Lutheran Church in Montgomery County).   Maria Catherina[1.3.2i], b. on May 16, 1755, baptized on June 8, 1755, and sponsored by Stophel Reitenauer and Maria Catharina Roth.

Johan/Jacob Frederick[1.3.3i], b. on Sep. 17, 1756, baptized on Oct. 3, 1756, and sponsored by Friedrich, son of Andreas Weiss, and Anna Catharina, daughter of Conrad Roth.

Maria Magdalena[1.3.4i], b. on Feb. 8, 1758, and baptized at New Hanover Lutheran Church in Montgomery County. She is presumed to have d. young.

Johannes[1.3.5i], b. on Aug. 27, 1758, baptized on Sep. 24, 1758, and sponsored by Johannes and Elisabeth Rietenauer.

Johannes Solomon[1.3.6i], b. on May 22, 1761, baptized on May 31, 1761, and sponsored by Johan Becker.

Johannes Daniel[1.3.7i], b. on Feb. 6, 1763, and baptized on Mar. 6, 1763.

Maria Barbara[1.3.8i], b. on Feb. 18, 1765, baptized on Apr. 5, 1765, and sponsored by Nichlaus and Maria Eva Smitt.

Maria Salome[1.3.9i], b. on May 1, 1768, and baptized at New Hanover Lutheran Church in Montgomery County.

Johan Peter[1.3.10i], b. on Aug. 18, 1770, baptized on Oct. 21, 1770, and sponsored by Peter and Elizabeth Weller.

Jonathan[1.3.11i], b. about 1771.

Maria Elisabetha[1.3.12i], b. on Jan. 3, 1772, and baptized at New Hanover Lutheran Church in Montgomery County.

Maria Susanna[1.3.13i], b. on Feb. 24, 1774, baptized on May 12, 1774, sponsored by Susanna Rietenauer, and m. Andrew Fry.

Johan Jacob Herb

Johan Jacob[1.3.1i] m. Catharina. They may be the Jacob and Catharina Herb that appear in the records of Frederick County, Maryland. Jacob and Catharina had the following children:

Elisabetha[1.3.1.1i], b. on Oct. 31, 1775, baptized at Oley Hill Church on Nov. 10, 1775, and sponsored by Paul and Elisabeth Moser.

Maria Catharina[1.3.1.2i], b. on Apr. 5, 1777, and baptized at New Hanover Lutheran Church in Montgomery County. She may be the Catharine that was confirmed at Oley Hill on May 19, 1792 aged 16 years (this Catherine probably m. Jacob Huter at New Hanover Lutheran on Apr. 2, 1795).

Anna Maria[1.3.1.3i], baptized at Middletown Evangelical Lutheran Church in Frederick County, Maryland, on Sep. 26, 1783. She has not been proven as a daughter.

Jacob[1.3.1.4i], b. about 1788, and m. Elizabeth Cronnickle in Frederick County, Middletown, Maryland, on May 8, 1810. He has not been proven as a son.

Maria Catherina Herb

Maria Catherina[1.3.2i] m. Andreas, son of Frederick and Catharina Nester. She d. in District Township on Sep. 16, 1795. He was b. on Apr. 14, 1748, and d. on Oct. 14, 1824. They are buried in Hill Church Union cemetery in Berks County, Pike Township. They had the following children in District Township (baptized at Oley Hill):

Friederich[1.3.2.1i], baptized on Jan. 27, 1774, and sponsored by Frederick Herb.

Maria Catherine[1.3.2.2i], b. on May 27, 1775, baptized on June 25, 1775, and sponsored by Jacob and Maria Catharina Herb.

Hanns Jacob[1.3.2.3i], b. on Dec. 25, 1777, and sponsored by Jacob Herb and wife.

Elizabeth[1.3.2.4i], b. on Feb. 26, 1778, baptized on Apr. 16, 1778, and sponsored by Jacob and Catharine Herb.

Christian[1.3.2.5i], b. on June 17, 1783, baptized on July 21, 1783, and sponsored by Christian Acker and Barbara Herb.

Georg[1.3.2.6i], b. on May 15, 1785, baptized on June 19, 1785, and sponsored by Georg Heit and Barbara Herb.

Jacob[1.3.2.7i], b. on Dec. 23, 1786, baptized on Apr. 1, 1787, and sponsored by Jacob Reitenauer and Barbara Herb.

Elizabeth[1.3.2.8i], b. on Sep. 20, 1790, baptized on Oct. 24, 1790, and sponsored by Adam and Elizabeth Frey.

Abraham[1.3.2.9i], b. on Jan. 22, 1793, baptized on Mar. 24, 1793, and sponsored by George Geres and Barbara Herb.

Susanna[1.3.2.10i], b. on Jan. 4, 1794, baptized the first Sunday after Trinity, and sponsored by Jacob and Catharine Herb.

Johan Frederick Herb

Johan Frederick[1.3.3i] m. Christina in Berks County in 1778, and Catherine Eklof in Montgomery County, New Hanover Lutheran Church, Pennsylvania, on Nov. 5, 1799. He was a cordwainer in Hereford Township. Frederick d. in Montgomery County, German

Township, Ohio, on Nov. 21, 1835. Frederick had the following children in Berks County, District Township, Pennsylvania (baptized at Oley Hill):

Johan Jacob[1.3.3.1i], b. on Apr. 2, 1780, baptized on May 28, 1780, and sponsored by Jacob and Catharina Herb.

Catharina Barbara[1.2.2.3.2i], b. on Dec. 4, 1781, baptized on Feb. 24, 1782, and sponsored by Christian Acker and Maria Barbara Herb.

Friedrich[1.3.3.3i], b. on Mar. 5, 1784, baptized on July 4, 1784, and sponsored by Andreas and Catharine Nestor.

Wilhelm[1.3.3.4i], b. on Sep. 5, 1786, and d. on Sep. 2, 1796.

Heinrich[1.3.3.5i], b. on Sep. 14, 1796, baptized on July 2, 1796, and sponsored by Jacob and Catharine Herb.

Johan Jacob Harp

Johan Jacob[1.3.3.1i] m. Elizabeth Bowman. She was b. on Jan. 21, 1781, and d. in Montgomery County, Germantown, Ohio, on Sep. 13, 1875. Jacob d. at Germantown, Ohio, on Aug. 7, 1857. They had the following children:

Catherine[1.3.3.1.1i], Fanny[1.3.3.1.2i], Abraham[1.3.3.1.3i], Frederick[1.3.3.1.4i].

Abraham Harp

Abraham[1.3.3.1.3i] m. Polly Peters on Dec. 7, 1844, and had the following children:

Jeremiah[1.3.3.1.3.1i]; Mariah[1.3.3.1.3.2i]; Leah[1.3.3.1.3.3i]; Henry[1.3.3.1.3.4i]; Sarah[1.3.3.1.3.5i]; David[1.3.3.1.3.6i].

Johannes Herb

Johannes[1.3.5i] m. Susanna Weiss (sister of Ehrhard Weiss). He was a cordwainer. He d. in Berks County, Earl Township, Pennsylvania, in Mar. 1800. They had the following children in District Township (baptized at Oley Hill):

Elizabeth[1.3.5.1i], b. on Nov. 23, 1776, baptized on Mar. 22, 1777, and sponsored by Erhard and Elisabeth Weiss.

Johannes[1.3.5.2i], b. on Oct. 21, 1778, baptized on Jan. 3, 1779, and sponsored by Erhard Weiss and Margaretha Spat.

Jacob[1.3.5.3i], b. on Sep. 7, 1785, baptized on Nov. 6, 1785, and sponsored by Henry Lehman and Eva Elizabeth Weiss.

Hans Georg[1.3.5.4i], b. on May 30, 1788, baptized on Aug. 17, 1788, and sponsored by Hans and Catharina Weiss.

Daniel[1.3.5.5i], b. on Sep. 14, 1790, baptized on Oct. 24, 1790, and sponsored by Michael and Margaretha Moser.

Henrich[1.3.5.6i], b. on Oct. 20, 1792, baptized on Dec. 9, 1792, and sponsored by Heinrich and Eva Lehmann.

David[1.3.5.7i], b. on June 13, 1797, baptized on July 30, 1797, and sponsored by Michael and Margaretha Moser.

Johannes Solomon Herb

Johannes Solomon[1.3.6i] m. Elizabeth. He was a cordwainer, and had the following children in District Township (baptized at Oley Hill):

Catharine[1.3.6.1i], b. on Dec. 19, 1783, baptized on Apr. 11, 1784, and sponsored by Daniel Herb and Rebecca Spat.

Jacob[1.3.6.2i], baptized on May 27, 1787, and sponsored by Daniel and Rebecca Herb.

Susanna[1.3.6.3i], b. on Feb. 18, 1790, baptized on Sep. 26, 1790, and sponsored by Friedrich Nester and Susanna Herb.

Jacob[1.3.6.4i], b. on Sep. 18, 1792, baptized on Oct. 20, 1792, and sponsored by Jacob and Catharine Herb.

Rebecca[1.3.6.5i], b. on Aug. 20, 1795, baptized on Nov. 21, 1795, and sponsored by Friedrich and Christina Herb.

Johannes Daniel Herb

Johannes Daniel[1.3.7i] m. Elizabeth Fronheiser Marcreda before May 1787. He m. Thesy Edward of Montgomery County, Franklin, Pennsylvania, in Berks County on Oct. 14, 1788. He then m. Rebecca before 1791, and Christina Neuman of Rockland Township, Berks County, Pennsylvania, on Dec. 11, 1792. Daniel had the following children in District Township (baptized at Oley Hill):

Jacob[1.3.7.1i], b. on June 16, 1788, baptized on July 6, 1788, and sponsored by Jacob Eyster and Barbara Herb.

Adam[1.3.7.2i], b. on Aug. 18, 1789, baptized on Aug. 30, 1789, and sponsored by Peter Schmidt and Elizabeth Herb.

Elizabeth[1.3.7.3i], b. on Nov. 27, 1791, baptized on Feb. 26, 1792, and sponsored by Peter Herb and Elizabeth Engel.

Maria Catherine[1.3.7.4i], b. on Aug. 2, 1793, baptized on Oct. 6, 1793, and sponsored by Jacob and Maria Catharina Herb.

Susanna[1.3.7.5i], b. on Mar. 12, 1796, baptized on May 22, 1796, and sponsored by Michael Lang and Susanna Herb.

Daniel[1.3.7.6i], b. on July 25, 1797, baptized on Nov. 19, 1797, and sponsored by Jacob and Catharine Herb.

Maria Barbara Herb

Maria Barbara[1.3.8i] m. Frederich Lobach about 1792, and Andreas Nester, widower of her sister, Maria Catherine, in Montgomery County, New Hanover Lutheran Church, Pennsylvania, on Feb. 11, 1796. Maria Barbara had the following children in District Township (baptized at Oley Hill):

Johan Jacob[1.3.8.1i], b. on Oct. 26, 1793, baptized on Feb. 12, 1794, and sponsored by Jacob and Catharina Herb.

Maria[1.3.8.2i], b. on June 26, 1797, baptized on Aug. 27, 1797, and sponsored by Johannes and Anna Elizabeth Wachter.

Anna Maria[1.3.8.3i], b. on Nov. 22, 1798, baptized on Mar. 10, 1799, and sponsored by Jacob and Catharine Herb.

Maria Salome Herb

Maria Salome[1.3.9i] m. Johann Daniel[1.4.4i], son of Johannes and Johanna Elisabetha[1.4i] (Herb) Reitenauer. Daniel was b. on Apr. 30, 1758, and d. in 1839. They had the following children in District Township (baptized at Oley Hill):

Catherine[1.3.9.1i], b. on June 20, 1788, baptized on Aug. 31, 1788, and sponsored by Jacob and Catherine Herb.

Elizabeth[1.3.9.2i], b. on Sep. 9, 1789, baptized on Oct. 28, 1789, and sponsored by Abraham Rietenauer and Barbara Herb.

Anna Maria[1.3.9.3i], b. on Jan. 21, 1791, baptized on Apr. 10, 1791, and sponsored by Abraham Frey and Barbara Herb.

Salome[1.3.9.4i], b. on Apr. 28, 1792, baptized on July 8, 1792, and sponsored by Jacob and Catharine Herb.

Daniel[1.3.9.5i], b. on Feb. 23, 1794, baptized on May 11, 1794, and sponsored by Abraham Reitenauer and Susanna Herb.

Johannes[1.3.9.6i], b. on Feb. 13, 1796, baptized on Mar. 13, 1796, and sponsored by Johannes and Elisabeth Reitenauer.

Jacob[1.3.9.7i], b. on Feb. 16, 1797, baptized on May 7, 1797, and sponsored by Adam and Elisabeth Frey.

Elizabeth[1.3.9.8i], b. on July 1, 1798, baptized on Nov. 4, 1798, and sponsored by Peter and Elisabeth Herb.

Johan Peter Herb

Peter[1.3.10i] m. Elisabetha, daughter of Michael and Anna Catharina (Geri) Hillegas, in Montgomery County, New Hanover Lutheran Church, Pennsylvania, on June 22, 1796. She was b. in Lehigh County, Pennsylvania, on Nov. 1, 1773, and d. in Montgomery County, Washington Township, Ohio, in 1826. Peter d. in Mercer

County, Dublin Township, Ohio, on Dec. 20, 1842, and is buried in the Old Frysinger cemetery. They had the following children in Berks County, District Township, Pennsylvania:

Johan Peter[1.3.10.11], b. on Feb. 24, 1797, baptized at Oley Hill on Apr. 9, 1797, and sponsored by Michael Hillegas and Susanna Herb. He m. Sarah, and d. in Ohio in 1844.

Wilhelm[1.3.10.21], b. on Mar. 29, 1798, baptized at Oley Hill on May 20, 1798, and sponsored by Daniel and Salome Reitenauer.

Jacob R.[1.3.10.31], b. about 1800, and m. Abijah Dunn in Miami County, Ohio, on Sep. 24, 1820.

Catherina[1.3.10.41], b. on July 4, 1803.

Joseph[1.3.10.51], b. in 1805.

Amos[1.2.2.9.61], b. in 1807.

Elisabeth Anna[1.3.10.71], b. in 1809.

Lydia[1.3.10.81], b. in Nov. 1813.

Jonas Henrich[1.3.10.91], b. on Mar. 20, 1814.

Johan Reuben[1.3.10.101], b. in 1816.

Wilhelm Harp

Wilhelm[1.3.10.21] m. Rhoda Martoin in Montgomery County, Ohio, on Dec. 12, 1822. She was b. in Kentucky on Mar. 31, 1802, and d. in Miami County, West Milton, Ohio, on Mar. 27, 1887. Wilhelm d. in West Milton on Mar. 1, 1867. They had the following children:

William B.[1.3.10.2.11], b. on Feb. 15, 1824, and m. Caroline Harper in Mercer County, Ohio, on Sep. 12, 1850. She was b. in 1831. They resided in Van Wert County, Wilshire, Ohio.

Andrew Jackson[1.3.10.2.21], b. on Dec. 15, 1825, and m. Eliza Ann Wertz. He d. in Feb. 1900.

George W.[1.3.10.2.31], b. in 1829, and m. Maria L. Tenney in Miami County in 1859.

Calvin Dunham[1.3.10.2.41], b. in 1833, and m. Elizabeth Durbin in Van Wert County, Ohio, in 1860.

Marquis Lafayette[1.3.10.2.51], b. on Mar. 27, 1835, and m. Mary Jane Harp, and Arabella C. Mast. Marquis d. on June 18, 1918.

Ann Eliza[1.3.10.2.61], b. in 1838, m. John Wesley Secrist, and d. in 1923.

Charles[1.3.10.2.71], b. in 1845.

Catherina Harp

Catherina[1.3.10.4i] m. William Frysinger in Montgomery County, Ohio, in 1816. She d. in Mercer County, Dublin Township, Ohio, on Sep. 17, 1853. They had the following children:

Nathan[1.3.10.4.1i], b. in Montgomery County, Germantown, Ohio, on July 3, 1816, m. Jane, daughter of Joseph and Lois (Petro) Ryan, in Mercer County, Ohio, on Nov. 1, 1844, and d. in Mercer County, Dublin Township, Ohio, on July 19, 1891. She was b. in Greene County, Ohio, on Sep. 18, 1826, and d. on Oct. 8, 1885.

Peter[1.3.10.4.2i], b. in Champaign County, Ohio, on Aug. 7, 1819, m. Sarah Ann Shindledecker in Mercer County on Nov. 22, 1846, and d. in Dublin Township on June 30, 1907.

John[1.3.10.4.3i], b. in Champaign County, Ohio, on Dec. 9, 1820, m. Sarah, daughter of Michael and Barbara (Kepler) Barton, in Mercer County, Ohio, on Apr. 8, 1852, and d. in Dublin Township on Dec. 18, 1897. She was b. in Knox County, Liberty Township, Ohio, on Jan. 15, 1832, and d. in Mercer County, Rockford, Ohio, on Feb. 20, 1913.

Elizabeth[1.3.10.4.4i], b. on Sep. 28, 1824, and d. on Feb. 18, 1836.

Sarah Ann[1.3.10.4.5i], b. on Apr. 9, 1825, and d. on Feb. 18, 1839.

Jacob[1.3.10.4.6i], b. on Jan. 30, 1826, m. Maria Shindledecker in Mercer County on Nov. 2, 1848, and d. in Dublin Township on Dec. 13, 1899.

Susanna[1.3.10.4.7i], b. on Apr. 8, 1829, and d. in Dublin Township on Mar. 11, 1845.

Cynthia Ann[1.3.10.4.8i], b. in 1831, and m. Jeremiah Dull.

Lydia[1.3.10.4.9i], b. on Oct. 1, 1832, and d. before 1836.

Catherine[1.3.10.4.10i], b. on Oct. 1, 1832, and d. on July 12, 1833.

William[1.3.10.4.11i], b. in 1835, served in the Civil War as a Private in Company E, 197th Regiment, and lost his left eye in battle. He m. Narcissus Wiley in Mercer County on Dec. 19, 1850, and d. in Mercer County, Shane's Crossing, Ohio, on Oct. 20, 1853.

Joseph Harp

Joseph[1.3.10.5i] m. Sarah Carmony in Montgomery County, Ohio, in 1823. Joseph d. in Mercer County, Dublin Township, Ohio, in Mar. 1836. They had the following children:

Catherine[1.3.10.5.1i], b. in Montgomery County, Ohio, about 1827, and m. Samuel/James Pope Hedges in Mercer County, Ohio, on Mar. 29, 1850.

Lydia[1.3.10.5.2i], b. in 1831.

Mary[1.3.10.5.3i], b. in 1836, and m. John Yant. He was b. in 1829. Mary d. in Mercer County, Black Creek Township, Ohio, on Apr. 4, 1881.

Amos Harp

Amos[1.3.10.6i] m. Margaret, daughter of Joseph and Margaretha (Lohr) Braun, in Miami County, Ohio, on Aug. 19, 1830, Anna Mille Overly in Auglaize County, Ohio, on Dec. 25, 1856, and Lucinda Goodwin in Mercer County, Ohio, on Apr. 23, 1865. Margaret was b. in Frederick County, Taneytown, Maryland, in 1808, and d. in Auglaize County, Noble Township, Ohio, between 1850 and 1856. Anna Mille d. before 1860. Lucinda d. before 1870. He resided in Auglaize County in 1860. Amos was a farmer, and d. in Mercer County, Dublin Township, Ohio, between 1870 and 1880. He is buried in Stringtown cemetery. Amos and Margaret had the following children:

Mary Ann[1.3.10.6.1i], b. in Mercer County, Dublin Township, Ohio, on Aug. 31, 1831, and m. Clayton Bice and Zacheriah Sutton. Zacheriah, son of John and Sarah Sutton, was b. in Butler County, Liberty Township, Ohio, on July 20, 1817. He m. Charity Donovan in Mercer County, Ohio, on June 25, 1839, Leah Buck in Mercer County in 1847, and Mary Ann Harp, in Auglaize County, Ohio, on Sep. 27, 1858. Charity was b. in 1823, and d. in Dublin Township on Feb. 22, 1846. She is buried in Chivington cemetery. Leah was b. in 1822, and d. in Dublin Township in 1856. She is buried in Stringtown cemetery. Mary Ann d. in Dublin Township on Mar. 6, 1913. Mary Ann m. Clayton Bice in Auglaize County, Ohio, in 1852. He d. about 1857/58. Zacheriah Sutton was a farmer in Dublin Township, and d. there on Feb. 19, 1885. He is buried in Stringtown cemetery.

Joseph Alonzo[1.3.10.6.2i], b. in Dublin Township on Mar. 13, 1835, m. Helena Koch in Auglaize County, Ohio, on May 23, 1858, and d. in Mercer County, Ohio, on Aug. 31, 1898.

Jonathan[1.3.10.6.3i], b. in Dublin Township on July 4, 1837, m. Caroline Bender in Mercer County, Ohio, on May 22, 1862, and Matilda Miller on Nov. 25, 1866. Matilda was b. in 1847, and d. in 1883. Jonathan d. in Mercer County, Black Creek Township, on Mar. 16, 1904.

Catherine[1.3.10.6.4i], b. in Auglaize County, Noble Township, Ohio, on May 14, 1840, and m. Ruel, son of George and Katherine A. (Stophlet) Roebuck, in Mercer County on Oct. 2, 1862. He was b. in Dublin Township on June 5, 1830. She d. in Dublin Township on Feb. 16, 1883. Ruel d. in Dublin Township on Sep. 20, 1887.

Margaret[1.3.10.6.5i], b. in Noble Township on Jan. 27, 1845(6), m. Cyrus Buck in Mercer County on Mar. 24, 1862, and d. in Dublin Township on Aug. 7, 1870. Cyrus was b. on Jan. 23, 1834, and d. on Apr. 5, 1870.

Elizabeth Ann Harp

Elizabeth Anna[1.3.10.7i] m. Nobel Baltzell in Mercer County, Ohio, on Sep. 12, 1839. He was b. in 1816, and d. in Dublin Township on Oct. 10, 1872. Elizabeth d. in Dublin Township on Dec. 5, 1865. They had the following children in Dublin Township:

Absalom[1.3.10.7.11], b. on Apr. 23, 1853, and d. in Dublin Township on Oct. 16, 1872.

Lydia Harp

Lydia[1.3.10.8i] m. William Hooks in Mercer County, Ohio, on Feb. 5, 1838. He was b. in 1810, and d. in Van Wert County, Liberty Township, Ohio, in Dec. 1881. Lydia d. in Liberty Township on Aug. 5, 1896. They had the following children:

Malinda[1.3.10.8.11], m. James/John Bevington, and Johan Johantgen in 1893.

Reuben[1.3.10.8.2i], b. in 1840, and m. Minerva Miller in 1866. Inman Henry[1.3.10.8.3i].

Mary Ann[1.3.10.8.4i], b. in 1857, and m. Philip Miller.

Abraham[1.3.10.8.5i], b. on Dec. 28, 1851, and m. Nancy Jane Dull.

Franklin[1.3.10.8.6i], b. about 1853, and d. in 1894.

Jonas Henrich Harp

Jonas Henrich[1.3.10.9i] m. Mary Ann Putman in Van Wert County, Ohio, on June 4, 1848. She was b. in Somerset County, Pennsylvania, in 1829, and d. in Van Wert County, Liberty Township, Ohio, on Mar. 6, 1902. Jonas d. in Liberty Township on Dec. 25, 1861. They had the following children in Liberty Township:

Commodore[1.3.10.9.11], b. on Apr. 25, 1849, m. Emeline Handwerck in 1875, and d. in Colorado in 1930.

Rosanna[1.3.10.9.2i], b. in 1853, m. Henry Flager in 1873, and d. in 1911.

Andrew Jackson[1.3.10.9.3i], b. on Oct. 30, 1855, and m. Loretta Elizabeth North on Nov. 5, 1885. She was b. in Van Wert County, Ohio, on Oct. 4, 1861, and d. in Van Wert County on Sep. 16, 1931. Andrew d. in Van Wert County on Dec. 21, 1938.

Lydia[1.3.10.9.4i], b. in 1859, m. Henry Brunni on Mar. 26, 1885, and d. in 1907.

William[1.3.10.9.5i], b. in 1861, m. Margaret R. Putman in 1887, and d. in Van Wert County, Ohio, in 1952.

Johan Reuben Harp

Johan Reuben[1.3.10.10i] m. Eleanor Rowland in Van Wert County, Ohio, on Jan. 31, 1843. He d. in Paulding County, Ohio, on June 9, 1895. They had the following children in Van Wert County, Liberty Township, Ohio:

Jonas H.[1.3.10.10.1i], b. on Mar. 26, 1844, and m. Hannah Waltz on Jan. 2, 1870. She was b. in 1850, and d. in Paulding County, Payne, Ohio, in 1881. Jonas d. in Payne on Feb. 10, 1880.

Alexander[1.3.10.10.2i], b. about 1846, and m. Dorothy A. Granger in 1869.

David[1.3.10.10.3i], b. about 1849.

William H./R.[1.3.10.10.4i], b. about 1851.

Andrew Jackson[1.3.10.10.5i], b. about 1854, and resided in Michigan.

Lydia Ann[1.3.10.10.6i], b. in 1856.

John Hines[1.3.10.10.7i], b. on Apr. 5, 1859, and m. Caroline Emeline Exline. She was b. in Erie County, Ohio, on Mar. 24, 1863, and d. on Aug. 11, 1921. John d. on Feb. 15, 1927.

Mary D.[1.3.10.10.8i], b. in 1862, and d. in 1862.

Commodore Alexander[1.3.10.10.9i], b. about 1866, and m. Netta (b. about 1873).

Jonathan Herb

Jonathan[1.3.111i] m. Susanna, resided in Northumberland County, Pennsylvania, in 1810, and had the following daughter:

Joseph[1.3.11.1i], b. about 1793, and baptized at Weissenberg Lutheran Church, Weissenberg Township.

Susanna[1.3.11.2i], b. in Lehigh County, Whitehall Township, Pennsylvania, on Apr. 18, 1794, and baptized at Schlosser's Reformed Church on June 8, 1794.

Hanna[1.3.11.3i], b. about 1795, and baptized at Lowhill Lutheran Church, Lowhill Township.

Peter[1.3.11.4i], b. on Jan. 9, 1797, and baptized at Lowhill Lutheran Church.

Anna Maria[1.3.11.5i], b. about 1800, and baptized at Lowhill Lutheran Church.

Maria Elisabetha Herb

Maria Elisabetha[1.3.12i] may have m. Adam Frey. She d. before 1806. Adam and Elisabetha Frey had the following children in District Township (baptized at Oley Hill):

Jacob[1.3.12.1i], b. on Dec. 19, 1792, baptized on Mar. 3, 1793, and sponsored by Jacob Frey and Barbara Herb.

Daniel[1.3.12.2i], b. on Apr. 2, 1794, baptized on May 11, 1794, and sponsored by Daniel and Salome Reitenauer.

Elizabeth[1.3.12.3i], b. on Apr. 16, 1795, baptized on July 26, 1795, and sponsored by Heinrich and Elisabeth Hees.

Johannes[1.3.12.4i], b. on Oct. 27, 1796, baptized on Mar. 12, 1797, and sponsored by Jacob and Catharina Herb.

Johanna Elisabetha Herb

Johanna Elisabetha[1.5i] m. Johannes, son of Johannes and Maria Catharina (Lehnhard) Reitenauer, in Berks County, Pennsylvania, in 1752. He was b. in Alsace, France, in Dec. 1723, and d. in District Township in Aug. 1805. Johannes Reitenauer, Sr., son of Nicholas and Susanna Reitenauer, was b. in Tieffenbach, Lower Alsace on Mar. 3, 1690, immigrated to America in 1739, and d. in Berks County on Nov. 3, 1755. Johannes m. Maria Catharina, daughter of Nicholas and Anna Barbara Lehnhard, in 1716. Maria Catharina was b. on June 5, 1696. Johanna Elisabetha d. in District Township on Jan. 20, 1808. They had the following children in District Township (baptized at Oley Hill):

Maria Elisabetha[1.5.1i], b. on May 17, 1752, and m. George Seibert.

Maria[1.5.2i], b. on Feb. 18, 1755, baptized on Mar. 16, 1755, and sponsored by Christoph and Maria Elisabeth, children of Hannes Reitenauer.

Catherine Barbara[1.5.3i], b. on Aug. 15, 1756, baptized on Sep. 12, 1756, and sponsored by Peter and Catharina Barbara Holl. She m. Michael Hoffman.

Johann Daniel[1.5.4i], b. on Apr. 30, 1758, baptized on May 21, 1758, and sponsored by Johan David and Anna Elizabeth Meier. He m. Maria Salome Harp[1.3.9i], and d. in 1839.

Johannes[1.5.5i], b. on Dec. 3, 1759, baptized on Dec. 16, 1759, and sponsored by Willhelm and Elizabeth Reichart. He d. in 1828.

Johannes Frederick[1.5.6i], b. on Apr. 4, 1762, baptized on Apr. 4, 1762, and sponsored by Johannes Herb and wife. He m. Catherine Muthart in Berks County, Pennsylvania, on Aug. 28, 1787, and d. in 1837. Catherine was b. in 1769, and d. in 1829.

Jacob[1.5.7i], b. on Sep. 18, 1764, baptized on Oct. 28, 1764, and m. Anna Margaret, and d. in 1833.

Elizabeth[1.5.8i], b. on July 5, 1765, and baptized on July 7, 1765.

Abraham[1.5.9i], b. about 1769, and m. Elizabeth Krumrein on Mar. 15, 1796.

Maria Susanna[1.5.10i], b. about 1771, and m. John Stoufer.

Maria Catherine[1.5.11i], b. on July 2, 1773, baptized on Aug. 2, 1773, and sponsored by Abraham and Gertraud Herb.

Johannes Herb

Johannes[1.6i] m. Anna Maria, and had the following children:

Johannes[1.6.1i], b. in 1750, and confirmed as a m. man at Oley Hill on May 19, 1792 aged 42 years.

Abraham[1.6.2i], b. in 1753, and confirmed at Oley Hill on May 19, 1792 aged 39 years. He has not been confirmed as a son, but seems to fit nowhere else.

Sebastian[1.6.3i], b. on Nov. 20, 1756, baptized at Falkner Swamp on Jan. 2, 1757, and sponsored by Sebastian Kuele and wife.

Johan Frederick[1.6.4i], baptized at Falkner Swamp on Mar. 12, 1759, aged 8 weeks, and sponsored by Frederick Weiss and wife.

Rosina[1.6.5i], b. on June 24, 1763, baptized at Oley Hill on Oct. 30, 1763, and sponsored by Jacob Walther and wife.

George[1.6.6i], b. on Nov. 8, 1765, and baptized in Berks County, Rockland Township, Mertz Church.

Jacob[1.6.7i], b. on Jan. 15, 1768, baptized at Oley Hill on May 1, 1768, and sponsored by Jacob and Rosina Walter.

Susanna Catharine[1.6.8i], b. on Feb. 18, 1770, baptized at Oley Hill on Aug. 18, 1770, and sponsored by Susanna Benvill and Catherine Ulrich. She m. (as Susanna) Peter Drollonger in Berks County, Hereford on Oct. 4, 1791.

Johannes Herb

Johannes[1.6.1i] m. Anna Maria Busch in Berks County, District Township, Pennsylvania, on Feb. 17, 1789. He was a cordwainer in District Township. They had the following children in Berks County (baptized at Oley Hill):

Anna Maria[1.6.1.1i], b. on Dec. 30, 1790, baptized on Jan. 16, 1791, and sponsored by George and Anna Haeusler.

Catherine[1.6.1.2i], b. on Nov. 13, 1792, baptized on Dec. 9, 1792, and sponsored by Friedrich Nestor and Catharine Busch.

Abraham[1.6.1.3i], b. on Sep. 30, 1796, baptized on Jan. 29, 1797, and sponsored by Abraham and Anna Herb.

Peter[1.6.1.4i], b. on July 31, 1798, baptized on Sep. 23, 1798, and sponsored by Peter Weller, Jr., and Elizabeth Seibert.

Abraham Herb

Abraham[1.6.2i] m. Charlotta, and had the following children in District Township (baptized at Oley Hill):

Maria Christina[1.6.2.1i], b. on Dec. 30, 1777, baptized at DeLong's Reformed Church on May 10, 1778, and sponsored by Philip Meyer and Christine Weyand. She was confirmed at Oley Hill on Nov. 1, 1794, aged 16 years. She m. David Klauser in Berks County, Alsace on Oct. 27, 1795.

Johannes[1.6.2.2i], b. in 1779, and confirmed at Oley Hill on Apr. 15, 1797, aged 18 years. He has not been proven as a son, but seems to fit nowhere else.

Charlotta[1.6.2.3i], b. in 1781, and confirmed at Oley Hill on Nov. 1, 1794 aged 13 years. She m. David Groh in Berks County, Rockland Township, on Dec. 11, 1804.

Abraham[1.6.2.4i], b. on Jan. 3, 1789, baptized on July 5, 1789, and sponsored by Heinrich and Elizabeth Hess.

Catharine[1.6.2.5i], b. on June 27, 1791, baptized on Nov. 6, 1791, and sponsored by Abraham Reitenauer and Catharine Wiant.

Sebastian Herb

Sebastian[1.6.3i] m. Anna Maria, and baptized the following son at DeLong's Reformed Church in Berks County:

Johan Conrad[1.6.3.1i], b. on Apr. 17, 1779, baptized on May 23, 1779, and sponsored by Conrad and Elizabeth Bader.

****

Herring

Unknown[1j], was the father of the following children, that are presumed to be brothers:

Johann Henrich[1.1j]; Johannes[1.2j].

Johann Henrich Herring

Johann Henrich[1.1j] m. Elisabeth Margaretha, and immigrated to America on the ship *Patience* on Sep. 9, 1751, and d. in York County, Paradise Township, Pennsylvania, in May 1779. Elisabeth d. before 1767. After Elisabeth's death, Henrich m. Ann Margaretha, widow of Dietrich Saltzgeber, in Christ's Lutheran Church on July 6, 1767. Anna d. before 1779. Henrich resided in Bucks County, Haycock Township, Pennsylvania, until Feb. 18, 1759, but had purchased 84 acres on the north side of Pigeon Hill's in York County, Paradise Township, Pennsylvania, on Jan. 2, 1759. This was part of a survey of 130 acres warranted to John Brady on July 5, 1745. The remaining portion of Brady's tract was deeded to Johann Phillip Herring, presumed nephew of Henrich. Henrich and his family moved to York County, in the spring of 1759. His will was written on Apr. 20, 1779, and probated on June 4, 1779. Henrich and Elisabeth had the following children:

Philip Wendel[1.1.1j], b. in 1727, and d. in 1812.

Maria Dorothea[1.1.2j], b. about 1730.

Johann Henrich[1.1.3j], b. in May 1732.

Maria Margaretha[1.1.4j], b. about 1734.

Catharina Dorothea[1.1.5j], b. about 1736.

Elisabeth[1.1.6j], b. about 1738.

Maria Christina[1.1.7j], b. about 1740, and m. Adam Fauster/Tauster.

Philip Wendel Herring

Philip Wendel[1.1.1j] m. Elisabeth, immigrated to America on the ship *Patience* on Sep. 9, 1751, and d. in Bucks County, Haycock Township, Pennsylvania, on Jan. 28, 1812. On May 30, 1768, he purchased 183 acres in haycock Township. He was a Collector of Arms in Haycock Township for the committee of Safety during the Revolutionary War (period ending July 10, 1776). They had the following children in Haycock Township:

Henrich[1.1.1.1j], b. on Oct. 2, 1753.

Johan Michael[1.1.1.2j], b. on May 3, 1756, and baptized at
Tohickon Lutheran on May 15, 1756, and sponsored by Johan Michael
Kronau and Catharina Dorothea Herring.

Peter[1.1.1.3j], b. about 1759.

Maria Susanna[1.1.1.4j], b. in 1762, baptized at Tohickon
Lutheran Church in Apr. 1762, and sponsored by Valentine Philipp.

Anna Elisabeth[1.1.1.5j], b. on Dec. 12, 1763, baptized at
Tohickon Lutheran on Oct. 28, 1763, and sponsored by George Desch
and Susanna Drach.

Susanna[1.1.1.6j], b. on Dec. 12, 1763, baptized at Tohickon
Lutheran on Oct. 28, 1763, and sponsored by George Desch and
Susanna Drach.

Johann[1.1.1.7j], b. about 1764.

Adam[1.1.1.8j], b. about 1768, and resided in Northumberland
(now Union) County, Mifflinburg, Pennsylvania, in 1800.

Johann Philip[1.1.1.9j], b. on Sep. 7, 1772, baptized at Trinity
Lutheran Church at Springfield, and sponsored by John Metzger and
Elisabeth Catharina Gares. He m. Priscilla before 1789, and d. in 1821.

Henrich Herring

Henrich[1.1.1.1j] m. Anna Margaretha, and d. in Clinton County,
Logan Township, Pennsylvania, on Dec. 1, 1840. She d. on Mar. 29,
1836. He served in the Revolutionary War from 1776 to 1779. He
farmed in Bucks County, Haycock and Springfield Townships, and in
1800, moved to Sugar Valley, Northumberland County, Miles
Township, Pennsylvania. This area became Clinton County, Logan
Township. They had the following children (baptized in Tohickon
Union):

Johann Heinrich[1.1.1.1.1j], b. in Haycock Township on Jan. 26,
1782 (sponsored by Philip Hering and wife), m. Margaret, and d. in
Clinton County, Green Township, Pennsylvania, in 1855. She was b. in
Pennsylvania in 1796. He was a shoemaker, and an Ensign in the
Centre County, Pennsylvania, Militia.

Susanna[1.1.1.1.2j], b. on Jan. 16, 1784, baptized on May 23,
1784, and sponsored by Rudolph Schoch and Susanna Herring.

Elisabetha[1.1.1.1.3j], b. on Mar. 1, 1786, baptized on Apr. 22,
1786, and sponsored by Michael and Ursula Werner.

Johannes[1.1.1.1.4j], b. on Dec. 18, 1789.

Son[1.1.1.1.5j], b. about 1791, and d. before 1835.

Catharina[1.1.1.1.6j], b. on June 27, 1793, baptized on Aug. 4, 1793, and sponsored by John Hering and Elizabeth Denman.

Margaretha[1.1.1.1.7j], b. on Mar. 31, 1796.

Johannes Herring

Johannes[1.1.1.1.4j] m. Sarah, daughter of Jacob and Catharine Wagner, and d. in Clinton County, Logan Township, Sugar Valley, Pennsylvania, before 1850. She was b. on Sep. 11, 1791. They had the following children:

Daniel W.[1.1.1.1.4.1j], b. on Feb. 5, 1824, m. Rebecca J. Donahay in Clinton County, Green Township, Pennsylvania, in 1850, and d. in Altoona, Pennsylvania, on Jan. 13, 1923. She was b. on Dec. 3, 1829, and d. in Centre County, Liberty Township, Eagleville, Pennsylvania, on Apr. 11, 1874.

Daughter[1.1.1.1.4.2j], b. about 1826.

Sarah[1.1.1.1.4.3j], b. on Oct. 13, 1829, m. George, son of Peter and Sarah Kahl, and d. on Mar. 1, 1914. He was b. on May 1, 1821, and d. on Feb. 2, 1904.

Son[1.1.1.1.4.4j], b. about 1831.

Daughter[1.1.1.1.4.5j], b. about 1833.

Johan Michael Herring

Michael[1.1.1.2j] m. Elisabeth, daughter of Jost and Margaretta Reese, and had the following children:

Daughter[1.1.1.2.1j], b. about 1781.

John[1.1.1.2.2j], b. on Dec. 16, 1783, baptized at Tohickon Union in Jan. 1784, and sponsored by Johan Peter and Catharina Schuck.

Catharine[1.1.1.2.3j], b. on Aug. 17, 1786, baptized at Tohickon Union on Sep. 20, 1786, and sponsored by Margaret Riese.

Son[1.1.1.2.4j], b. about 1789.

Son[1.1.1.2.5j], b. about 1792.

Son[1.1.1.2.6j], b. about 1795.

Mary Magdalena[1.1.1.2.7j], b. in Northampton County, Plainfield, Pennsylvania, on May 10, 1798, m. Jesse Worley in Northampton County, Easton on Apr. 17, 1817, and d. in Berks County, Mohnton, Pennsylvania, on Feb. 20, 1874. He was b. in 1788, and d. in Mohnton in 1838.

Son[1.1.1.2.8j], b. about 1803.

Daughter[1.1.1.2.9j], b. about 1805.

Peter Herring

Peter$^{1.1.1.3j}$ resided in Bucks County, Springfield Township, Pennsylvania, in 1783. He moved to Northumberland County, Pennsylvania, and then to Ohio. He had the following children:

Charles$^{1.1.1.3.1j}$, b. on Aug. 27, 1798.

Daniel$^{1.1.1.3.2j}$, b. in 1800.

Lewis$^{1.1.1.3.3j}$, b. in 1801.

Conrad$^{1.1.1.3.4j}$, resided in Summit County in 1840.

Adam$^{1.1.1.3.5j}$.

David$^{1.1.1.3.6j}$.

Kate$^{1.1.1.3.7j}$.

Christine$^{1.1.1.3.8j}$.

Elizabeth$^{1.1.1.3.9j}$.

Peter$^{1.1.1.3.10j}$, resided in Summit County, Ohio, in 1840.

Elias$^{1.1.1.3.11j}$.

Charles Herring

Charles$^{1.1.1.3.1j}$ m. Hannah Wiltrout on June 25, 1822. She was b. on Aug. 28, 1802. They had the following children:

Elizabeth$^{1.1.5.3.1.1j}$, b. about 1823, and m. ____ Whitmeyer.

Joel$^{1.1.1.3.1.2j}$, b. in 1824.

Daniel$^{1.1.1.3.1.3j}$, b. in 1828.

Diana$^{1.1.1.3.1.4j}$, b. in 1830, and m. ____ Dailey.

Sarah$^{1.1.1.3.1.5j}$, b. in 1832, and m. ____ Sweigart.

Allen$^{1.1.1.3.1.6j}$, b. in 1833.

Maria$^{1.1.1.3.1.7j}$, b. in 1836, and m. ____ Marsh.

Matilda$^{1.1.1.3.1.8j}$, b. in 1839, and m. ____ Dailey.

Hiram$^{1.1.1.3.1.9j}$, b. on Jan. 7, 1844, and m. Susan Foltz. She was b. on Dec. 4, 1843.

Anna Elisabeth Herring

Elisabeth$^{1.1.1.5j}$ m. Theobald Dresh, and d. in Schuylkill County, Lewistown Valley, Pennsylvania, on Aug. 12, 1833. He d. about 1817. They had the following children:

John$^{1.1.1.5.1j}$.

Dewalt/Theobald$^{1.1.1.5.2j}$.

Jacob$^{1.1.1.5.3j}$.

Charlotte$^{1.1.1.5.4j}$, b. on Sep. 11, 1796, m. Jacob Herring (1795-1861), and d. on Dec. 13, 1880.

Elisabeth$^{1.1.1.5.5j}$, b. on July 30, 1799, and d. in Lewistown on Feb. 17, 1886.

Maria$^{1.1.1.5.6j}$, b. on Dec. 23, 1801, m. Jonas Bankes (1806-1884), and d. in Lewistown on Dec. 15, 1856.

Susanna Herring

Susanna$^{1.1.1.6j}$ m. Jacob, son of Nicholas and Elisabeth (Hartman) Buck, in 1790, and d. in Bucks County, Jenkintown, Pennsylvania, about 1841. He was b. in Bucks County, Springfield Township, Pennsylvania, on May 1, 1770, and d. on July 24, 1843. They had the following children:

John$^{1.1.1.6.1j}$, b. on Apr. 26, 1791.
Jacob$^{1.1.1.6.2j}$, b. on Oct. 10, 1794.
Elisabeth$^{1.1.1.6.3j}$, m. Francis McCarty.
Nicholas$^{1.1.1.6.4j}$.
Samuel$^{1.1.1.6.5j}$, b. on July 30, 1807.
Catherine$^{1.1.1.6.6j}$, m. Jacob Zorfoss.
Joseph$^{1.1.1.6.7j}$.

Johann Herring

Johann$^{1.1.1.7j}$ m. Maria, daughter of Johan Philip and Catharina Schreyer, and d. in Columbiana County, Liberty Township, Ohio, sometime after 1850. She d. before 1850. John was a mason, sawmiller, and farmer. In 1816, he had 70 acres in Northumberland County, Chillisquaque Township, Pennsylvania, and by 1840, resided in Columbiana County, Ohio. They had the following children:

Samuel$^{1.1.1.7.1j}$, b. in Bucks County, Haycock Township, on Jan. 29, 1798, baptized on May 8, 1798, and sponsored by Philip and Priscilla Herring. He d. before 1810.

John$^{1.1.1.7.2j}$, b. in Haycock Township on Nov. 9, 1799, baptized at Tohickon Union on Dec. 26, 1799, and sponsored by Jacob Abel and wife. He m. Charlotte, and resided in Bucks County, Nockamixon Township, in 1825 and 1827.

David$^{1.1.1.7.3j}$, b. in 1801, and d. in 1871.
Anna Maria$^{1.1.1.7.4j}$, b. in 1804, and m. ____ Meyerly.
Daughter$^{1.1.1.7.5j}$, b. about 1808.
Reading$^{1.1.1.7.6j}$, b. about 1813, and d. about 1896.
Jared$^{1.1.1.7.7j}$, b. about 1818, and d. in 1879.

Maria Dorothea Herring

Maria Dorothea$^{1.1.2j}$ m. Johann Georg Gap about 1752, and Jacob Maak about 1763. Georg's probate inventory was filed in York County in 1757. Jacob was naturalized in York County on Apr. 10,

1760, and taxed in Paradise Township in 1762. Dorothea was alive in 1779. She had the following children:

Maria Margaretha$^{1.1.2.1j}$, b. in Bucks County on July 3, 1753, baptized at Tohickon Lutheran on July 22, 1753, and sponsored by Henry Herring and Maria Margaretha, both single (the mother is listed as Maria Dorothea Gab).

Dorothea$^{1.1.2.2j}$, b. about 1755.

Jacob$^{1.1.2.3j}$, baptized by RJL on July 15, 1764, and sponsored by Christian Michel and Anna Maria Mackin.

Johann Henrich Herring

Johann Henrich$^{1.1.3j}$ m. Juliana Salome, daughter of Ludwig and Maria Barbara Salomonmuller, in Apr. 1760, and d. in Manheim Township on June 29, 1801. He purchased 100 acres in Codorus Township on Aug. 8, 1795, that he sold to his son-in-law, Heinrich Miller on May 27, 1799. His will was written on Oct. 13, 1798, probated on July 18, 1801. She was b. on May 1741, and d. on Nov. 24, 1805. They are buried in Manheim Union Burial Ground. Heinrich and Juliana had the following children:

Ludwig$^{1.1.3.1j}$, b. about 1760, and was a communicant at Saint Jacob's Lutheran Church on Jan. 3, 1784.

Daughter$^{1.1.3.2j}$, b. about 1762, and d. young.

Johann Henrich$^{1.1.3.3j}$, b. on Nov. 11, 1764, baptized at St. Jacob's Lutheran Church on Mar. 3, 1765, and sponsored by Ludwig Salomonmuller. He d. young.

Maria Philippina$^{1.1.3.4j}$, b. on Apr. 23, 1766, m. Jacob Klein, and d. on Sep. 26, 1833. He was b. on Apr. 7, 1760, and d. on Oct. 17, 1836. They are buried in Mt. Olivet cemetery in Hanover.

Johannes$^{1.1.3.5j}$, b. on Jan. 7, 1768, and baptized at St. Jacob's on Feb. 7, 1768.

Johann Solomon$^{1.1.3.6j}$, b. on Oct. 7, 1769, and baptized at St. Jacob's on Nov. 12, 1769. He d. before 1798.

Anna Maria$^{1.1.3.7j}$, b. on Sep. 12, 1771, and baptized at St. Jacob's on Oct. 4, 1771. She m. Heinrich, son of Georg and Elisabeth (Herring) Miller.

Johann Jacob$^{1.1.3.8j}$, b. on Nov. 20, 1773, m. Eva, daughter of Michael and Margaretha (Matter) Ehrhard in York County in 1801, and d. in Centre County, Gregg Township, Pennsylvania, on Nov. 25, 1829. She was b. on Feb. 24, 1780, and d. on Dec. 23, 1848. They are buried in Heckman cemetery. In 1800, he was a Captain of the 5th Company, 124th Regiment, 1st Brigade, 5th Division Adams County Militia.

Anna Christina[1.1.3.9j], b. on June 17, 1776, and baptized at St. Jacob's on July 7, 1776.

Heinrich[1.1.3.10j], b. in 1778, and d. in Adams County, Conewago Township, McSherrystown, Pennsylvania, in 1855. He m. Loisa and Margaret. Loisa was b. on May 31, 1778, and d. on Mar. 6, 1842 (buried at Saint Matthew's Lutheran Church cemetery). Margaret was b. about 1782, and d. on Nov. 25, 1869 (buried at St. John's Lutheran Church, Abbottstown, Adams County). He was an Ensign in the 2nd Battalion, 61st Regiment, 5th Division of the York County Militia in 1808. In 1810, he was in Manheim Township; in 1820 in Maryland; in 1830/40 Adams County, Mount Pleasant Township, Pennsylvania; and in 1850, McSherrystown.

Georg[1.1.3.11j], b. on June 2, 1781, and d. on Dec. 7, 1806. He is buried at Manheim Union Burial Ground.

Johannes Herring

Johannes[1.1.3.5j] m. Christina, daughter of Mathias and Elizabeth Meyer, and had the following son:

Jacob[1.1.3.5.1j], b. on Feb. 19, 1794, and baptized at St. Jacob's on Mar. 23, 1794.

Maria Margaretha Herring

Maria Margaretha[1.1.4j] m. an unknown man, d. in York County, Paradise Township, before 1779, and had the following daughter:

Maria Catharina[1.1.4.1j], b. about 1757, and m. George Emler before 1779.

Catharina Dorothea Herring

Catharina Dorothea[1.1.5j] m. Johann Nicholas, son of Johann Nickel Michel. He resided in York County, Paradise Township, in 1769, and Dover Township in 1779. Catharina d. between 1779 and 1784. Nicholas m. Anna Maria before 1784. He served as a Captain in the Revolutionary War, and d. on May 11, 1812. His will was written in Dover Township on Apr. 1, 1784, and probated on Sep. 3, 1812 (it named only his wife Anna Maria, son Adam, and granddaughter, Anna Maria). They had the following children:

Adam[1.1.5.1j], b. about 1757.

Elisabeth Margaretha[1.1.5.2j], b. in Bucks County on Jan. 27, 1759, baptized at Tohickon Union on Feb. 18, 1759, and sponsored by Henry Herring and wife.

Catharina[1.1.5.3j], b. in Bucks County on June 20, 1761, baptized at Tohickon Union on July 5, 1761, and sponsored by John Owen and wife.

Anna Catharina[1.1.5.4j], baptized by Reverend Jacob Lischy on May 15, 1763, and sponsored by Christian Michel and Anna Catharina Bergheimerin.

Elisabeth Herring

Elisabeth[1.1.6j] m. George Miller. He was taxed in York County, Paradise Township, in 1762, and 1769. They had the following children:

Henrich[1.1.6.1j], b. about 1758, and m. Anna Maria, daughter of Johann Henrich Herring.

George[1.1.6.2j], b. about 1762.

Johannes Herring

Johannes[1.2j] m. Anna Margaretha, and immigrated to Pennsylvania on the ship *Neptune* on Sep. 24, 1751. In 1754, 56, 58, they were communicants at Trinity Lutheran Church in Bucks County, Springfield Township, Pennsylvania. They had the following children:

Anna Elisabeth[1.2.1j], b. about 1720.

Johann Jacob[1.2.2j], b. about 1727.

Johannes[1.2.3j], b. about 1729.

Johann Ludwig[1.2.4j], b. about 1731.

Anna Margaretha[1.2.5j], b. about 1733, and was a communicant at Trinity Lutheran Church in Bucks County, Springfield Township, Pennsylvania, in 1757.

Margaretha Barbara[1.2.6j], b. about 1735, and was a communicant at Trinity Lutheran Church in Bucks County, Springfield Township, Pennsylvania, in 1757.

Maria Elisabeth[1.2.7j], b. in 1737, and confirmed on Good Friday, 1753, at New Goshenhoppen Lutheran Church in Upper Hanover Township. She was a sponsor for a child of Jurg Henrich and Anna Elisabeth Joseph at Indianfield Lutheran Church on Aug. 5, 1753.

Johann Phillip[1.2.8j], b. about 1739.

Anna Elisabeth Herring

Anna Elisabeth[1.2.1j] m. Georg Heinrich Joseph. He immigrated to America on the ship *Patience* on Sep. 9, 1751, and was taxed in Paradise Township in 1762. His probate inventory was filed in

Paradise Township in 1766 (d. on Nov. 26, 1766). They had the following children:

Anna Catharina[1.2.1.1j], b. in Feb. 1740, and m. Johann Jonas, son of Heinrich Bott, at CLY on Sep. 16, 1760.

Christina[1.2.1.2j], b. on Sep. 21, 1744, m. Johan Georg Oderman, and d. in Paradise Township on Nov. 18, 1830. He was b. on Dec. 15, 1739, and d. on May 20, 1826.

Johannes[1.2.1.3j], b. in 1748, m. Catharina Elisabeth, daughter of Conrad Maul, and d. in Paradise Township in 1840.

Maria Elisabeth[1.2.1.4j], b. on June 3, 1753, baptized at St. Paul's Lutheran Church in Montgomery County, Pennsylvania, and sponsored by Maria Elisabeth Herring. She m. Johan Philip, son of Conrad Maul (see entry in Manchester section), and d. in 1836. He was b. in 1751, and d. in 1841.

Johann Jacob Herring

Johann Jacob[1.2.2j] immigrated to America on the ship *Two Brothers* on Sep. 28, 1753, and m. Maria Catharina Hackmann in Montgomery County, Upper Hanover Township, Pennsylvania, on Oct. 31, 1758. He was a communicant at Zion Reformed Church in Northampton County, Upper Milford Township, on Jan. 1, 1756, and Apr. 4, 1756. He purchased land in Northampton County, Allen Township, on May 17, 1777, that he sold on May 14, 1787. He resided in Northampton County, Hanover Township, Pennsylvania, in 1800, and d. before 1810. Maria Catharina was alive in 1810. They baptized the following children in St. Paul's Lutheran Church:

Johann Ludwig[1.2.2.1j], b. on May 1, 1759, and sponsored by Luddwig Herring at his baptism.

Anna Elisabetha[1.2.2.2j], b. on Mar. 27, 1760.

Anna Maria[1.2.2.3j], b. on Feb. 3, 1761.

Maria Catharina[1.2.2.4j], b. on Feb. 3, 1761, and sponsored by Maria Catharina, wife of Ludwig Herring at her baptism.

Anna Margaretha[1.2.2.5j], b. in 1764, and confirmed at St. Paul's (Blue) Church in Northampton (now Lehigh) County, Upper Saucon Township, Pennsylvania, on Apr. 5, 1776.

Anna[1.2.2.6j], b. in 1766, and confirmed at Zion (Stone) Church in Northampton County, Allen Township, on Nov. 5, 1780.

Andreas[1.2.2.7j], b. in 1767.

Andreas Herring

Andreas[1.2.2.7j] m. Maria, and had the following children:

Andreas[1.2.2.7.1j], b. on June 27, 1802, m. Sarah, daughter of Daniel and Margaret Spengler, and d. in Allen Township on Apr. 18, 1840. She was b. on Apr. 1, 1805, and d. on Aug. 13, 1879. They are buried in Greenwood cemetery.

Elisabeth[1.2.2.7.2j], b. about 1805.

Jacob[1.2.2.7.3j], b. on Sep. 16, 1807, m. Catharina Frevel on Jan. 27, 1834, and d. in Northampton County, Bushkill Township, on Nov. 2, 1862. He is buried in the Old cemetery at Bath. She was b. on Apr. 17, 1812, and d. on Mar. 1, 1902. She is buried in Nisky cemetery in Lehigh County, Eastern Salisbury.

Maria[1.2.2.7.4j], b. about 1809, m. Levi Barbar in Northampton County, Easton on Apr. 20, 1830, and d. in East Allen Township about 1834. He was b. on Feb. 7, 1808, and d. in Northampton County, Bath, Pennsylvania, on June 12, 1882. He is buried in Greenmount cemetery.

Johannes Herring

Johann[1.2.3j] immigrated to America on the ship *Neptune* on Sep. 24, 1751, m. Anna Elisabeth. He apparently resided in York County in 1763, but returned to eastern Pennsylvania. Johann d. in Berks County, Pennsylvania, before 1790, and his widow d. in Bucks County after 1800. They had the following children:

Margareth Elisabetha[1.2.3.1j], baptized at St. Paul's Lutheran Church in Montgomery County, Upper Hanover Township, Pennsylvania, on Feb. 8, 1752, and sponsored by Michael and Elisabeth Kabel.

Johann Henrich[1.2.3.2j], b. on Feb. 23, 1755, baptized at St. Paul's (Blue) Church, Northampton (now Lehigh) County, Upper Sauccon Township, Pennsylvania, on Mar. 30, 1755. He took the Oath of Allegiance in Berks County on June 7, 1778, and resided in Bucks County in 1800.

Johannes[1.2.3.3j], baptized in York (now Adams) County, Pennsylvania, at Littletown Christ's Reformed Lutheran Church on Oct. 16, 1763.

Johann Ludwig Herring

Johann Ludwig[1.2.4j] immigrated to America on the ship *Neptune* on Sep. 24, 1751, m. Maria Catharina, and d. in Montgomery County, Upper Hanover Township, Pennsylvania, between 1765 and 1769. They baptized the following children at St. Paul's Lutheran Church in Upper Hanover Township (except the last in Old Goshenhoppen in Upper Salford Township):

Johann Georg$^{1.2.4.1j}$, b. on Nov. 13, 1753, and d. on Apr. 25, 1776. He is buried at Goshenhoppen Church in Upper Salford Township.

Anna Christina$^{1.2.4.2j}$, b. on Jan. 14, 1756, and confirmed at Indian Creek Reformed Church in 1770.

Jacob$^{1.2.4.3j}$, b. in Montgomery County, Marlborough Township, on Oct. 28, 1758.

Eva Catharina$^{1.2.4.4j}$, b. on Jan. 8, 1761, and confirmed at St. Paul's on Feb. 14, 1774.

Johan Nickel$^{1.2.4.5j}$, b. on Feb. 16, 1763.

Johann Luttwig$^{1.2.4.6j}$, b. on Feb. 1, 1764.

Jacob Herring

Jacob$^{1.2.4.3j}$ m. Magdalena, daughter of Henry and Barbara (Nees) Guttelman, at St. John's on May 27, 1783, and d. in Bucks County, Rockhill Township, Pennsylvania, on Feb. 10, 1817. She was b. on Nov. 23, 1757, and d. on Apr. 26, 1842. They are buried in St. John's Lutheran Church, Ridge Valley. He was a cordwainer, and served as a Private in Captain John Schuler's Company, 5th Battalion during the Revolutionary War (1784-86). They had the following children in Montgomery County, Franconia Township:

Johan Georg$^{1.2.4.3.1j}$, b. on Dec. 28, 1784, baptized on Jan. 31, 1785, and d. in Bucks County, West Rockhill Township, on Aug. 14, 1825. He m. Catharina, daughter of Henry and Christina Dietz. She d. on June 1, 1860. They are buried at St. John's cemetery. He was a cordwainer.

Infant$^{1.2.4.3.2j}$, b. about 1786.

Johannes$^{1.2.4.3.3j}$, b. on June 1, 1788, baptized in 1790, and d. in Bucks County, West Rockhill Township, on May 10, 1880. He m. Christina Groff. She was b. on Feb. 8, 1795, and d. on Sep. 27, 1882. They are buried at St. John's cemetery.

Johan Jacob$^{1.2.4.3.4j}$, b. on Nov. 21, 1791, baptized on Feb. 7, 1792, and d. in Bucks County, West Rockhill Township, on Aug. 16, 1855. He m. Maria Magdalena, daughter of Abraham Bean. She was b. about 1792, and was alive in 1860. He is buried in Ridge Valley Lutheran cemetery.

Infant$^{1.2.4.3.5j}$, b. about 1793.

Maria Catharina$^{1.2.4.3.4j}$, b. on Mar. 11, 1795, baptized on May 10, 1795, and d. on Feb. 25, 1873. She m. Philip Berndt. He was b. on Feb. 1, 1796, and d. on Feb. 15, 1867. They are buried in Ridge Valley cemetery.

Samuel[1.2.4.3.5j], b. on Mar. 22, 1797, baptized on Apr. 17, 1797, and d. on Feb. 18, 1874. He m. Christina, daughter of Johannes and Christina Gilbert. She was b. on Oct. 27, 1800, and d. on Apr. 2, 1880. They are buried in Ridge Valley cemetery.

Peter[1.2.4.3.6j], b. on Mar. 22, 1797, baptized on Apr. 17, 1797, and d. in Northampton County, Upper Mt. Bethel Township, Pennsylvania, on Sep. 8, 1874. He m. Maria Berger in 1856. She was b. on Sep. 22, 1826, and d. at Centreville on July 26, 1899. They are buried in Stone Church cemetery.

Eva[1.2.4.3.7j], b. about 1800, and confirmed at Indianfield Lutheran Church in 1814.

Sarah[1.2.4.3.8j], b. on May 13, 1803, and d. on May 3, 1872. She is buried at Indianfield Lutheran Church.

Johan Nickel Herring

Johan Nickel[1.2.4.5j] m. Maria Hersh, and d. in Montgomery County, Marlborough Township, on July 27, 1839. She was b. on Mar. 16, 1760, and d. on Apr. 23, 1842. They are buried in St. Paul's cemetery. They had the following children in Montgomery County:

Catharina[1.2.4.5.1j], b. on May 19, 1785, m. Georg Neesz, and d. in Marlborough Township on Sep. 27, 1856. He was b. on Mar. 11, 1783, and d. on Mar. 31, 1857. They are buried at St. Paul's cemetery.

Mary[1.2.4.5.2j], b. about 1787, m. Martin Young on July 13, 1806, and was residing in Marlborough Township in 1839. He d. before 1839.

Johannes[1.2.4.5.3j], b. on Nov. 10, 1790, baptized on Dec. 19, 1790, and d. in Marlborough Township on Aug. 24, 1870. He m. Christina, daughter of Jacob Sheifley. She was b. on Nov. 6, 1795, and d. on May 17, 1861. They are buried at St. Paul's cemetery.

Maria[1.2.4.5.4j], b. on Oct. 23, 1793, baptized on Dec. 1, 1793, and d. on Dec. 2, 1864. She m. Abraham Herner. He was b. on Aug. 15, 1792, and d. on Aug. 29, 1859. They are buried in Ridge Valley Lutheran cemetery in Bucks County.

Lydia[1.2.4.5.5j], b. about 1797, was confirmed at Goshenhoppen in 1815, and was alive in 1839.

Sarah[1.2.4.5.6j], b. on Apr. 24, 1799, m. Henry Trumbauer, and resided in Marlborough Township in 1839.

Henrich[1.2.4.5.7j], b. on June 11, 1802, m. Hannah, daughter of Henry and Elisabeth (Brey) Heinrich, and d. on Sep. 23, 1878. She was b. on Dec. 10, 1808, and d. on Oct. 27, 1883.

Joseph[1.2.4.5.8j], b. on Aug. 28, 1807, m. Elisabeth, daughter of Abraham Brey, on Nov. 19, 1837, and d. in Marlborough Township on Apr. 22, 1888. She was b. on Jan. 26, 1806, and d. on Aug. 17, 1851. They are buried in St. Paul's cemetery. He was a whipstockmaker.

Johann Luttwig Herring

Johann Luttwig[1.2.4.6j] m. Barbara, and d. on Mar. 1, 1815. He is buried in Tohickon Reformed cemetery in Bucks County. He was a Private in Captain Schuler's Company, 4th Battalion in 1785/86. He had the following children:

Daughter[1.2.4.6.1j], b. about 1785.

Catharina[1.2.4.6.2j], b. on Dec. 22, 1787, m. David Schitz in Apr. 1811, and d. in Milford Township on Sep. 9, 1964. He was b. on Jan. 24, 1784, and d. on May 27, 1885. They are buried in St. John's cemetery.

Maria[1.2.4.6.3j], b. on Dec. 6, 1789, and d. on Mar. 6, 1840. She is buried in Ridge Valley cemetery in Bucks County.

Johannes[1.2.4.6.4j], b. on Aug. 10, 1794, m. Sarah Nesz, and d. in Bucks County, Rockhill Township, on Nov. 20, 1863. She was b. on Oct. 15, 1802, and d. on Feb. 8, 1863.

Jacob[1.2.4.6.5j], b. on Apr. 5, 1797, m. Christina, and d. in Bucks County, Spinnerstown, Pennsylvania. She was b. on Aug. 4, 1802, and d. on Mar. 26, 1880. She was buried at St. John's cemetery.

Johann Phillip Herring

Johann Phillip[1.2.8j] immigrated to America on the ship *Neptune* with his parents on Sep. 24, 1751. He m. Anna about 1766, and d. in Fairfield County, Amanda Township, Ohio, in 1823. His will was written on May 22, 1823, and probated in 1823. She d. in Amanda Township after 1800. Phillip was naturalized in Bucks County, Richland Township, Pennsylvania, on Aug. 8, 1765. In 1769, he was taxed in York County, Paradise Township, Pennsylvania.with two horses, and 46 acres. This was part of John Brady's Warrant on the North Side of Pigeon Hills. The other portion of this Warrant had been purchased by Philip's (presumed) uncle, Henry Herring, on Jan. 2, 1759. Phillip was taxed in Paradise Township in 1783, and in 1784, he moved to Dover Township. He served in the Revolutionary War as a Corporal in the York County, Militia in 1780 and 1782. In 1786, 1787, and 1788, he served in the York County, Militia in the 3rd Company of Foot, 3rd Battalion. Around 1803/04, he moved to Fairfield County, Amanda

Township, Ohio, where he had 183 acres of land. Phillip and Anna had
the following children:

Heinrich[1.2.8.1j], b. about 1767.

Elizabeth[1.2.8.2j], b. about 1769.

Philip[1.2.8.3j], b. about 1771.

Catherine[1.2.8.4j], b. in 1773.

John[1.2.8.5j], b. about 1775.

Anna Maria[1.2.8.6j], b. about 1777.

Catharine Barbary[1.2.8.7j], b. on Aug./June 28, 1779.

Eve[1.2.8.8j], b. on Feb. 27, 1783.

Heinrich Herring

Heinrich[1.2.8.1j] m. Margaret, daughter of Samuel and
Margaretha (Apfel) Wildasin, of York County, Manheim Township. She
was b. in 1771, and d. in Adams County, Straban Township,
Pennsylvania, on Oct. 5, 1846. Heinrich served in the York County
Militia in Captain John Sharp's 3rd Company of Foot, 3rd Battalion in
1786, 1787, and 1788. He d. in Dover Township in Aug. 1825. He was a
farmer and weaver. From 1824-27, he was taxed in Fairfield County,
Amanda Township, Ohio, as a non-resident for 61 acres that he
inherited from his father. Heinrich willed this land in Ohio to his son,
Philip. They had the following children:

Malli[1.2.8.1.1j], b. about 1788, and m. Jacob, son of Charles and
Barbara Mitman, in York County on Oct. 19, 1809.

Johannes[1.2.8.1.2j], b. on Mar. 3, 1790, baptized at Strayer's
on Aug. 2, 1790, and sponsored by Mattheis Mayer and Lizabeth
Haring.

Georg Michael[1.2.8.1.3j], b. on Feb. 12, 1792, baptized at
Strayer's on Apr. 6, 1792, and sponsored by Michael and Magdalena
Seifert.

John Philip[1.2.8.1.4j], b. on Nov. 7 (Sep. 17), 1793, baptized at
Strayer's on Mar. 31, 1794, and sponsored by John Philip and Anna
Hering.

Henry[1.2.8.1.5j], b. on Aug. 15, 1796.

Elizabeth[1.2.8.1.6j], b. in 1800.

Catharine[1.2.8.1.7j], b. on Apr. 3, 1802, and m. Henry
Bierbrauer in York County on Jan. 31, 1832.

Salome[1.2.8.1.8j], b. in 1805.

Isarah[1.2.8.1.9j], b. about 1807.

Jacob[1.2.8.1.10j], b. on Oct. 17, 1810.

Johannes Herring

Johannes[1.2.8.1.2j] m. Catharina. She d. in Ohio before 1825. Johannes had the following children:

Salome[1.2.8.1.2.1j], b. on Mar. 2, 1816, and m. Henry J. King in Guernsey County, Ohio, on Feb. 9, 1840.

Benjamin S.[1.2.8.1.2.2j], b. on Oct. 6, 1817, m. Sarah E., and d. in Guernsey County, Ohio, on July 4, 1894.

Louise[1.2.8.1.2.3j], b. in Dover Township on July 15, 1821.

Philip Herring

Philip[1.2.8.1.4j] m. Elizabeth, daughter of Johann Dieterich and Christina (Wolf) Rupert, in York County in 1817 and Elizabeth Hartman in Allen County, Ohio, on July 21, 1833. Elizabeth Rupert was b. on Feb. 21, 1797, and d. in Allen County, German Township, Ohio, on May 22, 1833. Elizabeth Hartman was b. in 1814, and d. in Allen County, German Township, in 1896. Philip inherited his father's land in Fairfield County, Amanda Township, Ohio, and moved there after his father's death. After spending a short time in Fairfield County, Philip and his uncle, John Herring, moved to Allen County, Ohio. Philip had the following children:

Emanuel[1.2.8.1.4.1j], b. in York County, Dover Township, on Nov. 30, 1818, m. Julia Ann Crites in Allen County, Ohio, on Dec. 27, 1849, and d. in Allen County, German Township, on May 15, 1852. After Emanuel's death, Julia m. Abraham Kesler in Allen County on Jan. 3, 1857.

Cassandra[1.2.8.1.4.2j], b. on July 16, 1820.

Rebecca[1.2.8.1.4.3j], b. about 1822, and m. Charles Miller in Allen County, Ohio, on May 28, 1843.

John Andrew[1.2.8.1.4.4j], b. on Oct. 8, 1824, and d. in Fairfield County, Amanda Township, Ohio, on Nov. 17, 1831.

Penrose R.[1.2.8.1.4.5j], b. in Fairfield County, Amanda Township, Ohio, on Aug. 24, 1829, m. Lydia Hunsaker in Allen County, Ohio, on Feb. 11, 1855, and d. in Allen County, German Township, on Apr. 7, 1874.

Gideon[1.2.8.1.4.6j], b. in Amanda Township on Aug. 11, 1832, m. Mary Bowsher in Allen County, Ohio, on Dec. 7, 1856, and d. in Allen County, German Township, on Dec. 9, 1915.

Saloma[1.2.8.1.4.7j], b. about 1834, and m. William Wurt in Allen County, Ohio, on Jan. 15, 1853.

William[1.2.8.1.4.8j], b. about 1836, and m. Phebe Jacobs in Allen County, Ohio, on Aug. 9, 1858.

Sarah[1.2.8.1.4.9j], b. about 1837, and m. David Piper in Allen County, Ohio, on Sep. 23, 1858.

Henry Herring

Henry[1.2.8.1.5j] m. Salome Bailey, and d. in York County, Fairview Township, on Dec. 14, 1861. She was b. on Jan. 12, 1806, and d. in Fairview Township on May 19, 1885. Henry was a Private in the War of 1812. They had the following children:

George Frederick[1.2.8.1.5.1j], b. in 1827, and d. in 1910.

Caroline[1.2.8.1.5.2j], b. in 1830, m. ____ Boyer, and d. in 1920.

Eliza[1.2.8.1.5.3j], b. in 1832, m. ____ Smyser, and d. in 1861.

Susanna[1.2.8.1.5.4j], b. in 1835, and d. on June 12, 1843.

Sarah Jane[1.2.8.1.5.5j], b. in 1838, m. ____ Gray, and d. in 1921.

Levi[1.2.8.1.5.6j], b. in 1840, and d. in 1916.

Rebecca[1.2.8.1.5.7j], b. on Dec. 25, 1842, and d. on May 31, 1890.

Henry B.[1.2.8.1.5.8j], b. on May 31, 1847, and d. on Mar. 20, 1848.

Malinda[1.2.8.1.5.9j], b. in 1850, m. ____ Hale, and d. in 1929.

Jacob Herring

Jacob[1.2.8.1.10j] m. Sarah Strayer in York County on Jan. 24, 1833, and d. in Greene County, Osborn (now Fairborn) Ohio. He was a Second Lieutenant in the York County, Militia. They had the following children:

Catherine[1.2.8.1.10.1j], b. in Dover Township on Apr. 2, 1834, m. William Bentzel in Adams County, Hanover, St. Matthew's Lutheran Church, Pennsylvania, on Aug. 24, 1862, and d. in York County, West Manchester Township, Pennsylvania, in 1892.

Lydia[1.2.8.1.10.2j].

Alvin[1.2.8.1.10.3j].

Jack[1.2.0.1.10.4j], b. in 1839, m. Maggie, and d. in Holmes County, Ohio, on Feb. 17, 1909. She d. in Holmes County on July 29, 1919.

Samuel Edward[1.2.8.1.10.5j], b. on Jan. 22, 1840, m. Catharine, daughter of Henry H. and Elizabeth (Peterman) Atticks, and d. in York, Pennsylvania, on Apr. 20, 1922. She was b. in Fairview Township on Jan. 13, 1840, and d. in York on July 2, 1926.

Elisabeth Herring

Elizabeth[1.2.8.2j] m. ____ Siford. He d. before 1823, and she d. in 1833. In 1833, the land in Fairfield County, Amanda Township, Ohio, she inherited from her father was divided between her heirs. She was taxed for this land in 1825, but she does not appear to have resided in Fairfield County. She had the following children:

Elisabeth[1.2.8.2.1j], m. Jacob Myers, and d. in Pennsylvania before 1833. She had 6 children.

Nancy[1.2.8.2.2j] (?unmarried in 1833).

Jacob[1.2.8.2.3j].

Joseph[1.2.8.2.4j].

Philip Herring

Philip[1.2.8.3j] m. Maria Eva, daughter of Jeremias and Maria Elizabeth Beer of Dover Township, before 1794. She was b. on Oct. 28, 1774, baptized at Strayer's on Nov. 26, 1774, and sponsored by Michael and Maria Eva Spaar. He was taxed in Dover Township in 1797, and d. before 1800. From 1824-1827, he (more properly, his estate) was taxed in Fairfield County, Amanda Township, as a non-resident for 61 acres that he inherited from his father. He had the following children:

Elizabeth[1.2.8.3.1j], b. about 1793.

Eve[1.2.8.3.1j], b. about 1795.

Peggy[1.2.8.3.3j], b. about 1797.

John[1.2.8.3.5j], b. about 1799, and possibly the John that m. Catharina Kring in Fairfield County, Ohio, on Apr. 6, 1825.

Catherine Herring

Catherine[1.2.8.4j] m. ____ Schaffer about 1794, ____ Hatten about 1804, ____ Briggs between 1812 and 1819 (he d. before 1820), and ____ Deeds between 1825 and 1850. She was on the 1820 census of Fairfield County, Amanda Township, and was taxed there in 1825. She d. in Allen County, Bath Township, Ohio, in 1856. Her will was written on Mar. 26, 1856, and probated on Apr. 5, 1856 (her son, Frederick Schaffer is the only one mentioned in the will). She had the following children:

Frederick Schaffer[1.2.8.4.1j], b. on July 12, 1795, and d. in Putnam County, Perry Township, Ohio, on Sep. 1, 1882. He resided in Fairfield County, Amanda Township, in 1830; Allen County, Bath Township, in 1840 and 1850; and Putnam County, Perry Township, Ohio, in 1859. He m. Ellener Scorkins about 1817, and Rosanna Eiche about 1849. Ellener was b. on Apr. 4, 1797, and d. on June 9, 1836 (there is a marker for her in Fairview cemetery in Putnam County). Rosanna was b. in Germany on May 13, 1816, and d. on Mar. 2, 1891. They are buried in Fairview cemetery.

Jacob Hatten[1.8.7.4.2j], b. about 1805.

David Hatten[1.8.7.4.3j], b. about 1807.

Ann Hatten[1.8.7.4.4j], b. about 1809 and resided in Fairfield County, Amanda Township, in 1830, with her brother George (she is the head of the household).

George Hatten[1.8.7.4.5j], b. about 1811, and m. Martha McClane in Fairfield County on Jan. 6, 1831.

John Herring

John[1.2.8.5j] m. Jane "Ginney" Poole in Fairfield County, Ohio, on June 16, 1807, and d. in Allen County, German Township, Ohio, in June 1847. She was b. in Maryland in 1775, and was residing in German Township in 1850. Jane's presumed brother, John Pool, m. Mary Claybaugh in Fairfield County on Oct. 25, 1811, and resided in Amanda Township in 1827 (taxed only for personal property) and 1830, and Allen County, German Township, in 1834. John Pool was b. between 1780 and 1790, and had a daughter about 1829; a son about 1827; a daughter about 1825; a son about 1823; and a son b. between 1815 and 1820. While in Amanda Township, he resided on 61 acres of land (R/T/S-20/13/14) that he inherited from his father. John Herring moved his family from Fairfield County, Amanda Township, to Allen County, German Township, Ohio, in 1833, and had land in Section 21 of German Township in 1834. John and Jane had the following children in Amanda Township:

Mary Jane[1.2.8.5.1j], b. in 1807.

Lewis[1.2.8.5.2j], b. in 1808.

David[1.2.8.5.3j], b. in 1810.

John[1.2.8.5.4j], b. on Sep. 10, 1811.

Henry[1.2.8.5.5j], b. in 1813.

Elizabeth[1.2.8.5.6j], b. in 1814.

Harriet[1.2.8.5.7j], b. about 1819, and m. Jacob Sours in Allen County, Ohio, on Feb. 1, 1849.

Susan[1.2.8.5.8j], b. in 1823, and was an unmarried woman living with her mother in 1850.

Mary Jane Herring

Mary Jane[1.2.8.5.1j] m. John/Jacob Stemen in Allen County, Ohio, on July 4, 1837. He d. in Allen County on Aug. 30, 1866. They had the following children:

Magdalene[1.2.8.5.1.1j], b. about 1838, and m. _____ Ditto.

Judith[1.2.8.5.1.2j], b. about 1840, and m. Eli Stevick in Allen County on Jan. 27, 1859.

Elizabeth[1.2.8.5.1.3j], b. about 1842, and m. F. D. Judkins in Allen County on Sep. 15, 1861.

John H.[1.2.8.5.1.4j], b. about 1844, and m. Emilene Leist in Allen County on July 15, 1866.

Enos M.[1.2.8.5.1.5j], b. about 1847, and m. Rachel A. Baxter in Allen County on Oct. 29, 1860.

Benjamin F.[1.2.8.5.1.6j], b. about 1850, and m. Sarah A. Bumgardner in Allen County on Feb. 17, 1876.

William A.[1.2.8.5.1.7j], b. about 1852, and m. Rachael John in Allen County on Dec. 21, 1871.

Mary Evaline[1.2.8.5.1.8j], b. about 1854, and m. Jacob J. Boggs in Allen County on July 8, 1875.

Noah S.[1.2.8.5.1.9j], b. about 1856.

Lewis Herring

Lewis[1.2.8.5.2j] m. Elizabeth, daughter of William and Elizabeth (Tester) Shope in Allen County, Ohio, on Apr. 28, 1835. She was b. in Fairfield County, Greenfield Township, Ohio, on Aug. 18, 1816. In 1850, Lewis was a farmer in German Township, and on Jan. 20, 1851, he purchased land in the southwest quarter of section thirty-four in Allen County, Amanda Township. He moved there between 1860 and 1870, and he and Elizabeth d. between 1870 and 1875. Lewis is buried in Elida, Trinity Lutheran cemetery, and Elizabeth may be buried there as well. They had the following children:

Mary Ann[1.2.8.5.2.1j], b. in Apr. 1836. She m. Jacob Little in Allen County on Dec. 30, 1860, and resided in Amanda Township in 1900. He was b. in Ohio in 1833.

John[1.2.8.5.2.2j], b. in 1840.

Nancy[1.2.8.5.2.3j], b. in 1842, and m. George Shock.

William[1.2.8.5.2.4j], b. in 1844.

Lavina[1.2.8.5.2.5j], b. in 1846. She m. Peter Allard in Allen County on Mar. 5, 1871, and resided in Amanda Township in 1880. He was b. in Ohio in 1846.

Samuel S.$^{1.2.8.5.2.6j}$, b. in 1849. He m. Elizabeth A. Raines in
Allen County on Jan. 9, 1868 and Kitturah Miller in Allen County on
June 4, 1874. He d. in Allen County, Amanda Township, in 1917.
Kitturah was b. in 1848, and d. in 1920.

Lewis J.$^{1.2.8.5.2.7j}$, b. in Oct. 1852, m. Ida A. Highland in
1890, and d. in Allen County, Amanda Township, in 1928. She was b. in
1862, and d. in 1925.

George$^{1.2.8.5.2.8j}$, b. in 1855. He m. Mary E. Miller about
1885, and d. in Allen County, Amanda Township, in 1936. She was b. in
1867, and d. in 1943.

Henry $^{1.2.8.5.2.9j}$, b. in 1858.

David Herring

David$^{1.2.8.5.3j}$ m. Susannah Van Wey in Allen County, Ohio,
on Aug. 1, 1841, and d. in Shelby County, Shelbyville, Illinois, before
1870. She was b. in Ohio in 1825, and was alive in 1870. They had the
following children:

Nancy Jane$^{1.2.8.5.3.1j}$, b. in Allen County in 1845, and m.
Jacob (Isaac) Rysacker in Allen County on Nov. 10, 1866.

Jacob Van Wey$^{1.2.8.5.3.2j}$, b. in Aug. 1847, m. Minerva
Swisher in Allen County on Sep. 1, 1866, and d. in Leavenworth
County, Leavenworth, Kansas, on Dec. 23, 1909.

Henry S.$^{1.2.8.5.3.3j}$, b. in Allen County, Bath Township, in
1849.

Manuel W.$^{1.2.8.5.3.4j}$, b. in Bath Township in 1851.

Abraham A.$^{1.2.8.5.3.5j}$, b. in Bath Township in 1852.

John$^{1.2.8.5.3.6j}$, b. in Bath Township in 1856.

William A.$^{1.2.8.5.3.7j}$, b. in Bath Township in 1858.

George$^{1.2.8.5.3.8j}$, b. in Shelby County, Shelbyville, Illinois, in
1863.

John Herring

John$^{1.2.8.5.4j}$ m. Catherine Bressler, widow of John Stuckey,
in Allen County, Ohio, on Nov. 2, 1848, and d. in Allen County,
German Township, on Sep. 23, 1873. She was b. in 1816, and d. on
Mar. 30, 1881. John Stuckey was the son of Christian and Mary
margaret (Harsh) Stuckey. John and Catherine Herring had the
following children:

Isaac$^{1.2.8.5.4.1j}$, b. on July 21, 1849, and d. on Sep. 17, 1863.

John W.$^{1.2.8.5.4.2j}$, b. in 1853, and m. Susanna Porter in
Allen County on Mar. 14, 1873.

Charles[1.2.8.5.4.3j], b. in 1856, and m. Catherine Bowersock in Allen County on Mar. 27, 1879.

Henry Herring

Henry[1.2.8.5.5j] m. Nancy, daughter of William and Elizabeth (Tester) Shope, in Allen County, Ohio, on Nov. 2, 1842 and Rachel Lowrey about 1854. Nancy was b. in Fairfield County, Greenfield Township, Ohio, on Nov. 2, 1820, and d. in German Township about 1853. Henry d. in German Township in Jan. 1886. He had the following children in German Township:

Rebecca[1.2.8.5.5.1j], b. in 1844.

David[1.2.8.5.5.2j], b. on June 15, 1845. He m. Mary M. Cremean in Allen County on Jan. 16, 1868 and Nanna Lowrey in Allen County on Mar. 27, 1884. He d. in Allen County, American Township, Ohio, on June 4, 1933.

Elizabeth[1.2.8.5.5.3j], b. in 1846, and m. Moses Thomas in Allen County on May 28, 1868.

Lewis[1.2.8.5.5.4j], b. in 1847, and d. before 1885.

Jeremiah[1.2.8.5.5.5j], b. in 1848.

June[1.2.8.5.5.6j], b. in 1852.

Hiram[1.2.8.5.5.7j], b. in 1855, and m. Isabele Johnson in Allen County on Jan. 3, 1878.

William[1.2.8.5.5.8j], b. in 1856, m. Mary Collins in Allen County on Oct. 10, 1878, and d. in Allen County, American Township, Ohio, in 1944. She was b. in 1856, and d. in 1942.

Henry E.[1.2.8.5.5.9j], b. in 1858, m. Mary M. Miller in Allen County on Dec. 19, 1878, and d. in Allen County, German Township, Ohio, on Mar. 11, 1880. She was b. in 1845, and d. in German Township on Aug. 30, 1881. This may be Henry, son of Lewis Herring.

Jane/Jennie[1.2.8.5.5.10j], b. in 1861, m. John A. Burget in Allen County on Apr. 26, 1883, and d. before 1885.

Nancy[1.2.8.5.5.11j], b. about 1862, and d. in German Township on Feb. 4, 1869.

Eleanor[1.2.8.5.5.12j], b. about 1864, and d. in German Township on Feb. 26, 1869.

Elizabeth Herring

Elizabeth[1.2.8.5.6j] m. Jacob Bressler in Allen County, Ohio, on Aug. 16, 1840, and d. in Allen County in 1896. He was b. in Pennsylvania in 1802. They had the following children:

Sarah Elling[1.2.8.5.6.1j], b. in 1838, and m. Samuel Crider in Allen County on May 11, 1856.

Henry[1.2.8.5.6.2j], b. in 1842, and m. Lavey Wallet in Allen County on Aug. 31, 1865.

William[1.2.8.5.6.3j], b. in 1844, and m. Hester A. Fisher in Allen County on Nov. 5, 1866.

Catherine L.[1.2.8.5.6.4j], b. in 1846, and m. John Thomas in Allen County on Dec. 15, 1870.

Marriann[1.2.8.5.6.5j], b. in 1848.

Daniel[1.2.8.5.6.6j], b. in 1849.

Anna Maria Herring

Anna Maria[1.2.8.6j] m. Philip Wollet in York County, Pennsylvania, about 1799. They resided in Fairfield County, Amanda Township, Ohio, until about 1833, and then moved to Allen County, Bath Township, Ohio. Philip's will was written on Dec. 3, 1835, and probated on Oct. 21, 1836. Anna Maria was alive in 1835. They had the following children:

Lydia[1.2.8.6.1j], b. in Dover Township in 1800, m. George W. Leach, and resided in Allen County, Bath Township, in 1850. He was b. in Virginia in 1793.

Mary[1.2.8.6.2j], b. in Dover Township in 1801, m. Harmon Webb in Fairfield County, Ohio, on Jan. 26, 1832, and resided in Allen County, Bath Township, in 1850. He was b. in Virginia in 1812.

Georg Michael[1.2.8.6.3j] in York County, Dover Township, in 1803, and baptized at Strayers. He m. Catherine, and resided in Allen County, Bath Township, in 1850. She was b. in Maryland in 1797.

Elizabeth[1.2.8.6.4j], b. about 1805, m. David Rowland about 1825, and d. before Sep. 3, 1835.

Daniel[1.2.8.6.5j], b. in Fairfield County, Amanda Township, in 1807, m. Hannah, and resided in Allen County, Bath Township, in 1850. She was b. in Pennsylvania in 1800.

Rebekah[1.2.8.6.6j], b. about 1809, and m. Solomon Donelen before 1835.

Catherine[1.2.8.6.7j], b. about 1811, and m. Henry Shenk before 1835.

Solomon[1.2.8.6.8j], b. in 1814, and m. Rebecca Ridenouer in Allen County, Ohio, in Jan. 1836, and Elizabeth Richards in Allen County in Sep. 1840. Elizabeth was b. in Ohio in 1823.

Samuel[1.2.8.6.9j], b. about 1816, and m. Phoeby Ridenouer in Allen County, Ohio, in Mar. 1837, and resided there in 1850.

Saloma Christina[1.2.8.6.10j], b. about 1818.
Nancy[1.2.8.6.11j], b. about 1820.

Catherine Barbary Herring

Barbary[1.2.8.7j] m. William, son of William Ward, and d. in
Fairfield County, Amanda Township, Ohio, on Nov. 5, 1850. She is
buried in Van Meter cemetery. He was b. in Virginia in 1780, was alive
in 1850, and d. in Allen County, Ohio, in 185?. They had the following
children:

William[1.2.8.7.1j], b. in 1814, and d. in Fairfield County,
Amanda Township, Ohio, in 1899. He is buried in Van Meter cemetery.

Eve Herring

Eva[1.2.8.8j] m. Peter, son of John and Salome (Zimmerman)
Stuckey, in Fairfield County, Ohio, on Oct. 6, 1805, and d. in Fairfield
County, Hocking Township, Muddy Prairie, Ohio, on Apr. 15, 1864. He
was b. in Lancaster County, Elizabeth Township, Pennsylvania, on Apr.
4, 1770, and d. in Hocking Township on Apr. 30, 1856. They had the
following children in Fairfield County (one daughter was the wife of
John Shaffer, and one was the wife of John Kerns):

Nancy[1.2.8.8.1j], b. in Sugar Grove, Ohio, on Mar. 6, 1805 (?),
m. John M. Stemen in Fairfield County on Nov. 24, 1824, and d. on
Apr. 28, 1836 (given the birth date, she may have been from a previous
marriage.

Hannah[1.2.8.8.2j], b. on Apr. 12, 1806, and d. on Nov. 12, 1850.
Susannah[1.2.8.8.3j], b. on June 19, 1813, and d. on Sep. 3,
1826.

Mary[1.2.8.8.4j], b. on July 4, 1815, and d. on July 10, 1894.
Eve[1.2.8.8.5j], b. on June 14, 1817, and d. on Feb. 28, 1819.
Franey[1.2.8.8.6j], b. on July 21, 1819, and d. on Mar. 1, 1824.
Catherine[1.2.8.8.7j], b. on Nov. 27, 1820.
Judith[1.2.8.8.8j], b. in 1823, and d. in 1907.

****

Hans Peter Hillegas

Hans Peter[1k] was b. in 1649, and m. Anna Regina. She was b.
in 1655, and d. in Sinsheim, Baden, Germany, on Sep. 7, 1708. Peter d.
in Sinsheim on Oct. 12, 1719. They had the following children:

Hans Konrad[1.1k], b. in Alsace Lorraine, France, about 1683.
Johann Frederich[1.2k], b. in Alsace Lorraine on Nov. 24, 1685.

Georg Peter[1.3k], b. in Alsace Lorraine about 1690.
Johann Jacob[1.4k], b. in Sinsheim on Jan. 12, 1692/93, and m.
Otilla Johanna Kaempler in Sinsheim on Jan. 30, 1719/20.
Georg Michael[1.5k], b. in Sinsheim on Feb. 14, 1695/96.
Johann Georg[1.6k], b. in Sinsheim on Oct. 1, 1702.

Johann Frederich Hillegas

Johann Frederich[1.2k] m. Elisabetha Barbara, daughter of Hans
Joerg and Anna Barbara (Metzer) Triegel in Baden, Heidelberg,
Eppingen, Germany, on Aug. 23, 1712. She was b. in Heidelberg,
Eppingen, on Oct. 24, 1694, and d. in Montgomery County,
Goshenhopen, Pennsylvania, on Mar. 4, 1759. Hans Joerg, son of Hans
Jacob and Elisabeth (Lang) Triegel, was b. in Heidelberg, Eppingen, in
1657, and m. Anna Barbara Metzer in Heidelberg on Aug. 28, 1691.
Hans Jacob, son of Hans Jacob (b. 1605) and Anna Margaretha Triegel,
was b. in Heidelberg in 1628, and m. Anna Elisabeth Lang in
Heidelberg on July 10, 1650. Friederich Hillegas arrived at Philadelphia
on the ship *William and Sarah* on Sep. 21, 1727, and d. at
Goshenhopen on Jan. 6, 1765. They had the following children:

Leopold[1.2.1k], b. in Sinsheim on Sep. 26, 1714, and resided in
Dutchess County, Esopus, New York, and m. Susanna.

Hans Adam[1.2.2k], b. in Sinsheim on Jan. 6, 1716/17.

Johan Frederick[1.2.3k], b. in Sinsheim on Apr. 2, 1719, and
resided in Dutchess County, Esopus, New York.

Johan Martin[1.2.4k], b. in Sinsheim on May 26, 1721, and d.
young.

Eva Elisabetha[1.2.5k], b. in Sinsheim on Nov. 16, 1723, and d. in
Montgomery County, Goshenhopen, Pennsylvania, in 1749.

Anna Margaretha[1.2.6k], b. in Sinsheim in Aug. 1726, m.
Matthias Richard, and d. in Montgomery County, Pennsylvania, on Jan.
6, 1773.

Anna Regina[1.2.7k], b. in Montgomery County, Upper Hanover
Township, Pennsylvania, in 1729.

Elisabetha Barbara[1.2.8k], baptized at the New Goshenhoppen
Reformed Congregation in Upper Hanover Township on June 4, 1732.

Georg Peter[1.2.9k], b. in Upper Hanover Township on Feb. 2,
1734/35, and baptized at the New Goshenhoppen Reformed
Congregation on May 9, 1736.

Conrad[1.2.10k], b. in Upper Hanover Township on Nov. 2, 1738.

Hans Adam Hillegas

Hans Adam[1.2.2k] m. Maria Margaretha, daughter of Johannes Hahlman, and Anna Catharine, daughter of Martin and Margaret Bitting (granddaughter of Henry and Anna Catharina Bitting), in 1754. Margaretha d. in Montgomery County, Upper Hanover Township, Pennsylvania, on Mar. 13, 1754. Anna Catherine was b. on Feb. 10, 1728, and d. on Feb. 26, 1810. Adam d. in Upper Hanover Township on Mar. 13, 1779. Adam had the following children in Upper Hanover Township (baptized at the New Goshenhoppen Reformed Congregation in Montgomery County):

Johan Michael[1.2.2.1k], baptized on Sep. 4, 1742.

August Johannes[1.2.2.2k], b. on June 6, 1743, and baptized at St. Paul's Lutheran Church.

Eve[1.2.2.3k], b. on July 16, 1745.

Johan Georg[1.2.2.4k], b. about 1748.

Catharina[1.2.2.5k], b. about 1751, and m. Johannes Griesemer.

Georg Adam[1.2.2.6k], b. on June 1, 1755.

Friderich[1.2.2.7k], b. on May 16, 1757.

Anna Margaretha[1.2.2.8k], b. on Feb. 26, 1758, baptized on May 15, 1758, and d. on June 25, 1821.

Johan Peter[1.2.2.9k], baptized on Nov. 28, 1759.

Elisabetha[1.2.2.10k], b. on Mar. 8, 1761.

Anna Christina[1.2.2.11k], baptized on May 10, 1761.

Anna Maria[1.2.2.12k], b. in Nov. 1765, m. Johannes Geyer at New Hanover Lutheran Church on May 17, 1789, and d. on May 19, 1813.

Johan Jacob[1.2.2.13k], b. on Apr. 26, 1772, m. Rosina Schultz, and d. on Feb. 2, 1828.

Johan Michael Hillegas

Johan Michael[1.2.2.1k] m. Catharina, daughter of Jacob and Anna Margaretha Gertrude (Griesemer) Geri, in Montgomery County, Goshenhopen, Pennsylvania, on Nov. 10, 1767. She was b. in Upper Hanover Township on Mar. 25, 1749. Michael d. in Berks County, District Township, Pennsylvania, in Nov. 1792, and his will was probated in Northampton County, Easton, Pennsylvania, on Nov. 2, 1792 (written on Oct. 10, 1782). After Michael's death, Catharina m. John Wagner before Oct. 24, 1797. Michael and Catharina had the following children in Lehigh County, Lower Milford Township, Pennsylvania, and baptized them at Great Swamp Reformed Church:

Rebecca$^{1.2.2.1.1k}$, baptized on Apr. 3, 1770, and sponsored by Jacob Geri and wife.

Johannes$^{1.2.2.1.2k}$, baptized on Jan. 16, 1772, and sponsored by Johannes Hillegas and wife.

Elisabetha$^{1.2.2.1.3k}$, baptized on Nov. 1, 1773, sponsored by Adam Geri and Elisabetha Neukomer, and m. Peter Harp/Herb.

Michael$^{1.2.2.1.4k}$, baptized on Nov. 15, 1775, and sponsored by Johann Cunius and wife.

Eva$^{1.2.2.1.5k}$, baptized on Dec. 20, 1777, and sponsored by Georg Horlacher and wife.

Anna Maria$^{1.2.2.1.6k}$, b. on Oct. 16, 1781.

August Johannes Hillegas

August Johannes$^{1.2.2.2k}$ m. Anna Maria, daughter of Jacob and Anna Margaretha Gertrude (Griesemer) Geri, in Montgomery County on Mar. 3, 1767. Johannes d. in Montgomery County on Mar. 4, 1803, and she d. in Upper Hanover Township on Mar. 29, 1795. They baptized the following children:

Maria Margreta$^{1.2.2.2.1k}$, b. on Aug. 3, 1769, and baptized at the New Goshenhoppen Reformed Congregation in Montgomery County.

Johan Georg$^{1.2.2.2.2k}$, b. about 1771, and baptized at Great Swamp Reformed Church in Lehigh County.

Catharina$^{1.2.2.2.3k}$, b. about 1775, and baptized at Great Swamp.

Eve Hillegas

Eve$^{1.2.2.3k}$ m. Georg, son of Hans Michael and Maria Veronica Horlacher, in Montgomery County on Oct. 11, 1763, and d. in Montgomery County on Nov. 23, 1821. Hans Michael and his wife arrived at Philadelphia on the ship *Pennsylvania Merchant* on Sep. 10, 1731, and settled on a farm partially in Montgomery County, New Hanover Township, and partially in Bucks County, Milford Township. Georg was b. in Bucks County on Oct. 6, 1738, and d. on Nov. 22, 1813. He is buried at great Swamp. They had the following children:

Catharina$^{1.2.2.3.1k}$, b. on Aug. 21, 1765, baptized at St. Paul's Lutheran Church, and d. at great Swamp on Mar. 11, 1821. She m. David Spinner on Nov. 26, 1782.

Eva$^{1.2.2.3.2k}$, b. on May 28, 1768, m. Johan Adam Levy, and d. at Great Swamp on Sep. 17, 1841. He was b. on Feb. 18, 1768, and d. on July 24, 1848.

Johann Georg[1.2.2.3.3k], b. in 1769.

Elisabetha[1.2.2.3.4k], b. on Jan. 11, 1772, baptized at the New Goshenhoppen Reformed Congregation, and d. on Apr. 3, 1854. She m. Jonathan Trexler on Apr. 3, 1792. He was b. on May 1, 1762, and d. on May 11, 1846. Elisabetha is buried on the Gonser farm.

Michael[1.2.2.3.5k], b. on Nov. 4, 1781, and d. on Mar. 31, 1823.

Johan Georg Hillegas

Johan Georg[1.2.2.4k] m. Elizabeth Jung in Montgomery County on Sep. 30, 1770, and d. in Montgomery County on Dec. 31, 1806. They baptized the following children at the New Goshenhoppen Reformed Congregation:

Johan Georg[1.2.2.4.1k], b. on Aug. 15, 1771.

Johannes[1.2.2.4.2k], b. on Feb. 11, 1773.

Eva[1.2.2.4.3k], b. on May 25, 1775.

Anna Margaretha[1.2.2.4.4k], b. about 1777, and baptized at Great Swamp Reformed Lutheran Church in Lehigh County.

Hans Adam[1.2.2.4.5k], b. on Nov. 12, 1780.

Michel[1.2.2.4.6k], b. on Nov. 30, 1781.

Heinrich[1.2.2.4.7k], b. on Aug. 20, 1783.

Infant[1.2.2.4.8k], b. on Oct. 31, 1784.

Elisabetha[1.2.2.4.9k], b. on Apr. 23, 1787.

Jacob[1.2.2.4.10k], b. on May 27, 1788.

Georg Adam Hillegas

Georg Adam[1.2.2.6k] m. and unknown woman about 1774, and Anna Schultz in Montgomery County, Pennsylvania, on July 2, 1776. Anna was b. in Oct. 1757. Adam d. in Montgomery County on July 31, 1823, and had the following children in Montgomery County:

Anna Maria Margaret[1.2.2.6.1k], b. on June 14, 1775.

Daughter[1.2.2.6.2k], b. on Apr. 27, 1777, and d. on May 6, 1777.

Georg Adam[1.2.2.6.3k], b. on June 1, 1786.

Georg Adam Hillegas

Georg Adam[1.2.2.6.3k] m. Maria Rebecca Gift. She was b. on Jan. 24, 1796, and d. on Feb. 17, 1871. George d. on Dec. 6, 1833. They had the following children:

Maria A.[1.2.2.6.3.1k], b. on Mar. 14, 1812, and d. on Nov. 11, 1818.

Maria Lavina[1.2.2.6.3.2k], m. Jacob A. Hillegas.

George Washington$^{1 \cdot 2 \cdot 2 \cdot 6 \cdot 3 \cdot 3k}$, b. on Jan. 12, 1818, m. Sarah Ann Hunter Fisher, and d. on Aug. 26, 1881.

Josiah$^{1 \cdot 2 \cdot 2 \cdot 6 \cdot 3 \cdot 4k}$, b. on Sep. 9, 1817, m. Esther C. Kepler, and Louise Doyle, and d. on Feb. 3, 1877.

William$^{1 \cdot 2 \cdot 2 \cdot 6 \cdot 3 \cdot 5k}$, b. on Apr. 25, 1820, m. Lucy Ann Schantz and Lydia Merkel, and d. on Sep. 1, 1902.

Caroline$^{1 \cdot 2 \cdot 2 \cdot 6 \cdot 3 \cdot 6k}$, b. in 1828, m. George L. Jacoby, and d. on Dec. 24, 1877.

Matilda$^{1 \cdot 2 \cdot 2 \cdot 6 \cdot 3 \cdot 7k}$, b. on Aug. 2, 1829, m. Isaac Potts, and d. on Sep. 3, 1874.

Friderich Hillegas

Friderich$^{1 \cdot 2 \cdot 2 \cdot 7k}$ m. Anna Huber, and d. on Mar. 21, 1827. They baptized the following children at the New Goshenhoppen Reformed Congregation:

Catharina$^{1 \cdot 2 \cdot 2 \cdot 7 \cdot 1k}$, b. on Mar. 13, 1781.

Friderich$^{1 \cdot 2 \cdot 2 \cdot 7 \cdot 2k}$, b. on Oct. 30, 1782.

Johan Peter Hillegas

Johan Peter$^{1 \cdot 2 \cdot 2 \cdot 9k}$ m. Susanna Heist, and d. in 1800. They baptized the following children at the New Goshenhoppen Reformed Congregation:

Catharine$^{1 \cdot 2 \cdot 2 \cdot 9 \cdot 1k}$, b. on Jan. 29, 1784, and baptized at Great Swamp Reformed Lutheran Church in Lehigh County.

Michael$^{1 \cdot 2 \cdot 2 \cdot 9 \cdot 2k}$, b. on Mar. 21, 1790.

Johan Peter$^{1 \cdot 2 \cdot 2 \cdot 9 \cdot 3k}$, b. on Dec. 7, 1791.

Jacob$^{1 \cdot 2 \cdot 2 \cdot 9 \cdot 4k}$, b. on May 4, 1792.

Maricha$^{1 \cdot 2 \cdot 2 \cdot 9 \cdot 5k}$, b. on Dec. 2, 1793.

Elisabetha Hillegas

Elisabetha$^{1 \cdot 2 \cdot 2 \cdot 10k}$ m. Johan Michael Huber, Jr., at New Hanover Lutheran Church on May 25, 1780, and d. on Jan. 18, 1839. They had the following children:

Elisabeth$^{1 \cdot 2 \cdot 2 \cdot 10 \cdot 1k}$, b. on Nov. 16, 1782, and baptized at the New Goshenhoppen Reformed Congregation.

Catharine$^{1 \cdot 2 \cdot 2 \cdot 10 \cdot 2k}$, b. on Feb. 24, 1785, and baptized at Falkner Swamp Reformed Church.

Georg Peter Hillegas

Georg Peter$^{1 \cdot 2 \cdot 9k}$ m. Anna Elisabetha Barbara Hornecker, and d. in Montgomery County on Sep. 24, 1810. They baptized the

following children at the New Goshenhoppen Reformed Congregation
in Montgomery County:

Johan Peter$^{1.2.9.1k}$, b. on Jan. 19, 1756, and m. Anna Maria
Maurer in Goshenhoppen on Mar. 16, 1779.

Friderich$^{1.2.9.2k}$, baptized on Apr. 26, 1759.

Anna Catharina$^{1.2.9.3k}$, b. on Jan. 23, 1761, baptized on Jan.
29, 1761, and m. Johannes Maurer at Falkner Swamp on May 30, 1780.

Elisabetha Barbara$^{1.2.9.4k}$, b. on Oct. 17, 1763.

Johannes$^{1.2.9.5k}$, b. on June 15, 1766.

Eva$^{1.2.9.6k}$, b. on Mar. 20, 1768.

Johan$^{1.2.9.7k}$, b. on Feb. 27, 1772.

Johan Jacob$^{1.2.9.8k}$, b. on Nov. 2, 1777.

Johan Friderich$^{1.2.9.9k}$, b. on Dec. 5, 1782.

Conrad Hillegas

Conrad$^{1.2.10k}$ m. Anna Maria Margaretha Schellenberger, and
d. in Montgomery County on Dec. 24, 1824. They baptized the
following children at the New Goshenhoppen Reformed Congregation
in Montgomery County:

Johannes$^{1.2.10.1k}$, baptized on July 13, 1760.

Elisabetha Barbara$^{1.2.10.2k}$, b. on Jan. 8, 1767, and m. Daniel
Jost at Falkner Swamp on Feb. 7, 1786.

Maria Margretha$^{1.2.10.3k}$, b. on Aug. 3, 1769.

Susanna$^{1.2.10.4k}$, b. on May 3, 1771, and m. Adam Jost at
Falkner Swamp on May 17, 1789.

Friedericus$^{1.2.10.5k}$, b. on Jan. 13, 1774.

Anna Maria$^{1.2.10.6k}$, b. on Aug. 18, 1775.

Magdalena$^{1.2.10.7k}$, b. on Mar. 8, 1778.

Maria Catharina$^{1.2.10.8k}$, b. on Jan. 27, 1783.

Georg Peter Hillegas

Georg Peter$^{1.3k}$ m. Anna Margaretha, d. in Philadelphia
County, Pennsylvania, in 1745, and had the following children at
Sinsheim:

Anne Margarethe$^{1.3.1k}$, b. on July 30, 1715, and m. Johan
Georg Passage/Passager.

Johan Jacob$^{1.3.2k}$, b. on Mar. 14, 1716/17.

Christof$^{1.3.3k}$, b. on Aug. 7, 1718.

Peter$^{1.3.4k}$, b. in 1721.

Catherine$^{1.3.5k}$, b. in 1723.

Elizabeth$^{1.3.6k}$, b. in 1725.

Susanna$^{1.3.7k}$, b. in 1727.

Georg Michael Hillegas

Georg Michael$^{1.5k}$, m. Margarete, d. in Philadelphia County, Pennsylvania, on Oct. 30, 1749, and had the following children:

Michael$^{1.5.1k}$, b. in Philadelphia on Apr. 22, 1729.

Hannah$^{1.5.2k}$, b. in Philadelphia on Feb. 21, 1739/40.

Michael Hillegas

Michael$^{1.5.1k}$ m. Hennretta Cox Bonde, and had the following children in Philadelphia:

Samuel$^{1.5.1.1k}$, b. on Feb. 17, 1754.

Michael$^{1.5.1.2k}$, b. on June 30, 1756.

William$^{1.5.1.3k}$, b. on Feb. 9, 1759.

Margaret$^{1.5.1.4k}$, b. on Nov. 21, 1760.

****

James Kiggin

James^{11} m. Sophia, daughter of Conrad and Anna Gertraud (Scharfenstein) Pickel, in Hunterdon County, New Jersey, on Dec. 2, 1780. She was b. in Hunterdon County, New Jersey, about 1760, and d. in Hunterdon County, Lebanon Township, New Jersey, in Nov. 1811. On Apr. 23, 1773, James (Kegan) was indentured to John Wilcox for four years in Philadelphia. He was taxed as a laborer on Ann Emlen's estate from 1781-3 in the Middle Ward (Moyamensing Township) of Philadelphia (Kaighn/Kaigen/Kaigen). On Oct. 1, 1785, he (Keggins) was a livery stabler on Chestnut Street between 5th and 6th Streets in Philadelphia. In 1786, he (Keggan) served in the Philadelphia County Militia under Colonel James Reed in Captain Peter Z. Lloyd's Company. From 1795-98, he (Keegan) was a tailor on the south west side of Dock Street #62, Philadelphia. James (Kaighn) d. in Philadelphia County, South Mulberry Ward, Pennsylvania, in 1798. His estate was administered in 1798 In 1800, a James Kigin appears on the census of South Mulberry Ward, Philadelphia. This was probably, the widow Sophia, with James Jr. listed as the head of the household. Sophia moved back to New Jersey about 1801, and was a householder there in 1802. Her will was written on Nov. 27, 1810, and probated in Nov. 1811. James and Sophia had the following children in Philadelphia:

James$^{1.11}$, b. about 1781.

Charles[1.21], b. about 1782.

Mary[1.31], b. about 1784, and m. James White in Hunterdon County, New Jersey, on Feb. 26, 1804. She received her mother's clothing, six silver teaspoons, and half of the proceeds from the sale of the household furniture.

Robert[1.41], b. in 1789.

Jonathan[1.51], b. on July 12, 1792.

James Kiggins

James[1.11] m. Mary. She was b. in Pennsylvania in 1783, and resided in Fort Bend County, Richmond, Texas, in 1850. In 1807, he resided in Fairfield County, Ohio, and in 1808, he was in Franklin County, Ohio. In 1810, he was residing in the Louisiana Territory, and in 1814, he was in Franklin County, North Gasconde Township, Missouri. James was said to have known Stephen F. Austin during a term in the Missouri legislature, and followed him to Texas. James d. in San Felipe de Austin (Washington County), Texas, in 1826. After James's death, Mary m. William Ross in San Felipe de Austin on June 21, 1830. He is presumed to have abandoned her, and she resumed the name, Kiggins. On Dec. 3, 1832, Mary was granted a league of land in what is now Brazos County, Texas. James and Mary had the following children:

James[1.1.11], b. about 1803 in Philadelphia, Pennsylvania, and m. Nancy Eads in Cole County, Missouri, on Dec. 17, 1823. He was granted a league of land in Washington County, Texas, on Mar. 23, 1831, and d. on the return home from San Jacinto (1836). His widow and children were residing in Washington County, Texas, after the Revolution. After James's death, Nancy m. William A. Brown in Washington County, Texas, on Nov. 16, 1839.

Nancy[1.1.21], b. about 1805, and m. Jacob Stevens in Missouri. He was granted a league of land in what is now Austin County, Texas, on Mar. 23, 1831, and was residing in Washington County, Texas, after the revolution.

John[1.1.3m], b. about 1811 in the Louisiana Territory.

Sarah[1.1.4m], b. in Franklin County, North Gasconde Township, Missouri, in 1813, and d. in Washington County, Texas, about 1845. She m. William Elliot Allcorn in Brazoria County, San Felipe de Austin, Victoria Pct., Texas, on July 2, 1829. William was granted a league of land in what is now Washington County, Texas, on Mar. 31, 1831, and d. there on Dec. 20, 1867. He was b. in Georgia in 1805.

Hamilton[1.1.51], b. in Franklin County, North Gasconde Township, in 1815.

Mahala[1.1.61], b. about 1817, and m. Uriah Anderson in Old Harrisburg County, Texas, on Aug. 7, 1837. He received a league of land in Fort Bend County after the revolution.

Washington S.[1.1.71], b. in Franklin County, North Gasconde Township, in 1820. He m. Elizabeth Fike in Fort Bend County, Texas, on Apr. 27, 1843. He received a third of a league of land in Fort Bend County, Texas, after the revolution.

John Kiggins

John[1.1.31] m. Clarinda Peavehouse in Fort Bend County, Texas, on Feb. 18, 1845. She was b. in Arkansas on June 24, 1824, and d. in Coleman County, Coleman, Texas, on Apr. 14, 1898. John d. in Coleman Texas (?after 1850). John received a third of a league of land in Fort Bend County after the revolution. He was one of the 750 volunteers that forced Woll to abandon San Antonio, and was imprisoned at Perote for two years. He opposed statehood, and is buried in Coleman, Texas. John and Clarinda had the following children in Fort Bend County, Richmond, Texas:

James B.[1.1.3.11], b. in 1847.
John F.[1.1.3.21], b. in 1848.
Mary[1.1.3.31], b. in 1849.

Hamilton Kiggins

Hamilton[1.1.51] and m. Margaret Hodge in Harris County, Houston, Texas, on Feb. 8, 1838. She was b. in Texas in 1819. They had the following children:

James C.[1.1.5.11], b. in 1840.
Sarah[1.1.5.21], b. in 1842.
Mary Ann[1.1.5.31], b. in 1844.
Alexander[1.1.5.41], b. on Mar. 5, 1846, m. Henrietta C., and d. in Fort Bend County on Dec. 21, 1914. She was b. on Feb. 19, 1847, and d. on Sep. 19, 1918. They are buried in Hodges Bend cemetery.
William[1.1.5.51], b. in 1848.
Margaret[1.1.5.6m], b. in 1851.
Nathan[1.1.5.7m], b. in 1853.
Lucy[1.1.5.8m], b. in 1857.

Charles Kiggins

Charles[1.21] m. Sophia, daughter of Jacob and Charity (Pickel) Apgar, sometime before Apr. 1814. She was b. in Hunterdon County, Lebanon Township, New Jersey, on Nov. 14, 1780, and resided in Hunterdon County, Reading Township, New Jersey, in 1840. Charles received half of the proceeds from the sale of his mother's furniture. Charles d. sometime before 1840. They had the following children:

Adam[1.2.11], b. in Hunterdon County, New Jersey, about 1819, and m. Elizabeth Hill in Hunterdon County on June 27, 1840.

Robert Kiggins

Robert[1.41] m. Mary, daughter of Ludwig and Rosina (Kern) Boyer, in Miami County, Ohio, on Nov. 24, 1814. She was b. in Rockingham County, Cub Run, Virginia, about 1793, and d. in Mercer County, Dublin Township, Ohio, before Sep. 1841. They had the following son:

John F.[1.4.11], b. in Miami County, Ohio, on Apr. 2, 1817.

John F. Kiggins

John F.[1.4.11] m. Sarah Ann McCloskey in Shelby County, Ohio, on Dec. 21, 1838. He d. in Shelby County, Sidney, Ohio, on Jan. 19, 1900, and is buried in Graceland cemetery. They had the following children:

Maggie[1.4.1.11].

William[1.4.1.21], b. about 1841, and served in the Civil War from Shelby County in the 20th OVI, Co. K, from Jan. 1862 to July 1862.

Emma T.[1.4.1.31].

Laura B.[1.4.1.41].

John Charles Fremont[1.4.1.51], b. on Sep. 3, 1855 in Shelby County, Orange Township, Ohio, and m. Laura Ella, daughter of Theodore Cozier, of Piqua, Ohio, in the Fall of 1884.

Jonathan Kiggins

Jonathan[1.51] m. Elizabeth, daughter of Ludwig and Rosina (Kern) Boyer, in Miami County, Ohio, on Oct. 21, 1813. She was b. in Rockingham County, Cub Run, Virginia, on July 10, 1790, and d. in Mercer County, Dublin Township, Ohio, on Oct. 8, 1840. Jonathan was a farmer, hunter and hewer of timbers (woodcutter). After his brother James brought him and his other brother, Robert, to Ohio, and soon after moved west, Jonathan made his way to Fort Hamilton (Ohio), where he was employed in killing game for the army. Between 1810 and 1813, he moved to Miami County, Ohio, and stayed there till 1816, when he moved to Shelby County. He remained in Shelby County till 1824, and then moved to Mercer County, Ohio. Jonathan d. in Dublin Township on Feb. 20, 1847. They are buried in Mount Olive cemetery. They had the following children:

Minerva Jane$^{1.5.11}$, b. in Miami County, Spring Creek Township, Ohio, on Dec. 25, 1810.

Mary$^{1.5.21}$, b. in Spring Creek Township on Mar. 20, 1814.

Lewis$^{1.5.31}$, b. in Spring Creek Township on May 5, 1816.

Rosina$^{1.5.41}$, b. in Spring Creek Township on May 5, 1816.

Sophia$^{1.5.51}$, b. in Shelby County, Perry Township, Ohio, about 1817, and m. Joseph Crow in Mercer County, Ohio, on Jan. 18, 1841.

James$^{1.5.61}$, b. in Shelby County, Orange Township, Ohio, on Mar. 25, 1819.

Margaret$^{1.5.71}$, b. in Shelby County, Orange Township, Ohio, on Sep. 19, 1821, and m. Ishmael, son of Ruel and Sarah (Jones) Roebuck.

Elizabeth$^{1.5.81}$, b. in Shelby County, Orange Township, Ohio, on Sep. 19, 1821.

Catherine$^{1.5.91}$, b. in Shelby County, Orange Township, in 1824.

Harriet$^{1.5.101}$, b. in Shelby County, Orange Township, in 1826.

Charlotte$^{1.5.111}$, b. in Mercer County, Dublin Township, Ohio, in 1829, and m. Thomas M. Elliot in Allen County, Ohio, on Apr. 11, 1848, and Michael Burns about 1849. Michael was b. in Ireland in 1824.

Minerva Jane Kiggins

Minerva Jane$^{1.5.11}$ m. Joseph Baltzell in Shelby County, Ohio, on Aug. 8, 1826. He was b. in 1806. Minerva d. in Mercer County, Dublin Township, Ohio, on May 30, 1892. She is buried in Mount Olive cemetery. They had the following son in Dublin Township:

Harrison$^{1.5.1.11}$, b. in 1833.

Harrison Baltzell

Harrison$^{1.5.1.11}$ m. Nancy Barton in Mercer County on Apr. 2, 1853. She was b. in Ohio in 1830. Harrison d. in Dublin Township on June 20, 1909. They had the following children in Dublin Township:

Melvina$^{1.5.1.1.11}$, b. in 1855.

James B.$^{1.5.1.1.21}$, b. in 1856.

Minerva Jane$^{1.5.1.1.31}$, b. in 1857.

John A.$^{1.5.1.1.41}$, b. in 1860.
George H.$^{1.5.1.1.51}$, b. in 1862.
Gilmore B.$^{1.5.1.1.61}$, b. in 1864.
Rebecca A.$^{1.5.1.1.71}$, b. in 1867.

Mary Kiggins

Mary$^{1.5.21}$ m. Andrew Clawson in Shelby County, Ohio, on Mar. 15, 1830. He was b. in 1808. They had the following children:

Jonathan$^{1.5.2.11}$, b. in Putnam County, Ohio, in 1833, and m. Mary Clawson on Oct. 12, 1856 in Allen County, Ohio.

Joseph$^{1.5.2.21}$, b. in Putnam County in 1835, and m. Sarah Ann Brown in Allen County, Ohio, on June 29, 1856.

Franklin$^{1.5.2.31}$, b. in Putnam County in 1838, and m. Elizabeth Brown in Allen County, Ohio, on July 12, 1857.

Harriet$^{1.5.2.41}$, b. in Putnam County in 1839, and m. Samuel Patton in Allen County, Ohio, on Oct. 21, 1858.

Matthew$^{1.5.2.51}$, b. in Putnam County in 1841, and m. Sarah Ann Moore in Allen County, Ohio, on Apr. 16, 1863.

Aaron$^{1.5.2.61}$, b. in Putnam County in 1843.

Thomas$^{1.5.2.71}$, b. in Allen County, Ohio, in 1845.

Mary$^{1.5.2.81}$, b. in Allen County in 1848.

Elizabeth$^{1.5.2.91}$, b. in Allen County in 1852.

Andrew$^{1.5.2.101}$, b. in Allen County in 1855.

Francis$^{1.5.2.111}$, b. in Allen County in 1858.

Lewis Kiggins

Lewis$^{1.5.31}$ m. Mary Ellen Shindledecker in Mercer County, Ohio, on Jan. 19, 1837. She was b. in Ohio in 1815. Lewis d. in Mercer County, Dublin Township, Ohio, on Feb. 26, 1887. He is buried in the New Frysinger cemetery. They had the following children in Dublin Township:

Alfred$^{1.5.3.11}$, b. in 1838, m. Delinda Wiley in Mercer County on Aug. 12, 1859, and d. in Dublin Township in 1907. He is buried in Mount Olive cemetery.

Luella$^{1.5.3.21}$, b. in 1840.
Minerva J.$^{1.5.3.31}$, b. in 1842.
William$^{1.5.3.41}$, b. in 1844.
Susan$^{1.5.3.51}$, b. in 1845.
Ellis$^{1.5.3.61}$, b. in 1847.
Harrieta$^{1.5.3.71}$, b. in 1847.
Armanda$^{1.5.3.81}$, b. in 1848.

John[1.5.3.91], b. in 1849.

Catherine[1.5.3.101], b. in 1849.

Maragret[1.5.3.111], b. about 1850, and d. on Sep. 22, 1851. She is buried in Mount Olive cemetery.

Elizabeth[1.5.3.121], b. on Aug. 31, 1852, and d. on Sep. 7, 1852. She is buried in Mount Olive cemetery.

Sarah[1.5.3.111], b. on Aug. 31, 1852.

James[1.5.3.121], b. in 1854.

Minerva J. Kiggins

Minerva J.[1.5.3.31] m. Alfred Boroff, and had the following children:

Lewis[1.5.3.3.11], b. in 1862.

Martha[1.5.3.3.21], b. in 1865.

James[1.5.3.3.31], b. in 1876.

Sarah G.[1.5.3.3.41], b. on Nov. 14, 1878.

John Kiggins

John[1.5.3.91] m. Sarah J. (b.1860), and had the following children in Dublin Township:

Mary A.[1.5.3.9.11], b. in 1879.

Rosina Kiggins

Rosina[1.5.41] m. Cyrus, son of Abraham and Rebecca (Hoover) Shindledecker, and grandson of Jacob and Abigail (Longstreet) Shindledecker, in Mercer County, Ohio, on Oct. 1, 1837. He was b. in Ohio on May 19, 1814, and d. in Dublin Township in 1894. Rosina d. in Dublin Township in 1907. They are buried in Mount Olive cemetery. They had the following children in Dublin Township:

Clayborn[1.5.4.11], b. in 1844.

Jeremiah[1.5.4.21], b. on Mar. 3, 1846, m. Josophene Lehman in Van Wert County, Ohio, on Mar. 14, 1883, and d. in Van Wert County on Feb. 21, 1935.

Cyrus[1.5.4.31], b. in Feb. 1848.

James[1.5.4.41], b. in 1851.

Harriet[1.5.4.51], b. in 1853.

Curtis[1.5.4.61], b. in 1854.

Milton[1.5.4.71], b. in 1858.

Mariah[1.5.4.81], b. in 1860.

Alvin[1.5.4.91], b. in 1863.

Cyrus Shindledecker

Cyrus[1.5.4.31] m. Celia A. (b. Oct. 1856), and had the following children in Dublin Township:

Arnold E.[1.5.4.3.11], b. in Mar. 1879.

Mary A.[1.5.4.3.21], b. in Jan. 1881.

Eva[1.5.4.3.31], b. in July 1885.

Clyde[1.5.4.3.41], b. in Feb. 1888.

Fredie[1.5.4.3.51], b. in Oct. 1890.

James Kiggins

James[1.5.61] m. Mercy Ann Clawson in Shelby County, Ohio, on Nov. 19, 1837. She was b. in Ohio on Feb. 22, 1819, and d. in Allen County, Marion Township, Ohio, on July 16, 1884. James d. in Marion Township on Nov. 4, 1895. They are buried in Hartshorn cemetery. They had the following children in Allen County, Marion Township, Ohio (the first three may have been b. in Shelby or Mercer County):

Elizabeth[1.5.6.11], b. on Feb. 23, 1839, m. Alexander Rayer, and d. in Marion Township on July 6, 1904.

Josiah[1.5.6.21], b. on Oct. 8, 1840, and m. Lucinda Bryan.

Lewis[1.5.6.31], b. on Oct. 2, 1842, m. Christina Alspaugh in Van Wert County, Ohio, on July 11, 1863, and d. in Allen County, Marion Township, on Nov. 19, 1871.

Alexander[1.5.6.41], b. on Mar. 6, 1845, m. Rebecca Catherine Brown, and d. in Van Wert County, Ohio, on Dec. 6, 1927. She was b. on Apr. 9, 1851, and d. on Feb. 4, 1932.

Louise Jane[1.5.6.51], b. on Jan. 9, 1847, and m. James Belt.

Rosina[1.5.6.61], b. on Apr. 23, 1849, and m. Vincent Carey.

James[1.5.6.71], b. on Aug. 27, 1851, m. Ellen Bryan in Allen County, Ohio, on May 11, 1872, and d. in Allen County, Delphos, Ohio, on Feb. 8, 1939.

Margaret Kiggins

Margaret[1.5.71] m. Ishmael, son of Ruel and Sarah (Jones) Roebuck, in Mercer County, Ohio, on Feb. 1835. She was b. in Shelby County, Orange Township, Ohio, on Sep. 19, 1821, and d. in Dublin Township on Apr. 17, 1901. Ishmael was a farmer. He was b. in Ross County, Ohio, on Sep. 15, 1809, and d. in Dublin Township on Jan. 15, 1853. Ishmael and Margaret are buried in Roebuck cemetery. After Ishmael's death, Margaret m. Justice Wells in Mercer County on Oct. 3, 1854. Justice was b. in Huron County, Ohio, on Aug. 23, 1826, and d.

in Dublin Township on June 18, 1893. Justice is buried in Roebuck cemetery. Ishmael and Margaret had the following children:

Vincent[1.5.7.1i], b. in 1836, and resided in Dublin Township in 1850.

Mary[1.5.7.2i], b. on Aug. 18, 1839, and d. on Oct. 30, 1851. She is buried in Roebuck cemetery.

William Jasper[1.5.7.3i], b. on July 3, 1841. He m. Catherine, daughter of George and Margaret (Snyder) Shaffer, in Van Wert County, Ohio, on Jan. 6, 1861, and Caroline Shindledecker in Mercer County on Mar. 27, 1870. Catherine was b. in Van Wert County, Liberty Township, Ohio, on Nov. 5, 1842, and d. in Dublin Township on Nov. 4, 1869. Caroline was b. in 1847, and d. about 1871 (I have not confirmed this death date, and I believe that she may be the Caroline Roebuck that m. Adam Binckley in Mercer County on May 9, 1872). William was a farmer, and d. in Dublin Township on Oct. 21, 1870. William and Catherine are buried in Roebuck cemetery.

Harriet[1.5.7.4i], b. on Nov. 9, 1842, and d. on May 31, 1849. She is buried in Roebuck cemetery.

Garrison[1.5.7.5i], b. in 1844, and d. in 1853.

Eliza Jane[1.5.7.6i], b. on Mar. 20, 1847. He m. Stephen N., son of John H. and Mary (Longbrake) Dysert, in Mercer County, Ohio, on Sep. 25, 1864. He was b. in Mercer County, Dublin Township, Ohio, on Feb. 4, 1840.

Sarah Ellen[1.5.7.7i], b. on Apr. 10, 1850. She m. George W., son of John H. and Mary (Longbrake) Dysert, in Mercer County on Dec. 30, 1868, and d. in Dublin Township on Sep. 13, 1874. She is buried in Roebuck cemetery. George was b. in Dublin Township on Jan. 20, 1843, and d. in Dublin Township on Sep. 9, 1912. After Sarah d., George m. Celia.

Henry N.[1.5.7.8i], b. on Mar. 13, 1852, and d. on Mar. 10, 1853. He is buried in Roebuck cemetery.

Elizabeth C.[1.5.7.9i], b. on Mar. 13, 1852, and d. on Feb. 16, 1853. She is buried in Roebuck cemetery.

Margaret (Kiggins) Roebuck and Justice Wells had the following children:

James Franklin[1.5.7.10m], b. in 1856.

Martha[1.5.7.11m], b. in 1859.

Florence[1.5.7.12m], b. in 1861, and m. David Archer.

Elizabeth Kiggins

Elizabeth[1.5.81] m. Alexander F. Irick in Mercer County, Ohio, on Feb. 10, 1839. He was b. in Rockingham County, Virginia, on Oct. 2, 1819. Elizabeth d. in Allen County, Marion Township, Ohio, in 1904. They had the following children in Allen County, Marion Township, Ohio (the first four in Mercer County, Dublin Township):

John F.[1.5.8.11], b. in 1839, and d. in the Civil War on Oct. 31, 1863.

William L.[1.5.8.21], b. in 1841, and m. Mary Canada.

Mary C.[1.5.8.31], b. in 1843, and m. Sebastian Alspaugh.

James Ishmael[1.5.8.41], b. on July 29, 1845, and m. Melvina Ditto on Nov. 6, 1866.

Margaret[1.5.8.51], b. about 1847, and d. about 1849.

Arminda[1.5.8.61], b. in 1850, and m. Charles Peltier.

Alexander F.[1.5.8.71], b. in 1852, and m. Rebecca Holmes.

Francis C.[1.5.8.81], b. about 1854.

Missouri[1.5.8.91], b. in 1855, and m. John Ludwig.

Dorisa/Denise[1.5.8.101], b. in 1858, and m. David Hoffman.

Jackson[1.5.8.111], b. about 1860, and m. Louise Hoffman.

Eliza E.[1.5.8.121], b. about 1862, and m. Emanuel Tucker.

Catherine Kiggins

Catherine[1.5.91] m. John Blackwell in Miami County, Ohio, on Apr. 15, 1847. He was b. in 1824. They had the following children:

George W.[1.5.9.11], b. in 1848.

Elizabeth E.[1.5.9.21], b. in 1849.

Harriet Kiggins

Harriet[1.5.101] m. Elijah Hooks in Mercer County, Ohio, on Feb. 13, 1841. Elijah was b. in Ohio in 1817. They moved to Grant County, Lima, Wisconsin, before 1843. They had the following children:

Arminda[1.5.10.11], b. in 1843. She m. William Redmond.

Mary C.[1.5.10.21], b. in 1845. She m. Hosea T. Mundon in Grant County on Dec. 16, 1866.

Minerva J.[1.5.10.31], b. in 1847. She m. David Barrett in Grant County on Mar. 1, 1866.

Calvin[1.5.10.41], b. in 1848, and m. Mary Jane Walker Robinson in Grant County on Jan. 26, 1878, and Elizabeth Clark nee Foot in Grant County on May 13, 1899.

Matilda[1.5.10.51], b. about 1851, and m. Reuben Green in Grant County on Oct. 2, 1869.

Emma$^{1.5.10.61}$, b. about 1854. She m. Charles C. Chesley in Grant County on July 3, 1875.

Albert$^{1.5.10.71}$, b. about 1862, and m. Caroline E. Bolzell in Grant County on July 8, 1883.

Laura$^{1.5.10.81}$, b. about 1865, and m. John Hutchcroft in Grant County on Mar. 10, 1886.

Samuel$^{1.5.10.91}$, b. about 1867, and m. Emma Hutchcroft in Grant County on Aug. 12, 1888.

Julia$^{1.5.10.101}$, b. about 1869, and m. Isaac J. Hull in Grant County on May 27, 1891.

****

Hans Pickel

Hans^{1m} m. Veronica, and had the following son:
Balthasar$^{1.1m}$.

Balthasar Pickel

Balthasar$^{1.1m}$ m. Anna Eva, daughter of Hans Mullier of Neuleiningen near Grunstadt, in Bad Durkheim, Germany, on Jan. 22, 1677/78. He d. in Germany before Nov. 18, 1704, and Anna Eva m. Mattheus, son of Elias and Clara Reinboldt, at Durkheim on Nov. 18, 1704. Anna Eva immigrated to America in 1709, and resided in Hunterdon County, New Jersey, in 1717. They had the following children:

Anna Magdalena$^{1.1.1m}$, b. on Nov. 6, 1679.
Hans Michael$^{1.1.2m}$, b. on June 1, 1681.
Johan Nicholas$^{1.1.1m}$, b. on Sep. 14, 1683.
Balthazar$^{1.1.2m}$, b. in 1686.
Frantz Wilhelm$^{1.1.3m}$, b. about 1689.

Johan Nicholas Pickel

Johan Nicholas$^{1.1.1m}$ m. Johanna, and had the following children in Hunterdon County, Lebanon Township, New Jersey:

Johan Balthazar$^{1.1.1.1m}$, b. about 1720.
Conrad$^{1.1.1.2m}$, b. about 1725.

Johan Balthazar Pickel

Johan Balthazar$^{1.1.1.1m}$ m. Barbara, and had the following children:

Nicholas$^{1.1.1.1.1m}$, m. Rebecca.
Mary$^{1.1.1.1.2m}$, m. ____ Bodine.

Conrad Pickel

Conrad$^{1.1.1.2m}$ m. Anna Gertraud, daughter of Matthais and Anna Gertraud (Schuld) Scharfenstein, in Hunterdon County, New Jersey, on Apr. 11, 1751. Anna d. in Lebanon Township in 1802, and Conrad d. there in June 1801. They had the following children in Lebanon Township:

Catherine$^{1.1.1.2.1m}$, b. in 1752.
Hannah Charity$^{1.1.1.2.2m}$, b. about 1754.
Nicholas$^{1.1.1.2.3m}$, b. about 1756.
Matthias$^{1.1.1.2.4m}$, b. about 1758.
Sophia$^{1.1.1.2.5m}$, b. about 1760, and m. James Kiggins.
Sarah$^{1.1.1.2.6m}$, b. in 1763, m. William Hoffman in Hunterdon County in 1786, and d. in Hunterdon County on June 5, 1841.
Georg$^{1.1.1.2.7m}$, b. about 1765.

Catherine Pickel

Catherine$^{1.1.1.2.1m}$ m. William Apgar in Hunterdon County, Cokesbury on Apr. 17, 1774, and d. in Lebanon Township on Dec. 9, 1831. He was b. in Clinton, New Jersey, in 1752, and d. on Apr. 9, 1836. They had the following children:

Johanna Gertrude$^{1.1.1.2.1.1m}$, b. on Mar. 3, 1775.
Hannah$^{1.1.1.2.1.2m}$, b. on Mar. 3, 1776.
Elisabeth$^{1.1.1.2.1.3m}$, b. in 1777.
Nicholas P.$^{1.1.1.2.1.4m}$, b. on June 29, 1779.
James$^{1.1.1.2.1.5m}$, b. on Jan. 28, 1781.
William$^{1.1.1.2.1.6m}$, b. on Oct. 29, 1782.
Elisabeth$^{1.1.1.2.1.7m}$, b. on June 12, 1785, and m. William Mettler.
Sarah$^{1.1.1.2.1.8m}$, b. on June 12, 1785, and m. Isaac Bloom.
Catherine$^{1.1.1.2.1.9m}$, b. on Aug. 2, 1789.
Nancy$^{1.1.1.2.1.10m}$, b. on July 12, 1792, and m. Samuel Manning.
William$^{1.1.1.2.1.11m}$, b. on July 15, 1794.
George P.$^{1.1.1.2.1.12m}$, b. in 1799, and m. Elisabeth McPherson.

Nicholas P. Apgar

Nicholas P.$^{1.1.1.2.1.4m}$ m. Catherine Manning, and had the following children:

James$^{1.1.1.2.1.4.1m}$; George$^{1.1.1.2.1.4.2m}$; John$^{1.1.1.2.1.4.3m}$; Catherine$^{1.1.1.2.1.4.4m}$; Maria$^{1.1.1.2.1.4.5m}$.

Hannah Charity Pickel

Hannah Charity$^{1.1.1.2.2m}$ m. Jacob Apgar in Hunterdon County in 1769, and resided in Lebanon Township in Apr. 1814. Jacob was b. on July 18, 1746, and d. on May 6, 1814. They had the following children:

Anna$^{1.1.1.2.2.1m}$, b. on Feb. 1, 1770, and m. Herman Henry.

Frederick$^{1.1.1.2.2.2m}$, b. on June 11, 1772.

Catherine$^{1.1.1.2.2.3m}$, b. on Feb. 6, 1774, and m. George Kreamer.

Conrad$^{1.1.1.2.2.4m}$, b. on Apr. 8, 1776.

Nicholas$^{1.1.1.2.2.5m}$, b. on Oct. 9, 1778.

Sophia$^{1.1.1.2.2.6m}$, b. on Nov. 14, 1780, and m. Charles Kiggins.

Matthias S.$^{1.1.1.2.2.7m}$, b. about 1782.

Sallie$^{1.1.1.2.2.8m}$, b. on June 16, 1785, and m. McClosky Skureman.

Effie Elisabeth$^{1.1.1.2.2.9m}$, b. on Dec. 26, 1787, and m. John S. Melick.

John Casper$^{1.1.1.2.2.10m}$, b. on Apr. 6, 1790.

Jacob$^{1.1.1.2.2.11m}$, b. on Apr. 6, 1794.

Adam$^{1.1.1.2.2.12m}$, b. about 1796.

Frederick Apgar

Frederick$^{1.1.1.2.2.2m}$ m. Eve, daughter Harmon Hoffman, and d. on Jan. 20, 1840. She was b. on Dec. 25, 1775, and d. on Feb. 28, 1858. They had the following children:

Anna$^{1.1.1.2.2.2.1m}$, b. in 1794, and m. George Hoffman.

Jacob$^{1.1.1.2.2.2.2m}$, b. in 1794, and m. Catherine Apgar, daughter of William.

Conrad P.$^{1.1.1.2.2.2.3m}$, b. in 1800, and m. Mary Apgar, daughter of William.

Nicholas$^{1.1.1.2.2.2.4m}$, b. on Mar. 10, 1803, and m. Delilah Apgar, daughter of Wm..

Frederick$^{1.1.1.2.2.2.5m}$, b. on May 1, 1806, and m. Kate Trimmer, widow of Wm. Apgar.

Charity$^{1.1.1.2.2.6m}$, b. in 1809, and d. in 1831.

Sallie$^{1.1.1.2.2.7m}$, m. Aaron Alpaugh.

Mary$^{1.1.1.2.2.8m}$, b. in 1818, and m. Elijah Apgar, son of Herbert.

Conrad Apgar

Conrad$^{1.1.1.2.2.4m}$ m. Elisabeth Cramer, and d. on Mar. 1, 1836. She was b. on Apr. 23, 1776, and d. on Jan. 16, 1848. They had the following children:

Elisabeth$^{1.1.1.2.2.4.1m}$, m. Peter Rowe and Peter P. Apgar, son of Peter.

William C.$^{1.1.1.2.2.4.2m}$, m. Catherine Felmley, daughter of David.

Jacob$^{1.1.1.2.2.4.3m}$, b. in 1802, m. Mary Farley (1802-1887), and d. in 1830.

Frederick$^{1.1.1.2.2.4.4m}$, m. Catherine, daughter of James Todd.

Charity$^{1.1.1.2.2.4.5m}$, m. William, son of John Alpock.

Conrad$^{1.1.1.2.2.4.6m}$, m. Elisabeth, daughter of George Hoffman.

Mariah$^{1.1.1.2.2.4.7m}$, m. Allen, son of Watson Crague.

Harmon$^{1.1.1.2.2.4.8m}$, m. Effie, daughter of George Eick.

Nicholas Apgar

Nicholas$^{1.1.1.2.2.5m}$ m. Mary, daughter of Peter Bunn, and had the following children:

Jacob$^{1.1.1.2.2,5.1m}$, m. Margaret Trimmer.

Peter N.$^{1.1.1.2.2.5.2m}$, m. Isabel, daughter of Frederick Hoffman.

Abraham$^{1.1.1.2.2.5.3m}$, m. Mary A., daughter of John Apgar.

Elisabeth$^{1.1.1.2.2.5.4m}$, m. Peter J., son of John Philower.

Charity$^{1.1.1.2.2.5.5m}$, m. Andrew Stout.

Catherine$^{1.1.1.2.2.5.6m}$, m. Morris Teats.

Anna$^{1.1.1.2.2.5.7m}$, m. Oliver Farley.

Martha$^{1.1.1.2.2.5.8m}$, m. William Alpaugh.

Matthias S. Apgar

Matthais S.$^{1.1.1.2.2.7m}$ m. Catherine Skureman (no children), and Elsie, daughter of Frederick Hoffman. Matthias and Elsie had the following children:

Amanda$^{1.1.1.2.2.7.1m}$, m. Joseph Lommerson.

Mary$^{1.1.1.2.2.7.2m}$, m. Simon, son of Conrad Apgar.

John L.$^{1.1.1.2.2.7.3m}$, m. Eliza, daughter of Daniel Potter.
Huldah$^{1.1.1.2.2.7.4m}$, m. Aaron, son of Minert Farley.

John Casper Apgar

John Casper$^{1.1.1.2.2.10m}$ m. Elizabeth, daughter of Andrew Best, and Nancy, daughter of John Carlisle. John Casper had the following children:

Jacob B.$^{1.1.1.2.2.10.1m}$, m. Elisabeth, daughter of Andrew Schuyler.

Ann$^{1.1.1.2.2.10.2m}$, m. Daniel Seals.

Elisabeth$^{1.1.1.2.2.10.3m}$, m. John P., son of Peter Sutton.

Polly$^{1.1.1.2.2.10.4m}$.

John R.$^{1.1.1.2.2.10.5m}$, m. Susan, daughter of Andrew Schuyler.

Casper P.$^{1.1.1.2.2.10.6m}$, m. Rachel, daughter of Phillip Philhower.

Andrew$^{1.1.1.2.2.10.7m}$, m. Eliza Brown.

Immanuel$^{1.1.1.2.2.10.8m}$, m. Hannah, daughter of Matthias Hellebrant.

Jacob Apgar

Jacob$^{1.1.1.2.2.11m}$ m. Hannah, daughter of Conrad Apgar, and had the following children:

Matthias$^{1.1.1.2.2.11.1m}$.

Ann$^{1.1.1.2.2.11.2m}$, m. William Apgar, son of Herbert.

James$^{1.1.1.2.2.11.3m}$, m. a daughter of Peter Lance.

John$^{1.1.1.2.2.11.4m}$, m. Ann, daughter of Frederick Hoffman.

Peter$^{1.1.1.2.2.11.5m}$.

Mary$^{1.1.1.2.2.11.6m}$, m. Nicholas, son of Jacob Apgar.

Adam Apgar

Adam$^{1.1.1.2.2.12m}$ m. Mary, daughter of Christopher Philhower, and Betsey Parks. Adam had the following children:

Nathan$^{1.1.1.2.2.12.1m}$, m. Catherine, daughter of Frederick Apgar.

Charity$^{1.1.1.2.2.12.2m}$.

Matthias$^{1.1.1.2.2.12.3m}$, b. on Apr. 7, 1823, and m. Amanda Linaberry.

Benjamin$^{1.1.1.2.2.12.4m}$.

Frederick$^{1.1.1.2.2.12.5m}$.

Adam$^{1.1.1.2.2.12.6m}$, m. Elizabeth Lance.

Nicholas$^{1.1.1.2.2.12.7m}$.
Catherine$^{1.1.1.2.2.12.8m}$, m. _____ Orts.
Emma$^{1.1.1.2.2.12.9m}$.

Nicholas Pickel

Nicholas$^{1.1.1.2.3m}$, m. Elizabeth about 1789, and had the following children at Hunterdon County, High Bridge:
Johannes$^{1.1.1.2.3.1m}$, b. on July 6, 1790.
Mary$^{1.1.1.2.3.2m}$, b. on Sep. 22, 1796, and m. _____ Barnes.
Jonathan$^{1.1.1.2.3.3m}$, b. on Oct. 2, 1798, and m. Hannah Person in New Jersey on May 12, 1821.

Matthias Pickel

Matthias$^{1.1.1.2.4m}$ m. Adelyna, and had the following children in Lebanon Township:
Anna$^{1.1.1.2.4.1m}$, b. about 1784.
Anna Elisabetha$^{1.1.1.2.4.2m}$, b. on Jan. 6, 1787.
Catherine$^{1.1.1.2.4.3m}$, b. about 1790.

Georg Pickel

Georg$^{1.1.1.2.7m}$ m. Elizabeth about 1789, and had the following children:
Jacob$^{1.1.1.2.7.1m}$; Sarah$^{1.1.1.2.7.2m}$, m. _____ Hummer; Nicholas$^{1.1.1.2.7.3m}$; William Apgar$^{1.1.1.2.7.4m}$.

Balthazar Pickel

Balthazar$^{1.1.2m}$ m. Anna Gertrude Reiterin on Aug. 16, 1718, d. in Hunterdon County, New Jersey, on Dec. 5, 1765, and had the following children in Hunterdon County:
Maria Catherine$^{1.1.2.1m}$, b. on July 15, 1719.
Balthazar$^{1.1.2.2m}$, b. on Sep. 8, 1720.
Anna Eva$^{1.1.2.3m}$, b. about 1727, and m. Johannes Helfrich Schaum in Hunterdon County on Dec. 3, 1750.
Henry$^{1.1.2.4m}$, b. in 1729.

Balthazar Pickel

Balthazar$^{1.1.2.2m}$ m. Sophia. She was b. in 1726, and d. in 1764. Balthazar d. on Nov. 25, 1786. They had the following children:
Baltus$^{1.1.2.2.1m}$, b. about 1747.
Nicholas$^{1.1.2.2.2m}$, b. about 1749.

Frederick$^{1.1.2.2.3m}$, b. about 1751.
Abraham$^{1.1.2.2.4m}$, b. about 1753.

Baltus Pickel

Baltus$^{1.1.2.2.1m}$ m. Mary, and had the following daughter:
Catharina$^{1.1.2.2.1.1m}$, b. in 1789, and m. William Metler in
Hunterdon County on Mar. 24, 1808.

Nicholas Pickel

Nicholas$^{1.1.2.2.2m}$ m. Anna, and had the following children in
Hunterdon County, New Germantown:
Sarah$^{1.1.2.2.2.1m}$, b. in 1781.
Peter Regintine$^{1.1.2.2.2.2m}$, b. on Apr. 24, 1783.

Frederick Pickel

Frederick$^{1.1.2.2.3m}$ m. Elizabeth, d. in 1820, and had the
following children:
Mary Rose$^{1.1.2.2.3.1m}$; Margaret$^{1.1.2.2.3.2m}$;
Catherine$^{1.1.2.2.3.3m}$; Baltis$^{1.1.2.2.3.4m}$; Elisabeth$^{1.1.2.2.3.5m}$;
Hannah$^{1.1.2.2.3.6m}$; Charity$^{1.1.2.2.3.7m}$; George$^{1.1.2.2.3.8m}$, b. in 1784.

George Pickel

George$^{1.1.2.2.3.8m}$ m. Sarah Howell, and Mary, and d. in 1864.
George and Sarah had the following children:
Marietta$^{1.1.2.2.3.8.1m}$, m. John Rowe.
Frederick$^{1.1.2.2.3.8.2m}$, m. Mary Hildebrandt.
Isaac$^{1.1.2.2.3.8.3m}$, m. Margaret Gulicks.
Ruth$^{1.1.2.2.3.8.4m}$, m. John Davis.
Matthias$^{1.1.2.2.3.8.5m}$, m. Maria Smith.
Alfred$^{1.1.2.2.3.8.6m}$, m. Sarah Crater and ____ Sutton.
Samuel$^{1.1.2.2.3.8.7m}$, m. Deborah Bartles and Elisabeth
Walters.
Henry$^{1.1.2.2.3.8.8m}$, m. Mary Evert.
George$^{1.1.2.2.3.8.9m}$, m. Jane Beavers.

Abraham Pickel

Abraham$^{1.1.2.2.4m}$ m. Peggy Farley, d. in 1823, and had the
following children:
Abraham$^{1.1.2.2.4.1m}$; Adrain$^{1.1.2.2.4.2m}$; Minard$^{1.1.2.2.4.3m}$;
Margaret$^{1.1.2.2.4.4m}$.

Henry Pickel

Henry$^{1.1.2.4m}$ d. in 1765, and had the following children:

Baltus$^{1.1.2.4.1m}$, b. in 1760, and d. in Hunterdon County in 1765.

Henry$^{1.1.2.4.2m}$, b. about 1762.

Elisabeth$^{1.1.2.4.3m}$, b. about 1764.

Gertraut$^{1.1.2.4.4m}$, b. about 1765.

Henry Pickel

Henry$^{1.1.2.4.2m}$ m. Maria, and had the following children in Hunterdon County:

Johannes$^{1.1.2.4.2.1m}$, b. on Feb. 12, 1784.

Elisabeth$^{1.1.2.4.2.2m}$, b. on Nov. 27, 1785.

Henry F.$^{1.1.2.4.2.3m}$, b. on Sep. 28, 1789.

Christina$^{1.1.2.4.2.4m}$, b. on Oct. 23, 1791.

Jacob$^{1.1.2.4.2.5m}$, b. about 1793.

****

Matthias Scharfenstein

Matthias^{1n} m. Dorothea Maria, daughter of Johannes Wilhelm Weyer, on Nov. 6, 1713, and Anna Gertraud, daughter of Johan Gerhard Schuld, in Muscheid, Germany, on Oct. 15, 1731. Dorothea was b. in 1678, and was buried in Feb. 1726. Matthias was a freeholder in Reading Township, Hunterdon County, New Jersey, in 1741. He was naturalized on Dec. 8, 1744. Matthias d. in Hunterdon County, Reading Township, New Jersey, in Oct. 1756. His will was written on Oct. 16, 1750, and probated on Oct. 6, 1756. Anna was alive in 1750. Matthias had the following children:

Johann Moritz$^{1.1n}$, b. on Aug. 8, 1714, baptized at Urbach, and sponsored by Johannes Thomas, Moritz Henn, and Anna Loysa Stroder.

Eva Christina$^{1.2n}$, b. on May 11, 1715, baptized at Urbach, and sponsored by Eva Margaretha Klein, Anna Christina Dils, and Johannes Mathias Thomas. She m. Philip Eick, and d. in Hunterdon County, Leban Township, New Jersey, on Feb. 12, 1792. She is buried in Lebanon cemetery.

Johann Peter$^{1.3n}$, baptized at Urbach in Oct. 1716, and sponsored by Johannes Hoffmann, Peter Noll, and Magdalena Schmid. He was confirmed at Urbach in 1731, and naturalized in Hunterdon County, New Jersey, on Aug. 14, 1750. He purchased 210 acres of the

Logan Tract in German Valley on Dec. 8, 1749. Estate papers were submitted by his widow, Anne, in Morris County, Roxbury Township, New Jersey, on June 2, 1760.

Elisabetha[1.4n], b. on Sep. 7, 1718, baptized at Urbach, and sponsored by Elisabeth Gertraut Langsdorf, Eulalia Hoffman, and Johan Jacob Ahlbuh. She was confirmed at Urbach in 1731.

Son[1.5n], b. on May 12, 1721, baptized at Urbach, sponsored by Arnd Bettgenhauser, Joannis Scharfenstein, and Maria Catharina Kaule, and buried in Mar. 1722.

Son[1.6n], b. on Apr. 8, 1723, baptized at Urbach, and sponsored by Herbert Henn, Fridericus Ziggenhauser, and Anna Margaretha Kalbitzer.

Son[1.7n], b. on Feb. 8, 1726, baptized at Urbach, sponsored by Theil Schmidt, Johan Theil Wers, and Anna Maria Enders, and buried Feb. 12, 1729.

Anna Gertraud[1.8n], b. in Uberdorff/Muscheid, Germany, about 1732, and m. Conrad Pickel.

Johann Georg[1.9n], baptized at Readington, New Jersey, on Mar. 17, 1734, and sponsored by Johan Georg Eyk, Jacob Eyk, and Eva Thomasse.

Matthias[1.10n], b. in 1738, and m. Elisabeth Hagar in Morris County, New Jersey, in 1760.

Maria Catharina[1.11n], b. in 1740, and m. Peter Jung.

Peter[1.12n], b. in 1742, and m. Rebecca in 1767.

Jacob[1.13n], b. about 1744, and m. Sarah in 1767.

Sophia[1.14n], b. about 1746, and m. John Mills.

Johan Moritz Scharfenstein

Johann Moritz[1.1n] was naturalized on Aug. 14, 1750, and was a blacksmith. He resided in Tewksbury Township in 1764, and bought 361 acres in Upper German Valley in 1767. His will was written on Sep. 12, 1781, and probated in Morris County, New Jersey, on Sep. 21, 1781. He m. Catharina, who d. on Apr. 18, 1806, aged 85. She is buried in Basking Ridge Presbyterian cemetery. They had the following children:

Matthias[1.1.1n], b. in 1735.

Christina[1.1.2n], b. in 1737, and m. Hermanes Dilts in 1766.

Anna[1.1.3n], b. in 1739.

Elisabeth[1.1.4n], b. in 1741.

Johan[1.1.5n], b. in 1743.

Dorothy[1.1.6n], b. in 1745, and m. Wilhelm Welsch in Morris County in 1770.

Morris[1.1.7n], b. about 1747.

Anna Mary[1.1.8n], b. on Sep. 11, 1754.

****

Johann Peter Schuch

Johann Peter[1o] m. Ann Maria Kappel, and had the following children at Baumholder, Germany:

Sara Catharina[1.1o], b. at Rathsweiler, Palatinate, baptized at Baumholder, Rheinland on Jan. 19, 1690, and m. Christoffel Doll.

Johann Christian[1.2o], baptized at Ulmet on May 4, 1690.

Johann Christian Schuch

Johann Christian[1.2o] m. Anna Catharina, daughter of Georg Christoffel of Patersbach, Germany, on June 5, 1714, and immigrated to America on the ship *Samuel* in 1739. They settled in Bucks County, Springfield Township, Pennsylvania. On Oct. 3, 1739, he was granted a tract in Springfield on a branch of Cook's Creek near Durham. On June 30, 1747, Reverend Michael Schlatter preached at a place called Springfield/Schuggenhause. On Sep. 29, 1747, Christian was present at the first meeting of the Coetus of Pennsylvania at Philadelphia. On Nov. 12, 1763, he gave 1 acre and 56 perches to the church. Anna Catharina d. between 1758 and 1761. They had the following children baptized at Ulmet:

Juliana Elisabetha[1.2.1o], baptized on Jan. 29, 1716.

Maria Margaretha[1.2.2o], baptized on June 24, 1718.

Elisabetha Catharina[1.2.3o], baptized on Aug. 4, 1720, and was buried in Northampton County, Easton at Mount Bethel on Feb. 1, 1802. She was unmarried.

Anna Sara[1.2.4o], baptized on Aug. 30, 1722.

Anna Maria[1.2.5o], baptized on Jan. 23, 1725.

Johan Peter[1.2.6o], baptized on Nov. 14, 1726, and d. on Jan. 14, 1731.

Johan Georg[1.2.7o], baptized on July 9, 1729, and d. on Jan. 12, 1731.

Maria Elisabetha[1.2.8o], baptized on Oct. 7, 1731.

Johan Peter[1.2.9o], baptized on Feb. 7, 1734.

Anna Catharina[1.2.10o], baptized on Sep. 28, 1736.

Johan Peter Schuch

Johan Peter[1.2.9o] m. Anna Maria, and was buried in
Northampton County, Easton, Pennsylvania, on Aug. 13, 1794. They
had the following children in Bucks County, Springfield Township,
Pennsylvania:

Johan Christian[1.2.9.1o], b. on Oct. 19, 1763, baptized at Trinity
Union Church on Nov. 2, 1763, and sponsored by Christian Schuck and
the wife of Michael Werler.

Anna Margaretha[1.2.9.2o], b. on Nov. 9, 1769, baptized at
Trinity Union Church on Dec. 10, 1769, and sponsored by Jacob
Guckert and wife.

Anna Catharina[1.2.9.3o], b. on June 21, 1771, baptized at
Trinity Union on July 21, 1771, and sponsored by Bernhard and Maria
Catharina Derr.

Johan Heinrich[1.2.9.4o], baptized at Trinity Union on July 23,
1775, and sponsored by Henry Weyerbach and Maria Elisabeth Geres.

****

Johann Michael Stophlet

Johann Michael[1p] was b. in France in 1730. He m. Elisabeth
Engel. He served as a Captain during the Revolutionary War. Michael
d. in Montgomery County, Douglas Township, Pennsylvania, in 1782.
They had the following children in Montgomery County:

Johannes[1.1p], b. in 1750.

Margaret[1.2p], b. about 1754, and m. David Gerlin in
Montgomery County New Hanover Lutheran Church on June 9, 1775.

Anna Catherine[1.3p], b. on July 2, 1755.

Johann Henrich[1.4p], b. on Oct. 7, 1757 (Sep. 29, 1752
tombstone), and sponsored by Heinrich Engle and wife.

Eva Frederica[1.5p], b. on Sep. 4, 1759, and sponsored by
Frederick Locser and wife.

Jacob[1.6p], b. on Aug. 23, 1765, and sponsored by Jacob and
Eva Eppele.

Elizabeth[1.7p], b. on Apr. 3, 1767, baptized at Falkner Swamp
on Sep. 6, 1767, and m. Henry A. Wann in Berks County, Amity
Township, Amityville, Pennsylvania, on Apr. 13, 1794.

Ludwig[1.8p], b. about 1769.

Anna Maria[1.9p], b. on May 9, 1771.

Johannes Stophlet

Johannes[1.1p] m. Elisabeth Schuman in Montgomery County, New Hanover Lutheran Church, Pennsylvania, on Apr. 30, 1776. Johannes d. at New Hanover on Feb. 4, 1802, and Elisabeth Sometie after 1810. They had the following children at New Hanover:

Margaretha[1.1.1p], b. in 1772, and confirmed in 1790 at age 18.

Barbara[1.1.2p], b. on Jan. 31, 1777, sponsored by Georg Kraft and Barbara Schuman, and d. on July 28, 1781.

Johan Georg[1.1.3p], b. on Nov. 14, 1778, and sponsored by Georg and Susanna Gilbert.

Johannes[1.1.41], b. on Feb. 22, 1781.

Jacob[1.1.5p], b. on May 12, 1783, and sponsored by Jacob and Elisabetha Engel.

Elisabeth[1.1.6p], b. on Mar. 10, 1794, and d. on Oct. 14, 1800.

Michael[1.1.7p], b. about 1796.

Johan Georg Stophlet

Johan Georg[1.1.3p] m. Maria Werthain in Montgomery County, New Hanover Lutheran Church on Jan. 25, 1807, and resided in Douglas Township in 1810. They had the following children:

Samuel[1.1.3.1p], b. on Oct. 30, 1809, and confirmed in 1825. He m. Judith Dotterer at Falkner Swamp on Aug. 2, 1835.

Esther[1.1.3.2p], b. on Oct. 25, 1823.

Johannes Stophlet

Johannes[1.1.4p] m. Elisabeth Herbst in Montgomery County on Feb. 14, 1808, and resided in New Hanover in 1810. They had the following children:

Sarah[1.1.4.1p], b. on June 16, 1809, and sponsored by Samuel and Sarah Uetter.

Johannes[1.1.4.2p], b. on Dec. 1, 1814, and sponsored by John and Maria Herbst.

Michael Stophlet

Michael[1.1.7p] m. Catherine Reigner in Montgomery County on May 26, 1816, and had the following children in Montgomery County:

Elisabeth[1.1.7.1p], b. on Nov. 27, 1816.

Herman[1.1.7.2p], b. on Sep. 27, 1817.

Heinrich[1.1.7.3p], b. on Oct. 9, 1819.

Sarah[1.1.7.4p], b. on Feb. 14, 1824.

Johann Henrich Stophlet

Johann Henrich[1.4p] m. Apollonia, and d. in Northampton County, Plainfield, Pennsylvania, on Aug. 20, 1828. She was b. in Aug. 1762, and d. in Aug. 1833. They are buried in Forks Churchyard cemetery. They had the following children in Northampton County, Plainfield, Pennsylvania (Henrich was residing in Montgomery County in 1780, and Plainfield in 1800):

Samuel[1.4.1p], b. on May 4, 1781 (not confirmed, but seems to fit nowhere else).

Elizabeth[1.4.2p], b. on Oct. 21, 1783, and baptized at St. Peter's Lutheran Church in Plainfield Township.

Anna Maria[1.4.3p], b. on Mar. 11, 1786, and baptized at St. Peter's.

Henry[1.4.4p], b. on Oct. 5, 1787, and baptized at St. Peter's. He resided in Northampton County, Plainfield in 1820, and may be the Henry Stoffle, who was residing in Allegheny County, Allegheny Township, Pennsylvania, in 1830.

Barbara[1.4.5p], b. on May 21, 1789, and baptized at the German Evangelical Lutheran Church of Easton.

Jacob[1.4.6p], b. on Nov. 7, 1790, and baptized at Dryland Lutheran Church in Lower Nazareth Township. He resided in Northampton County, Forks Township, in 1830.

David[1.4.7p], b. about 1791 (not confirmed, but seems to fit nowhere else). He resided in Clermont County, Washington Township, Ohio, in 1818 when he purchased lot #40 in Neville. In 1819, he purchased lot #151 in Batavia, and lot #55 in Neville. He was treasurer from 1820-22. He was a property holder in 1826. There was a Julia Ann Stophlet who m. Winslow Fletcher in Clermont County on Aug. 29, 1832. She may have been a widow or a daughter of David.

Margaret[1.4.8p], b. on May 21, 1797, and baptized at St. Peter's.

Samuel Stophlet

Samuel[1.4.1p] served in the War of 1812 as a Private in the U.S. Volunteer Calvary Light Dragoons under Captain Joseph Markle, and Major James V. Ball from Sep. 12, 1812 to Sep. 12, 1813 from Westmoreland County, Pennsylvania. He m. Mary Williams about 1806. She was b. in Pennsylvania on Feb. 6, 1783. Samuel moved from Westmoreland County, South Huntingdon Township, Pennsylvania, to Wayne County, Franklin Township, Ohio, between 1812 and 1818.

Samuel and Mary were residing in Holmes County, Salt Creek Township, Ohio, in 1860. They had the following children:

Samuel$^{1.4.1.1p}$, b. in 1807.

Katherine A.$^{1.4.1.2p}$, b. on Apr. 3, 1809.

Jane$^{1.4.1.3p}$, b. about 1811, m. David H. Baker in Holmes County, Ohio, on Dec. 24, 1829, and d. in Holmes County, Ohio, before 1850.

Sarah$^{1.4.1.4p}$, b. about 1818, and m. George W. Galloway in Holmes County, Ohio, on Oct. 8, 1839.

David F.$^{1.4.1.5p}$, b. in Holmes County, Salt Creek Township, Ohio, on Jan. 2, 1824.

Samuel Stophlet

Samuel$^{1.4.1.1p}$ m. Adelaide Ferry in Allen County, Fort Wayne, Indiana, on Mar. 21, 1836, and Mary McMaken in Fort Wayne on Dec. 16, 1841. Mary was b. in 1819, and d. in Fort Wayne on Mar. 18, 1884. Samuel had a tailor shop on the north west corner of Barr and Columbia 182?-3?, was a 3rd Sergeant in the militia sent to suppress the rebellion among laborers on the Wabash and Erie Canal, a vestryman at Trinity Protestant Episcopal on May 27, 1839, a probate judge from Nov. 9, 1840-44, an assessor in 1840, a representative from 1844-46, and took over as post master in 1849 (and moved the post office further down Calhoun) while residing in Fort Wayne, and moved to Allen County, Delphos, Ohio, sometime after 1850. He d. in Delphos on Oct. 14, 1865. He has not been confirmed as Samuel's son, but seems to fit here. He had the following children in Fort Wayne:

Francis$^{1.4.1.1.1p}$, b. in 1842, and resided in Kansas City in 1884.

John Walpole$^{1.4.1.1.2p}$, b. on Apr. 25, 1845.

Joseph W./H.$^{1.4.1.1.3p}$, b. in 1848, m. Agnes H. Fowles in Fort Wayne on Jan. 23, 1872, and resided in Falls City, Pennsylvania, in 1884.

Samuel$^{1.4.1.1.4p}$, m. Adelaide Ferry in Fort Wayne on Mar. 21, 1836.

Anna L.$^{1.4.1.1.5p}$, m. Henry T. Simpson in Fort Wayne on May 18, 1876.

John Walpole Stophlet

John W.$^{1.4.1.1.2p}$ m. Lizzie Underhill in Fort Wayne on Sep. 10, 1873. In July 1886, he moved to Toledo, Ohio, and became known as one of Ohio's best known traveling salesmen. John d. on Jan. 20, 1905. They had the following children in Fort Wayne, Indiana:

Eddie G.[1.4.1.1.2.1p], b. on Oct. 18, 1878, and d. on Oct. 23, 1878.

David F. Stophlet

David F.[1.4.1.5p] m. Sarah Williams in Holmes County in 1845, and Ruth about 1857. David had the following children in Holmes County, Fredericksburg, Ohio:

Marquis Lafayette[1.4.1.5.1p], b. in 1846, and m. Elizabeth Heller in Wayne County, Ohio, on Aug. 10, 1873.

Elwood[1.4.1.5.2p], b. about 1850.

Olive F.[1.4.1.5.3p], b. in 1852, and m. Thomas G. Morgan in Holmes County on Apr. 14, 1870.

Samuel W.[1.4.1.5.4p], b. in Sep. 1854, and m. Alice Latha Braden in Wayne County, Orrville on Aug. 1, 1883, and Laura Gailey at Orrville on May 11, 1892.

William E.[1.4.1.5.5p], b. about 1856.

Frank[1.4.1.5.6p], b. about 1858.

Taymer[1.4.1.5.7p], b. about 1859.

Gertrude[1.4.1.5.8p], b. in 1861.

Kate[1.4.1.5.9p], b. about 1863.

Catherine[1.4.1.5.10p], b. in 1865.

Francis[1.4.1.5.11p], b. in 1867.

Etta[1.4.1.5.12p], b. in 1871.

Gainor[1.4.1.5.13p], b. in 1879.

Katherine A. Stophlet

Katherine A.[1.4.1.2p] m. George, son of Ruel and Sarah (Jones) Roebuck, in Mercer County, Dublin Township, Ohio, on Mar. 15, 1829. She has not been confirmed as Samuel's daughter, but in all likelihood she is Samuel Jr.'s sister. George Roebuck's father, Ruel, was a keel boat operator on the St. Mary's River between Fort Wayne and Shane's Crossing (now Rockford), Ohio. It is very probable that Katherine and George met in Fort Wayne, if George was working with his father, or at Shane's Crossing, which was the stopping point on the way to Fort Wayne. George was, b. in Ross County, Ohio, on Oct. 30, 1807. Katherine d. in Dublin Township on Mar. 11, 1875. George d. in Dublin Township on Jan. 26, 1846. They are buried in Roebuck cemetery. They had the following children in Dublin Township:

Ruel$^{1.1.1.2.3.1.1i}$, b. on June 5, 1830. He m. Catherine, daughter of Amos and Margaret (Broun) Harp, in Mercer County on Oct. 2, 1862. She was b. in Auglaize County, Noble Township, Ohio, on May 14, 1840, and d. in Dublin Township on Feb. 16, 1883. Ruel d. in Dublin Township on Sep. 20, 1887.

Samuel$^{1.1.1.2.3.1.2i}$, b. in 1833. He m. Mary Jane Wolf in Tippecanoe County, Indiana, on Dec. 14, 1857. She was b. in Indiana in Oct. 1838. Samuel d. in Tippecanoe County, Wabash Township, Indiana.

John Alexander$^{1.1.1.2.3.1.3i}$, b. on Mar. 14, 1835. He m. Gemima Davis in Mercer County, Ohio, on Mar. 14, 1851. She was b. in Oct. 1841, and d. in Dublin Township in 1915. John Alexander d. in Dublin Township on Oct. 10, 1899.

Eliza$^{1.1.1.2.3.1.4i}$, b. in 1837. She m. Emanuel Putman in Mercer County on Sep. 21, 1858. He was b. in Bedford County, Pennsylvania, on Apr. 24, 1832, and d. in Dublin Township on Apr. 29, 1916. He came to Mercer County in 1849, with his mother, Lizzie Jane (b.1800), and brothers, William (b.1831), and Philip (b.1835). Eliza d. in Dublin Township in 1869.

Susan$^{1.1.1.2.3.1.5i}$, b. on Oct. 4, 1839, and m. John, son of Peter and Catharina (Schlater) Dull, in Mercer County on Jan. 1, 1860.

Mahala J.$^{1.1.1.2.3.1.6i}$, b. in 1843. She m. William Black in Mercer County on Sep. 26, 1867, and David F. Thomas in Mercer County on Oct. 30, 1884. He d. in Dublin Township on Feb. 10, 1874. Mahala d. in Dublin Township in 1918.

Jacob Stophlet

Jacob$^{1.6p}$ m. Eva Mayer in Montgomery County, New Hanover Township, Pennsylvania, on Apr. 4, 1786. They may have had the following children in Lehigh County, Pennsylvania:

Susanna$^{1.6.1p}$, b. on June 8, 1788.
Maria$^{1.6.2p}$, b. on Nov. 22, 1792.
Jonas$^{1.6.3p}$, b. on Dec. 10, 1798.

Ludwig Stophlet

Ludwig$^{1.8p}$ m. Susanna, and had the following children in Lehigh County, Pennsylvania:

Magdalena$^{1.8.1p}$, b. on Sep. 25, 1790.
Sarah$^{1.8.2p}$, b. on Jan. 26, 1792.
Catherine$^{1.8.3p}$, b. on Oct. 22, 1794.

William$^{1.8.4p}$, b. on Aug. 16, 1798.
George$^{1.8.5p}$, b. in Sep. 1799 (this has not been confirmed).

****

William Wartenbe

William^{1q} was b. in about 1667, and had the following children in London, England (he may have m. Mrs. Mary Welby in Wartenby, Leicestershire on Oct. 21, 1700):

Edward$^{1.1q}$, b. about 1688, m. Elizabeth Duckworth in London, and d. in Chester County, Pennsylvania, in 1715.
William$^{1.2q}$, b. about 1690.

William Wartenbe

William$^{1.2q}$ m. Ann (possibly Ann Pelle/Peal in Wartenby on Apr. 28, 1700), d. in Philadelphia County, Bristol Township, Pennsylvania, in Mar. 1732/33. Ann d. in Bristol Township in 1741. They had the following children:

John$^{1.2.1q}$, b. about 1710.
Ann$^{1.2.2q}$, b. about 1713, and m. ____ Pratt.
Mary$^{1.2.3q}$, b. about 1716, and m. Bryan Hughs in Christ's Church of Philadelphia on Sep. 16, 1736.
Robert$^{1.2.4q}$, b. about 1719.
William$^{1.2.5q}$, b. about 1722.

John Wartenbe

John$^{1.2.1q}$ m. Elizabeth Taylor, and had the following children:
Rebecca$^{1.2.1.1q}$, b. about 1731.
Ann$^{1.2.1.2q}$, b. about 1733.

Robert Wartenbe

Robert$^{1.2.4q}$ m. Susanna Crane about 1740, and d. in Philadelphia County, Bristol Township, Pennsylvania, in 1760. They had the following children:

Robert$^{1.2.4.1q}$, b. about 1741, and d. in Bristol Township in Mar. 1766.
Richard$^{1.2.4.2q}$, b. about 1743.
John$^{1.2.4.3q}$, b. about 1745.
William$^{1.2.4.4q}$, b. about 1747.
Elizabeth$^{1.2.4.5q}$, b. about 1749.

Eleanor[1.2.4.6q], b. about 1751, and m. Peter Taylor of Bristol Township. Peter d. in Montgomery County, Chaltenham, Pennsylvania, in 1784.

Susanna[1.2.4.7q], b. about 1753.

Richard Wartenbe

Richard[1.2.4.2q] m. Mary, and d. in Bristol Township in 1792. They had the following son:

Robert[1.2.4.2.1q].

John Wartenbe

John[1.2.4.3q] m. Elizabeth Keeper, and had the following son:

John[1.2.4.3.1q], m. Sarah Dilworth before 1791.

William Wartenbe

William[1.2.4.4q] was a bricklayer in Philadelphia, when he signed his share of his father's property to his brother, Richard on Mar. 13, 1777. He resided in Kent County, Delaware in 1788, and had the following daughter:

Mary[1.2.4.4.1q].

William Wartenbe

William[1.2.5q] m. Sarah Hellings in Philadelphia County, St. Michael's Zion Lutheran Church of Pennsylvania on Apr. 4, 1755, and Eva Hellings at St. Michael's on Mar. 29, 1756. William was taxed in Middlesex County, New Brunswick Township (South Ward of New Brunswick), New Jersey, in 1772. According to tradition, William and Eva d. of smallpox in Middlesex County, New Brunswick Township, New Jersey, while their son was serving in the Revolutionary War. He supposedly came home on furlough, and found them dead. "He was so mortified that they could not be handled with hands. Consequently, he rolled them up in sheets, hauled them out and dug a hole, and buried them both in one grave. In so doing, he buried the last one of the name, himself excepted." (Quotes from Stewart Patterson Wartenbe.) They had the following children:

William[1.2.5.1q], b. about 1757.

Jacob[1.2.5.2q], b. about 1759, and was taxed in Somerset County, New Jersey, in 1780.

Nicholas[1.2.5.3q], b. about 1769, and resided in Brooke County, Virginia, in 1790.

William Wartenbe

William$^{1\cdot2\cdot5\cdot1q}$ m. Catherine White ("a short heavy girl" (SPW)) about 1778. She was b. on Jan. 31, 1761, and d. in Muskingum County, Salt Creek Township, Ohio, on May 19, 1839. Catherine is buried in Salt Creek Baptist cemetery. During the Revolutionary War, William was a Private in Captain James Morgan's Company, 2nd Regiment, Middlesex County, Militia from Sep. 8, to Oct. 8, 1777, Nov. 14 to Dec. 7, 1777. He received a certificate on June 10, 1784 for 9£ and 3 shillings "for depreciation of his continental pay". William was taxed in Middlesex County, New Brunswick Township (South Ward of New Brunswick), New Jersey, in 1778 and 1780. In 1785, he purchased 110 acres in Ohio (now Brooke) County, Virginia, on Buffalo Creek (near Fowlersburg), and was taxed there from 1788 to 1813. He owned a grist mill and a saw mill. In 1797, he received a grant for 38 acres in Ohio County, and in 1802, he purchased 180 acres in Section 33, Township 10, Range 4 in Jefferson County, Ohio. In 1814, he purchased 80 acres near Muskingum County, Zanesville, Ohio, and moved there. He was a millwright and mill owner. Catherine was a member of the Salt Creek Baptist Church as early as 1823. William d. in Salt Creek Township in July 1821. They had the following children (the first three in Middlesex County, New Jersey, and the rest in Brooke County, Wellsburg, Virginia):

Catherine$^{1\cdot2\cdot5\cdot1\cdot1q}$, b. on May 28, 1779, and m. Joseph Mitten and John Gray (before 1818).

John$^{1\cdot2\cdot5\cdot1\cdot2q}$, b. on Nov. 22, 1780.

Francis David$^{1\cdot2\cdot5\cdot1\cdot3q}$, b. on Apr. 28, 1783.

Margaret$^{1\cdot2\cdot5\cdot1\cdot4q}$, b. on Aug. 31, 1785, and m. Otho Baker in Brooke County, Virginia, on Mar. 11, 1802.

Mary$^{1\cdot2\cdot5\cdot1\cdot5q}$, b. on June 27, 1787.

Sarah$^{1\cdot2\cdot5\cdot1\cdot6q}$, b. on Mar. 15, 1789, and m. ____ Holly.

Jane$^{1\cdot2\cdot5\cdot1\cdot7q}$, b. on Nov. 23, 1790, and d. before 1801.

William$^{1\cdot2\cdot5\cdot1\cdot8q}$, b. on Jan. 12, 1792.

Isaac$^{1\cdot2\cdot5\cdot1\cdot9q}$, b. on Jan. 24, 1794.

Nancy Ann$^{1\cdot2\cdot5\cdot1\cdot10q}$, b. on May 19, 1796, and m. James Watson in Muskingum County, Ohio, on Oct. 5, 1821.

Elizabeth$^{1\cdot2\cdot5\cdot1\cdot11q}$, b. on Dec. 23, 1797.

Joseph$^{1\cdot2\cdot5\cdot1\cdot12q}$, b. on Oct. 17, 1799.

Mary Jane$^{1\cdot2\cdot5\cdot1\cdot13q}$, b. in 1801, and m. Nathan Smith in Muskingum County, Ohio, on Apr. 13, 1820.

Mercy$^{1\cdot2\cdot5\cdot1\cdot14q}$, b. on Mar. 18, 1803, and m. James Crane in Muskingum County, Ohio, on Sep. 26, 1822.

Susanna$^{1.2.5.1.15q}$, b. on Feb. 22, 1806, and m. Daniel Cumstock in Muskingum County, Ohio, Oct. 17, 1822.

John Wartenbe

John$^{1.2.5.1.2q}$ m. Ruth Baker in Brooke County, Virginia, in 1802, and d. in Muskingum County, Perry Township, Ohio, on Jan. 13, 1851. Ruth was b. on Jan. 6, 1789, and d. in Perry Township on Feb. 6, 1850. John moved to Muskingum County, Perry Township, Ohio, in 1809, and built a sawmill on Salt Creek in the southwest corner of section 22 in 1810. He built a grist mill in 1812. They had the following children (the first four in Virginia, and the rest in Muskingum County, Ohio):

William Baker$^{1.2.5.1.2.1q}$, b. on Jan. 23, 1804.

Agnes$^{1.2.5.1.2.2q}$, b. on Oct. 7, 1805, and m. Henry Bliss in Muskingum County on Nov. 23, 1831.

Cassandra$^{1.2.5.1.2.3q}$, b. on Dec. 24, 1808, m. Abraham Haines in Muskingum County on Nov. 11, 1834, and d. on June 21, 1893.

Samuel W.$^{1.2.5.1.2.4q}$, b. on Mar. 18, 1810.

Catherine W.$^{1.2.5.1.2.5q}$, b. on Aug. 28, 1812, and d. on July 29, 1839.

Elizabeth Ann$^{1.2.5.1.2.6q}$, b. on Aug. 18, 1815, m. Hiram Wilson, and resided in Vinton County, Ohio.

Francis$^{1.2.5.1.2.7q}$, b. on Mar. 29, 1818, and m. Frances Ellen Gabriel.

Nancy$^{1.2.5.1.2.8q}$, b. on Dec. 9, 1821, m. Benjamin Fulkison in Muskingum County on Apr. 12, 1841, and d. on Aug. 18, 1890.

Salina$^{1.2.5.1.2.9q}$, b. on July 26, 1823, and m. James Judah Allison.

Caroline$^{1.2.5.1.2.10q}$, b. on Apr. 3, 1826, and d. in Perry Township on Sep. 28, 1936.

Ruth Baker$^{1.2.5.1.2.11q}$, b. on Jan. 18, 1829, m. Valentine Renner, and d. in Vermillion County, Danville, Illinois, on Sep. 30, 1920.

Harriet$^{1.2.5.1.2.12q}$, b. on Mar. 1, 1833, and d. on June 1, 1849.

William Baker Wartenbe

William Baker$^{1.2.5.1.2.1q}$ m. Elvira Westbrook in Muskingum County, Ohio, on May 28, 1826, and had the following children:

Abraham$^{1.2.5.1.2.1.1q}$, b. in Nov. 1829, and d. in 1845.

Elizabeth Ann$^{1.2.5.1.2.1.2q}$, b. on Apr. 5, 1831.

Edith$^{1.2.5.1.2.1.3q}$, b. on Dec. 28, 1834, and m. ___ Wycoff.

Robert P.$^{1.2.5.1.2.1.4q}$, b. on June 25, 1837, and d. before 1850.

Samuel W.$^{1.2.5.1.2.1.5q}$, b. on Mar. 15, 1843, m. Harriet M. (b. in Ohio in Aug., 1853), and resided in Ohio in 1900.

Joseph Baker$^{1.2.5.1.2.1.6q}$, b. on Mar. 30, 1845, and m. Mary Margaret Humphreys in Jackson County, Ohio, on June 2, 1870.

Samuel W. Wartenbe

Samuel W.$^{1.2.5.1.2.4q}$ m. Lorinda Ballou in Morgan County, Ohio, on Sep. 22, 1838, and d. in Hamilton County, Cincinnati, Ohio, on June 20, 1851. She was b. in Muskingum County, Chandelersville, Ohio, on Jan. 7, 1815, and d. in Licking County, Granville, Ohio, in Mar. 1916. They had the following children in Muskingum County, Duncan Falls, Ohio:

Laura$^{1.2.5.1.2.4.1q}$, b. on July 18, 1839, and m. William Wing Spellman.

Emma$^{1.2.5.1.2.4.2q}$, b. on Sep. 22, 1841, and d. on Sep. 29, 1916.

Welcome$^{1.2.5.1.2.4.3q}$, b. on June 8, 1844, and d. in Muskingum County, Ohio, on Feb. 1, 1850.

Edith$^{1.2.5.1.2.4.4q}$, b. on Jan. 13, 1850, m. James Brayton in Licking County, Granville, Ohio, on Aug. 28, 1873, and d. in Los Angeles County, Pasadena, California in 1939. He was b. in Kings County, Brooklyn, New York, on Sep. 1, 1849, and d. in Licking County, Granville, Ohio, on Oct. 23, 1874.

Francis David Wartenbe

Frances David$^{1.2.5.1.3q}$ m. Catherine Callendine in Brooke County, Virginia, on Sep. 29, 1807, and Hannah Douherty about 1820. Francis moved to Armstrong County, Pine Creek, Pennsylvania, about between 1836 and 1840, and d. there sometime before 1840. Catherine was b. on Dec. 31, 1788, and d. in Muskingum County, Salt Creek Township, Ohio, on Jan. 13, 1814. Hannah resided in Armstrong County in 1840. William had the following children:

Mary$^{1.2.5.1.3.1q}$, b. about 1808, and d. about 1809.

Daniel$^{1.2.5.1.3.2q}$, b. in 1809.

Sarah$^{1.2.5.1.3.3q}$, b. on Sep. 18, 1812, and m. Robert Vincent in Muskingum County, Ohio, on June 1, 1836.

Catherine$^{1.2.5.1.3.4q}$, b. about 1821, and m. ___ Hall.

David Francis$^{1.2.5.1.3.5q}$, b. on Oct. 23, 1823.
Mordecai$^{1.2.5.1.3.6q}$, b. about 1825.

Daniel Wartenbe

Daniel$^{1.2.5.1.3.2q}$ m. Ellen Umstead in Muskingum County, Ohio, on Dec. 31, 1833, and d. on Oct. 6, 1853. They had the following children:

William Elmore$^{1.2.5.1.3.2.1q}$, b. in 1836, and d. before 1850.
Samuel$^{1.2.5.1.3.2.2q}$, b. about 1842, and m. Mary E. Mills in Muskingum County, Ohio, on Dec. 16, 1863.

David Francis Wartenbe

David Francis$^{1.2.5.1.3.5q}$ m. Mary Forsythe about 1847, and Sara Jane Lafferty O'dell in Buffalo County, Wisconsin, on May 17, 1890. Mary was b. in Armstrong County, Pennsylvania, on June 26, 1818, and d. in Pepin County, Pepin, Wisconsin, on Jan. 15, 1875. They had the following son:

Francis David$^{1.2.5.1.3.5.1q}$, b. in Armstrong County, Kittaning, Pennsylvania, on Nov. 2, 1848. He m. Hannah Broatch on July 22, 1875, and d. in La Crosse County, La Crosse, Wisconsin, on Apr. 23, 1925.

Mary Wartenbe

Mary$^{1.2.5.1.5q}$ m. Edward Holly in Brooke County, Virginia, on May 23, 1805, and had the following children:

Samuel$^{1.2.5.1.5.1q}$; Isaac$^{1.2.5.1.5.2q}$; Enoch$^{1.2.5.1.5.3q}$; George$^{1.2.5.1.5.4q}$; Thomas$^{1.2.5.1.5.5q}$; Wilson$^{1.2.5.1.5.6q}$; Mercy$^{1.2.5.1.5.7q}$; Penelopy$^{1.2.5.1.5.8q}$; Mary$^{1.2.5.1.5.9q}$.

William Wartenbe

William$^{1.2.5.1.8q}$ m. Susanna, daughter of Edward and Martha (Nott) Richmond, in Morgan County, Ohio, on Apr. 12, 1821. She d. in Williams County, Farmer Township, Ohio, about 1835. William d. there in 1841. William was a volunteer in the War of 1812 from Brooke County, Virginia. They had the following children in Muskingum County, Salt Creek Township, Ohio (except the last two in Williams County):

William$^{1.2.5.1.8.1q}$, b. in 1821.
Jefferson$^{1.2.5.1.8.2q}$, b. in 1824.
Martha Jane$^{1.2.5.1.8.3q}$, b. in 1826.
David$^{1.2.5.1.8.4q}$, b. on Jan. 20, 1827.

Joseph$^{1.2.5.1.8.5q}$, b. in 1828. The family lost knowledge of he when went west at the time of the Klondyke gold find. He resided in Defiance County, Ohio, in 1850.

Mary A.$^{1.2.5.1.8.6q}$, b. in 1833.

Ephraim B.$^{1.2.5.1.8.7q}$, b. in 1835. I suspect he is listed as Sebastian, b. in 1823, residing with his sister, Jane Marshall in 1850, because David claims that there is only seven in the family, and Ephraim is nowhere to be found in 1850.

William Wartenbe

William$^{1.2.5.1.8.1q}$ m. Catherine A. Greene in Williams County, Ohio, on June 23, 1842, and d. in Defiance County, Farmer Township, Ohio, between 1860 and 1870. Catherine was b. in Maryland in 1818, and was alive in 1870. They had the following children in Farmer Township:

William David$^{1.2.5.1.8.1.1q}$, b. in 1842. He m. Harriet Maria, daughter of Jacob Israel and Lydia (Spangler) Frager, in Defiance County, Ohio, on June 18, 1868, and d. in Grant County, South Dakota, in Nov. 1910. She was b. in Williams County, Ohio, on Sep. 4, 1848, and d. in Grant County, South Dakota, on Dec. 10, 1915. William served in the Civil War.

Temperance$^{1.2.5.1.8.1.2q}$, b. in 1843, and m. Albert Lovejoy in Defiance County, Ohio, on Aug. 23, 1862.

Mary Stone$^{1.2.5.1.8.1.3q}$, b. on Dec. 3, 1848. She m. Leander, son of Jacob Israel and Lydia (Spangler) Frager, in Defiance County, Ohio, on July 26, 1866, and d. in Washington County, Washington, Kansas, on June 12, 1928. He was b. in Williams County, Farmer Township, Ohio, on Sep. 12, 1845, and d. in Washington, Kansas, on Jan. 12, 1927.

James$^{1.2.5.1.8.1.4q}$, b. in 1849.

Sarah E.$^{1.2.5.1.8.1.5q}$, b. in 1851, and m. David Weidler in Defiance County on June 18, 1868.

Robert H.$^{1.2.5.1.8.1.6q}$, b. in 1853.

Ada R.$^{1.2.5.1.8.1.7q}$, b. in 1855.

Luther$^{1.2.5.1.8.1.8q}$, b. in 1859, and d. before 1870.

Orin$^{1.2.5.1.8.1.9q}$, b. in 1861.

Jefferson Wartenbe

Jefferson$^{1.2.5.1.8.2q}$ m. Sarah Mochmar in Williams County, Ohio, on Feb. 18, 1845, and d. in Allegan County, Dorr Township, Michigan, before 1880. Sarah was b. in Ohio in May 1830, and resided in Newaygo County, Bridgeton, Michigan, in 1910. They had the following children:

Eliza J.$^{1.2.5.1.8.2.1q}$, b. in Defiance County, Farmer Township, Ohio, in 1847.

Mary$^{1.2.5.1.8.2.2q}$, b. in Farmer Township in 1849.

David$^{1.2.5.1.8.2.3q}$, b. in Farmer Township in May 1852, m. Dealea about 1881 and Addeline about 1906, and d. resided in Newaygo County, Bridgeton, Michigan, in 1910.

Wesley Ephraim$^{1.2.5.1.8.2.4q}$, b. in Farmer Township in 1854, m. Sarah E. about 1883, and resided in Wayne County, Detroit, Michigan, in 1920.

Sarah$^{1.2.5.1.8.2.5q}$, b. in Williams County, St. Joseph Township, Ohio, in 1857.

Ella$^{1.2.5.1.8.2.6q}$, b. in St. Joseph Township in Jan. 1859, and m. Robert Osterhout in Allegan County, Michigan, on Nov. 28, 1878.

Georgia Estella$^{1.2.5.1.8.2.7q}$, b. in Allegan County, Dorr Township, Michigan, in 1866, and m. Henry Elfers in Allegan County on Dec. 21, 1882.

Martha Jane Wartenbe

Martha Jane$^{1.2.5.1.8.3q}$ m. James Marshall in Williams County, Ohio, on June 23, 1842, and d. in Defiance County, Milford Township, Ohio, between 1850 and May 1859. James was b. in Pennsylvania in 1816. They had the following children in Williams County, Farmer Township, Ohio:

Samuel J.$^{1.2.5.1.8.3.1q}$, b. in 1844.

Bartley$^{1.2.5.1.8.3.2q}$, b. in 1846.

David Wartenbe

David$^{1.2.5.1.8.4q}$ m. Margaret, daughter of Thomas and Sabra Ann (Mercer) Mercer, in Marshall County, Indiana, on May 3, 1860. She was b. in Jackson County, Scioto Township, Ohio, on Dec. 29, 1825, and d. in Marshall County, Walnut Township, Indiana, on Mar. 1, 1909. In 1848, David moved to Champaign County, Homer, Illinois, and until 1857, moved back and forth between Homer and Defiance County, Ohio (he was residing in Defiance County in 1850). On Aug. 8, 1857, he settled near Argos, Indiana, and worked at the Conkley Mill. He was working as an engineer in 1860. His obituary stated that this grandfather moved from Virginia because of his opposition to slavery, and that David's family consisted of seven children, six that were deceased, and the seventh had been lost to the family upon his immigration to California at the time of the Klondyke Gold find. His obituary also stated that his father d. when David was 14, and his mother d. while he was in "babyhood". David d. in Walnut Township, at the home of his daughter, Jane, on July 5, 1917. They are buried in Maplegrove cemetery. They had the following children in Walnut Township:

Thomas Lincoln[1.2.5.1.8.4.1q], b. on Mar. 8, 1861. He m. Magdalena "Maggie", daughter of Moses and Polly (Mullican) Black, in Wilson County, Prairie Township, Kansas, at the home of Maggie's stepfather, John Spangle, on Jan. 14, 1886. Around Feb. 1885, Thomas went west, and settled in Fredonia, Kansas, and made numerous trips between Fredonia and Argos, Indiana. On Aug. 27, 1885, he was visiting in Argos with intentions of returning to Kansas and commence improvements on his Homestead. Thomas entered 160 acres of Homestead land in Meade County, Kansas, sometime prior to Aug. 1885 at the cost of $14. They resided in Benedict, Kansas, on July 7, 1887. Thomas d. in Howard County, Kokomo, Indiana, on May 27, 1943. Maggie d. in Marshall County, Argos, Indiana, on June 5, 1936.

Mary E.[1.2.5.1.8.4.2q], b. on Aug. 23, 1862, and d. on Nov. 8, 1862.

Martha Jane[1.2.5.1.8.4.3q], b. on Aug. 4, 1865. She m. Clinton F. Bodey in Marshall County, Indiana, on Sep. 15, 1885. He was b. in Marshall County, Indiana, in Dec. 1863. They resided in Marshall County, Walnut Township, Indiana, in 1920.

Orley E.[1.2.5.1.8.4.4q], b. on July 21, 1868, and d. in Walnut Township on Mar. 7, 1887. He was a teacher.

Mary A. Wartenbe

Mary A.[1.2.5.1.8.6q] m. Henry N. Swetland in Defiance County, Ohio, on Jan. 21, 1860, and d. in DeKalb County, Stafford Township, Indiana, about 1881. He was b. in New York in 1833. They had the following children in DcKalb County, Indiana:

Adelbert[1.2.5.1.8.6.1q], b. in 1861.

Carrie V.[1.2.5.1.8.6.2q], b. in 1863, and m. Wallace G. Dietsman in DeKalb County, Indiana, on Jan. 1, 1903.

Ida[1.2.5.1.8.6.3q], b. in 1875.

Irene[1.2.5.1.8.6.4q], b. in 1877, and m. Frank P. Bradley in DeKalb County on May 7, 1899.

Ephraim B. Wartenbe

Ephraim B.$^{1.2.5.1.8.7q}$ m. Amanda Ellen Hollinger in Allen County, Indiana, on Feb. 8, 1863. She was b. in Stark County, Ohio, on Sep. 28, 1842, and d. in Allen County, Fort Wayne, Indiana, on May 22, 1935. Ephraim served in the Civil War in Company F, 142nd Indiana Infantry, and d. in Fort Wayne on May 19, 1882. Amanda filed for her husband's pension on Sep. 29, 1888. They are buried in New Haven I.O.O.F. cemetery. They had the following children (the first four in Allen County, Springfield Township, and the rest in Fort Wayne):

Eva S.$^{1.2.5.1.8.7.1q}$, b. in 1864, and d. in Fort Wayne on July 31, 1885.

Infant$^{1.2.5.1.8.7.2q}$, b. about 1866, and d. in Aug. 1870.

Infant$^{1.2.5.1.8.7.3q}$, b. about 1868, and d. in Sep. 1870.

William E.$^{1.2.5.1.8.7.4q}$, b. in 1871. He m. Etta Grace Tait in Allen County, Indiana, on June 22, 1892, and d. in Fort Wayne on Sep. 24, 1941. Etta was b. in Indiana in 1875.

Charles M.$^{1.2.5.1.8.7.5q}$, b. on Feb. 12, 1874, and d. in Fort Wayne on May 9, 1903.

Claude$^{1.2.5.1.8.7.6q}$, b. on Mar. 27, 1882, and d. in Fort Wayne on Dec. 4, 1957.

Isaac Wartenbe

Isaac$^{1.2.5.1.9q}$ m. Mercy Pierce, daughter of Aaron and Marcy (Pierce) Robinson, in Muskingum County, Ohio, on Aug. 6, 1817 and Eliza Dawson, widow of ___ Guthrie, in Defiance County, Ohio, on July 16, 1840. Isaac d. in Defiance County, Hicksville, Ohio, on Mar. 19, 1860. Mercy was b. in Brooke County, Virginia, on Feb. 7, 1793, and d. in Defiance County, Farmer Township, Ohio, on Oct. 20, 1838. Isaac moved to Williams County, Farmer Township, Section 10 in 1834, and was one of the first three families in the Township. He was Justice of the Peace, member of the Disciples Church, and taught music. Isaac had the following children (the first seven in Muskingum County, Salt Creek Township, and the rest in Williams/Defiance County, Farmer Township):

Angeline$^{1.2.5.1.9.1q}$, b. on May 9, 1818, m. Daniel Coy in Williams County, Ohio, on Sep. 6, 1838, and d. in Defiance County, Hicksville, Ohio, on May 1, 1895.

Aaron Robinson$^{1.2.5.1.9.2q}$, b. on Mar. 29, 1821.

Jane$^{1.2.5.1.9.3q}$, b. on Aug. 19, 1823, m. James M. Evans in Williams County on Apr. 29, 1841, and may have resided in Michigan.

Mercy$^{1.2.5.1.9.4q}$, b. on May 23, 1826, m. Nathaniel Crary in Williams County on Feb. 13, 1844, and d. in Defiance County on Oct. 26, 1854.

Mary$^{1.2.5.1.9.5q}$, b. in 1829, and d. in Franklin County, Columbus, Ohio, about 1880.

Amanda M.$^{1.2.5.1.9.6q}$, b. on July 8, 1831, and m. William J. Henry in Defiance County on Oct. 30, 1856.

Mergeline A.$^{1.2.5.1.9.7q}$, b. on Aug. 8, 1834, m. Stephen W. Strong in Defiance County on Jan. 2, 1851, and d. in Defiance County on July 10, 1885.

Anna Eliza$^{1.2.5.1.9.8q}$, b. about 1841, m. Wayne Koons in Defiance County on Nov. 15, 1863, and resided in Defiance County, Sherwood, Ohio.

Nancy M.$^{1.2.5.1.9.9q}$, b. on Nov. 29, 1842, and m. Francis Rice in Williams County on Apr. 30, 1874.

Sarah$^{1.2.5.1.9.10q}$, b. on June 25, 1845, and m. Gilbert O. Coburn in Defiance County on Mar. 26, 1865.

Nathan$^{1.2.5.1.9.11q}$, b. on Feb. 1, 1847, and d. on Apr. 24, 1863.

Caroline$^{1.2.5.1.9.12q}$, b. about 1849, m. Martin Moudy in Defiance County on June 16, 1869, and resided in Williams County, West Unity, Ohio.

Aurilla$^{1.2.5.1.9.13q}$, b. on Oct. 1, 1851, m. Albert Lovejoy, and d. on Oct. 4, 1921.

Candace$^{1.2.5.1.9.14q}$, b. on Oct. 19, 1853, m. Frank Gillespie and Jasper Perkins, and d. on Apr. 4, 1904.

Isaac Wesley$^{1.2.5.1.9.15q}$, b. on Aug. 7, 1854, m. Susan H. Hunter in Williams County on June 3, 1877 and Ella Wyatt about 1899, and d. in Defiance County, Hicksville, Ohio, on July 5, 1931.

Laurena$^{1.2.5.1.9.16q}$, b. about 1856, and m. Charles Newman.

Aaron Robinson Wartenbe

Aaron Robinson$^{1.2.5.1.9.2q}$ m. Elizabeth Dawson in Williams County, Ohio, on July 31, 1845, Mary Jane Bradshaw, widow of ____ Ault, before 1850 (probably in Berrien County, New Buffalo, Michigan), and Amanda Calhoun in Cherokee County, Texas, on Mar. 14, 1866. Amanda was b. in Mississippi in 1840. Aaron d. in Van Zandt County, Texas, about 1877. Aaron had the following children:

Martin Chandler$^{1.2.5.1.9.2.1q}$, b. in Berrien County, New Buffalo, Michigan, on Mar. 22, 1850. He m. Lora Lavina Fails in

DeKalb County, Newville, Indiana, on July 3, 1873, and d. in Carter County, Grandin, Missouri, on May 9, 1938.

Frances Mergeline$^{1.2.5.1.9.2.2q}$, b. in LaPorte County, Michigan City, Indiana, in 1852.

Albines Delescus$^{1.2.5.1.9.2.3q}$, b. in Michigan City on Jan. 15, 1853, m. Mary Elizabeth Hellinger, and d. on June 17, 1935.

Arminda$^{1.2.5.1.9.2.4q}$, b. in Michigan City in 1855.

Melissa$^{1.2.5.1.9.2.5q}$, b. in Michigan City about 1857, and m. J. D. Wages in Van Zandt County, Texas, on May 25, 1879.

Amasa$^{1.2.5.1.9.2.6q}$, b. in Van Zandt County, Texas, about 1872, and m. C. E. Hubbard in Van Zandt County on Jan. 20, 1895.

Luch$^{1.2.5.1.9.2.7q}$, b. in Van Zandt County about 1874, and m. D. N. Johnson in Van Zandt County on May 2, 1895.

Clara$^{1.2.5.1.9.2.8q}$, b. in Van Zandt County about 1876, and m. J. I. Davis in Van Zandt County on Sep. 12, 1897.

Elizabeth Wartenbe

Elizabeth$^{1.2.5.1.11q}$ m. Solomon Johnson in Muskingum County, Ohio, on Nov. 16, 1820, and d. in Muskingum County, Chandelersville, Ohio, in 1864. They had the following son:

William Wartenbe$^{1.2.5.1.11.1q}$, d. in Lawrence County, Irontown, Ohio.

Joseph Wartenbe

Joseph$^{1.2.5.1.12q}$ m. Nancy, daughter of Martin and Lydia (Shaver) Smith, in Muskingum County, Ohio, on June 20, 1820, and d. in Defiance County, Farmer Township, Ohio, on Feb. 16, 1854. She was b. in Frederick County, Virginia, on Dec. 5, 1801, and d. in DeKalb County, Stafford Township, Indiana, on Dec. 13, 1888. Joseph was a carpenter. They had the following children (the first five in Muskingum County, Salt Creek Township, and the rest in Williams/Defiance County, Farmer Township):

Martin Smith$^{1.2.5.1.12.1q}$, b. on Aug. 29, 1820, m. Catherine Griffith in Guernsey County, Ohio, on Oct. 17, 1839, and d. in Defiance County, Farmer Township, on Dec. 26, 1866.

Stewart Patterson$^{1.2.5.1.12.2q}$, b. on Mar. 29, 1823. He m. Cordelia Wanamaker in DeKalb County, Indiana, on Feb. 3, 1859, and d. in DeKalb County, Stafford Township, Indiana, on Apr. 7, 1905.

Rebecca$^{1.2.5.1.12.3q}$, b. on Mar. 5, 1825, m. John Slough in Williams County on Feb. 2, 1843, and Henry Battershell in Defiance County on Sep. 12, 1850.

Mary Ann[1.2.5.1.12.4q], b. on May 13, 1827, m. Lorenzo H. Sales in Defiance County on Aug. 31, 1845, and resided in Buchanan County, St. Joseph, Missouri.

John Smith[1.2.5.1.12.5q], b. on June 1, 1829, m. Sarah Ann Sawyer in Defiance County on Oct. 20, 1850, and d. in Decatur County, Grande River, Iowa, on July 13, 1866.

Elizabeth[1.2.5.1.12.6q], b. on Jan. 13, 1832, m. Cuyler Cornelius Sawyer in Defiance County on Oct. 15, 1850, and resided in Clayton County, Luana, Iowa.

Lydia J.[1.2.5.1.12.7q], b. on July 6, 1835, m. Harmon William Henkle, and d. in Keokuk County, Keota, Iowa, on Apr. 15, 1923.

Catherine[1.2.5.1.12.8q], b. on July 6, 1835, m. William Stewart in Defiance County on Jan. 23, 1859, and d. on Oct. 28, 1883.

Eliza M.[1.2.5.1.12.9q], b. on Dec. 11, 1838, m. Elias Spangler in Williams County on Apr. 9, 1859, and d. on Feb. 22, 1864.

Nathan S.[1.2.5.1.12.10q], b. on Mar. 4, 1841, and d. in Cobb County, Kennesaw, Georgia, on June 25, 1864.

Nancy Annetta[1.2.5.1.12.11q], b. on Apr. 30, 1843, m. Benoni Clark in Defiance County on Oct. 15, 1863, and d. in Missouri on Aug. 9, 1873.

****

INDEX